T3-BOX-267

ts

ENTEREDOCT 1 7 1996

Learning Through Folklore Series

Norma J. Livo, Series Editor

Of Bugs and Beasts: Fact, Folklore, and Activities. By Lauren J. Livo, Glenn McGlathery, and Norma J. Livo. 1995.

Who's Afraid...? Facing Children's Fears with Folktales. By Norma J. Livo. 1994.

Who's Endangered on Noah's Ark? Literary and Scientific Activities for Teachers and Parents. By Glenn McGlathery and Norma J. Livo. 1992.

Of Bugs and Beasts

Fact, Folklore, and Activities

Lauren J. Livo

Glenn McGlathery

Norma J. Livo

Illustrated by
David Stallings

Photography by
Lauren J. Livo
Steve Wilcox

Columbia College Library
600 South Michigan Avenue
Chicago, IL 60605

1995
TEACHER IDEAS PRESS
A Division of
Libraries Unlimited, Inc.
Englewood, Colorado

*Dedicated to the animals of the air, water,
and earth, who enrich our lives even
though they may not be appreciated.*

—LJL, GEM, and NJL

Copyright © 1995 Lauren J. Livo, Glenn Edward McGlathery,
and Norma J. Livo
All Rights Reserved
Printed in the United States of America

No part of this publication may be reproduced, stored in a retrieval system, or
transmitted, in any form or by any means, electronic, mechanical, photocopying,
recording, or otherwise, without the prior written permission of the publisher. An
exception is made for individual library media specialists and teachers who may make
copies of activity sheets for classroom use in a single school. Other portions of the
book (up to 15 pages) may be copied for in-service programs or other educational
programs in a single school.

TEACHER IDEAS PRESS
A Division of
Libraries Unlimited, Inc.
P.O. Box 6633
Englewood, CO 80155-6633
1-800-237-6124

Production Editor: Louisa M. Griffin
Copy Editor: Diane Hess
Proofreader: Eileen Bartlett
Interior Design and Layout: Kay Minnis

Library of Congress Cataloging-in-Publication Data

Livo, Lauren J.
　　Of bugs and beasts : fact, folklore, and activities / Lauren J.
Livo, Glenn McGlathery, Norma J. Livo ; illustrated by David
Stallings.
　　xxi, 217 p. 22x28 cm.
　　Includes bibliographical references and index.
　　ISBN 1-56308-179-2
　　1. Animals. 2. Animals--Folklore. 3. Animals--Study and
teaching--Activity programs. I. McGlathery, Glenn, 1934-
II. Livo, Norma J., 1929-　　. III. Title.
QL50.L776 1994
591--dc20　　　　　　　　　　　　　　　　　94-25874
　　　　　　　　　　　　　　　　　　　　　　　CIP

TMC. 591 L788o

Livo, Lauren J.

Of bugs and beasts

Contents

OF THE AIR

OF THE WATER

OF THE EARTH

Preface

Most amphibia are abhorrent because of their cold body, pale color, cartilaginous skeleton, filthy skin, fierce aspect, calculating eye, offensive smell, harsh voice, squalid habitation, and terrible venom; and so their Creator has not exerted his powers [to create] many of them.

Linnaeus, writing in the 10th
Systema Naturae (1758)

In the eighteenth century, when Swedish naturalist Linnaeus wrote about his abhorrence of "amphibia," he expressed a negative attitude that unfortunately remains common to this day.[1] In fact, the number of animals we *don't* consider "abhorrent" sometimes seems surprisingly limited.

When we began work on this book, we had an idea of the types of animals we wanted to profile. Basically, we wanted to write about animals with reputations out of proportion to the actual or potential harm they do—animals that make people react with an "Ugh!"

We distributed a survey that illustrated 40 different types of animals (see appendix C). Some creatures we expected people to like, some to dislike. We used preliminary results from this survey to fine-tune our selection of animals to profile.

We have tried to avoid being stuffy about the animals we profile. For example, we use the colloquial term *buzzard* when writing about the group that includes turkey vultures and black vultures. We prefer the informal term *packrat* for the animal most biologists call "woodrat." The correct common names are noted when our usage diverges from more formal usage.

Throughout the book we occasionally use terms like *class*, *family*, or *genus*. These are names that biologists use to organize, or classify, living creatures into hierarchical groups. For an explanation of the biological classification of animals in this book, please see appendix B.

Learning about an animal—including its adaptations and the ways it interacts with other organisms—can only increase our respect for the creature. We expect this book to be useful to children, their parents, and their teachers. We hope it helps lessen any disdain you might feel toward the organisms.

You can't escape at least some encounters with the animals profiled in this book. Perhaps it will be a slug creeping over a piece of fallen fruit, a moth trembling against a screen door, or a snake disappearing into a rocky wall. We hope this book helps prepare you and the children in your life for these encounters. Whatever the circumstances, may all your encounters be both interesting and informative.

NOTES

1. Linnaeus's "amphibia" included both amphibians and reptiles. Not only did Linnaeus write without regard to the role of these creatures in ecosystems, he underestimated their numbers. While few forms of reptiles and amphibians live in Sweden's northerly climes, tremendous diversity exists in the tropics.

Acknowledgments

I ask forgiveness of all the ants I have stepped on (on purpose or accidentally), of all the leeches I have recoiled from in disgust, and of any other unlovables I may have wounded (include slugs here).

N.J.L.

Thanks to my students at the University of Colorado at Denver. They willingly completed surveys, had their students and friends complete surveys, and tried some of the activities in this book.

G.E.M.

Thanks to the teachers who distributed our survey to their students, including Mamie Garceo (Horace Mann Middle School, Denver Public Schools), and Richard Irwin and Charles Counts (International Baccalaureate Program, George Washington High School, Denver Public Schools). Jody Wilcox Livo helped draw the creatures featured in our survey. Todd Livo Wilcox, my in-house paper-folding specialist, helped make the origami models featured in some activities. Tom Nesler, of the Colorado Division of Wildlife, gave us information about the razorback sucker. Dr. Shi-Kuei Wu of the University of Colorado Museum reviewed early drafts of the chapters on clams and slugs. Christopher Nagano, entomologist with the U.S. Fish and Wildlife Service, and Monique Born, of the California Department of Fish and Game, provided information about the Kern primrose sphinx moth. Dexter Sear's enthusiam for cultural entomology aided my explorations in this new terrain. Editing by Louisa Griffin and Diane Hess helped improve this book. Steve Wilcox shared camera duties with me and more besides. I worked on portions of this book while an artist-in-residence at Rocky Mountain National Park; I thank Corky Hays, coordinator of this wonderful program.

L.J.L.

Grateful acknowledgment is made for permission to use the following copyrighted material:

"The Bat," copyright 1938 by Theodore Roethke. "Dying Man," copyright 1956 by Atlantic Monthly Co. "Interlude," copyright 1938 by Theodore Roethke. "The Marrow," copyright 1962 by Beatrice Roethke, Administratrix of the Estate of Theodore Roethke, from *The Collected Poems of Theodore Roethke* by Theodore Roethke. Used by permission of Doubleday, a division of Bantam Doubleday Dell Publishing Group, Inc.

"Straighten Up and Fly Right," by Nat "King" Cole and Irving Mills. Copyright 1944 (Renewed 1972) AMERICAN ACADEMY OF MUSIC, INC. c/o EMI MILLS CATALOG, INC. All rights reserved. Reprinted by permission of CPP/BELWIN, INC., Miami, FL.

"The Moth and the Star," by James Thurber. Copyright 1940 James Thurber. Copyright 1968 Helen Thurber. From *Fables for Our Time*, published by Harper & Row.

"On Societies as Organisms," copyright 1971 by The Massachussetts Medical Society, from *The Lives of a Cell* by Lewis Thomas. Used by permission of Viking Penguin, a division of Penguin Books USA Inc.

Furtive Fauna by Roger Knutson. Copyright 1992 by Roger Knutson; Illustrations copyright 1992 Viking Penguin, a division of Penguin Books USA Inc. Used by permission of Penguin, a division of Penguin Books USA Inc.

"Taking off Pitch Gloves" from *The Pinon Pine: A Natural and Cultural History* by Ronald M. Lanner. Copyright 1981. University of Nevada Press.

Introduction

> *. . . all the meaner things: the rat, and the owl,*
> *and the bat—the moth, and the fox, and the*
> *wolf. . . .*
>
> Professor Van Helsing
> *Dracula* by Bram Stoker

PERCEPTIONS OF ANIMALS

Some of the animals profiled in this book are found worldwide, others exclusively on this continent, but all have at least some representatives in North America. We wanted to describe not only animals often feared or disliked, but ones that readers could potentially observe.

The coyote and razorback sucker accounts in this book profile single animal species. Most accounts—buzzards, clams, moths, and so on—discuss groups of animals that contain from a handful to hundreds of species.

People often perceive the animals profiled in this book as creatures cloaked in evil—among the "meaner things." The reputations that precede them, however, are often much more fearsome than the animals themselves. The way we perceive these animals depends, in part, on our own cultural biases.

Many cultures incorporate animals such as bats, coyotes, snakes, toads, and spiders into stories, myth, and folklore. These animals have varying roles, from functioning as minor but important components (leeches in *The Younger Brother*, pages 46-47) to creative heros (*Clamshell Boy*, page 56), the butt of jokes (*Coyote and the Lizards*, pages 125-26), and object lessons (*A Snake in the Road*, pages 88-89). Interestingly, some of the least popular creatures—such as jellyfish—tend to have the fewest associations with cultural traditions. Many people don't even like to *think* about some of these lowly creatures.

Beyond their roles in stories and myth, however, is another dimension: the real animal functioning within its habitat and responding to the challenges of growth, reproduction, and survival. The animals profiled in this book each have novel adaptations, from a skunk's pungent spray to a snake's heightened sense of smell. And they have interesting interactions with the organisms around them, from the cooperative pollination of the yucca blossom by the yucca moth to a clam's parasitic dependence on native fish that act as hosts for its larvae.

Both fact and folklore have roles in shaping our thoughts and feelings about wildlife. Our personal observations of animals, together with the reactions of others, also help to mold our responses. According to Stephen R. Kellert of Yale University's School of Forestry and Environmental Studies, what we know about animals affects the types of attitudes we hold and the degree to which we feel a kinship to animals.

Frequently, we use loaded words to describe animals. The ones we like, we term appealing, graceful, regal, cuddly, majestic, noble, attractive. We call the creatures we fear clammy, creepy, slimy, slithery, disgusting, vile, nasty, repulsive. The most frightening ones we call beastly, as though they could be something else.

We also use animals to characterize people. "She's a real fox," an appreciative teenage boy might say to another about a girl. Meanwhile, the girl in question might think the boy is a "skunk" or a "toad" who hangs on to her "like a leech." A person with bad vision might be described (incorrectly) as "blind as a bat." Someone who has trouble resisting temptation might be called a worm or a jellyfish.

In all instances, *we* imbue the animals with characteristics based on our biases. Coyote, the trickster god of the Navajo, becomes the vicious predator of the Wyoming shepherd. The wise and patient slug of the Lummi becomes the terror of the suburban garden.

The following table shows the results of our survey on the popularity of animals (most unpopular and most popular animals listed first):

10 Least Popular Animals	**10 Most Popular Animals**
1. leech	1. eagle
2. slug	2. dog
3. ant	3. deer
4. jellyfish	4. fox
5. tarantula	5. bluebird
6. moth	6. bear
7. buzzard	7. coyote
8. razorback sucker	8. robin
9. skunk	9. box turtle
10. worm	10. raccoon

As is obvious, invertebrates fared more poorly in terms of popularity than vertebrates, accounting for 7 of the 10 least popular animals. This is despite the fact that invertebrates were only about a third of the animals illustrated on the survey. All 10 of the most popular animals were vertebrates. One animal profiled in this book, the coyote, was among the 10 most popular animals in this survey. We included it because of its history of being maligned. Also, because most of our survey participants are urban, we felt that attitudes about coyotes might be quite different in rural populations. For example, in a survey by Stephen Kellert, the coyote was one of the least-liked animals. (For more information about the survey, see appendix C.)

Some animals, including many of those profiled in this book, tend to make people squeamish. One telephone movie review service (Reel Review) even warns the squeamish about the on-screen appearance of snakes or other creepy-crawlies, as well as the more usual details about the sex and violence content of movies. Just why do so many of us react so strongly to certain kinds of animals?

The more alien the world the animal inhabits, the more likely we are to view it with skepticism or dismay. Bats and moths, for example, are active at night, when we—organisms dependent on sight—are at a disadvantage. Some of the animals in this book live in the water, an environment in which we are short-term visitors at best.

Slimy animals—or those thought of as slimy—also seem inherently disgusting. Many people, for example, believe that snakes are slimy. Even during nature presentations that confront them with a living, breathing—and *dry*—snake, they sometimes refuse to change their attitude. "I don't care," they say, "they *look* slimy." In general, people prefer animals with fur or feathers versus scales or "slimy" skins.

Other animals perform what we regard as disgusting chores. Some, such as buzzards and slugs, are part of nature's cleanup crew, active, respectively, in disposing of dead animals or decomposing materials. Suckers behave like "scum-sucking bottom feeders"; they spend their days vacuuming invertebrate prey from the bottoms of rivers, lakes, and streams.

Parasites, which fill themselves with us, fill *us* with revulsion. Yet we may owe even these creatures a debt. According to Roger Knutson: "We were probably prepared for reading and writing by those early efforts to see small dark creatures against the skin of others. And there was certainly natural selection among those early humans for enhanced powers of persuasion. Someone who can talk another person into looking them over for tiny ectoparasites would have no trouble selling veg-o-matics to the unwary."[1]

We also tend to dislike animals with very different body plans, as exemplified by snakes and spiders. The first has too few and the latter too many legs for our comfort. And we can't even begin to make sense of the body of a jellyfish, with its radial instead of bilateral symmetry.

It's often said that what we don't know, we fear. This seems true of many of our unlovable animals, creatures whose lives are mysterious and alien yet beautiful in their own ways. Some believe that we have an inherited aversion to certain creatures. As biologist E. O. Wilson notes, "People acquire phobias . . . to the objects and circumstances that threaten humanity in natural environments: heights, closed spaces, open spaces, running water, wolves, spiders, snakes. They rarely form phobias to the recently invented contrivances that are far more dangerous, such as guns, knives, automobiles, and electric sockets."[2]

Author Desmond Morris agrees and says we prefer animals with features such as hair, rounded outlines, flat faces capable of expressions, the ability to manipulate objects, and vertical posture. "Snakes," he writes "are disliked because they are 'slimy and dirty' and spiders are repulsive because they are 'hairy and creepy.' "[3] Often, Morris continues, the animals we fear are at least potentially dangerous.

Many consider at least some of the animals in this book as dangerous. According to an article in *Men's Health* magazine, about 200 people in the United States die each year in encounters with animals.[4] What animal is responsible for the majority of these deaths? Unpopular animals such as tarantulas, slugs, leeches?

No. The top three killers are deer (about 131 deaths per year), bees (43 deaths), and dogs (14 deaths). Deer are usually involved in human fatalities through traffic accidents, when deer wander onto roadways. Dogs (often in packs) and bees take a more direct approach when involved in human mortalities.

Despite their roles in human deaths, deer and dogs were among the most preferred animals in our survey (bees weren't among the animals on the survey form); tarantulas, slugs, and leeches—who didn't cause any deaths—were the least popular. All the human deaths combined attributed to animals in this book about equal the number of deaths per year attributed to dogs and remain far below the numbers for bees and deer.

Something is dreadfully wrong here. Certainly, some of the animals profiled in this book cause occasional harm. The tarantula has an overblown reputation, but other spiders such as black widows can cause deaths. Rattlesnakes, coral snakes, and other venomous serpents can kill. Coyotes have attacked and maimed vulnerable individuals, especially unsupervised toddlers.

The lesson from these harmful interactions isn't to persecute the animals. It is to treat these and other animals—including ones we like—with sufficient respect and caution. For example, keep an eye on young children when camping or in other places frequented by wild animals. Don't catch snakes unless you know they are harmless varieties. Never handle large boas and pythons alone (owners with the scent of prey on their hands have been strangled by pet snakes). Let wild animals find their own food. Not only can human food harm the animals directly, it can reduce their fear of humans. Such dependence on people for food has cost many bears in national parks their lives when they turn into "problem bears." The same may be true of the coyotes that have attacked people.

OVERCOMING
OUR FEARS

If, as several authors suggest, we have inherited a kernel of squeamishness or fear of certain animals, we are flexible enough that we can overcome some of these feelings through education. For example, J. Mark Morgan and James H. Gramann examined four teaching strategies used to change students' attitudes about snakes:

- *Mere exposure.* For example, students can view a snake in a terrarium;

- *Modeling.* For example, an adult handles a snake while the students watch;

- *Direct contact.* For example, students can touch a snake; and

- *Information.* For example, students listen to a presentation about snakes.[5]

They found that simply providing information about snakes was not enough to change attitudes. In fact, information alone, or mere exposure alone, may make phobias about snakes somewhat worse. Various combinations of strategies—especially those that included modeling—helped change attitudes, but the largest increase in positive attitudes resulted when Morgan and Gramann combined all four strategies.

Morgan and Gramann's study emphasized attitudes about snakes, but their strategies probably are effective for changing attitudes about other types of animals. Having animals in a classroom presents opportunities for all four types of teaching strategies. If an animal is a long-term visitor to the class, students can also encourage one another to interact with the animal as they take care of it.

Of course, some students may remain especially fearful of one or more animals. Neither adults nor other students should ever thrust an unwelcome animal at anybody. This would simply reinforce the fearful person's already negative feelings.

WHY BOTHER CARING?

Still, the question remains for some: Why should anyone care about the animals in this book? There are some highly practical reasons that these and other lowly creatures deserve some respect. Consider the following:

- A scientist, studying a common type of moth, discovered a new class of antibiotics called cecropins.

- Secretions from a tropical frog contain a peptide called adenoregulin, which has potential for treating disorders such as depression, stroke, and seizures.

- Leeches produce substances that may one day have medical applications, including anesthetic compounds and various chemicals that prevent or dissolve blood clots.

- Many snake venoms contain proteins called disintegrins, which may help doctors prevent blood platelets from clumping together in patients with blood clots.

- Venom from a snake called the jararaca contains a peptide that may help control blood pressure.

- A protein called Bat-PA, obtained from vampire bats, may be another promising cardiovascular drug.

This list is an example of what biologists call "chemical prospecting"—investigating plants and animals for the novel chemicals they produce. Organisms face many challenges as they grow, obtain food, protect themselves, and produce offspring. For example, it makes sense that the blood-feeding leech has developed substances to help it obtain a steady flow of blood. By investigating chemicals produced by such animals, chemists can learn about their effects and eventually develop useful drugs and materials.

More important, the animals profiled in this book play roles—often important ones—in ecosystems. Just a few of these "ecosystem services" include moths pollinating flowers, ants dispersing plant seeds, buzzards recycling dead animals, coyotes keeping rodent populations under control, and clams acting as sentinels of a river's health. Ecological research has demonstrated that ecosystems containing large numbers of species are more stable, even after disturbance, than simpler ecosystems. So even when we don't yet know what specific role an animal plays, it very likely contributes to the general health of its habitat through interactions with other organisms.

However, even when an animal serves a vital function in its ecosystem, people may be unwilling to help protect and conserve it if the animal doesn't fit our ideals of what is desirable. Popular animals such as pandas, whooping cranes, and Florida panthers are known in conservation circles as "charismatic megafauna." When endangered, these kinds of animals are much more likely to receive a disproportionate share of public attention and funding for recovery efforts. A recent public opinion poll, conducted by Don Coursey of the University of Chicago, indicated that this was just fine with many people. Only about a third of the people believed that all endangered species deserve equal protection regardless of the type of animal. As nature writer Gary Gerhardt noted, "Green and slimy critters, and insects and rodents can kiss their existence goodby."[6]

The animals profiled in this book are part of our biological heritage, and we need to be responsible stewards for future generations. As Stephen Kellert writes, although we "must start with creatures we can empathize with readily—the larger, charismatic vertebrates—eventually we will need to extend our appreciation to the grandeur found within all living organisms."[7]

HOW TO USE THIS BOOK

We have organized this book into three parts—"Of the Air," "Of the Water," and "Of the Earth." The air, water, and earth play integral roles in stories about creation worldwide. In the Iroquois creation story, Sky Woman fell from the sky and the Sky People changed into water animals and the muskrat dove to the bottom of the water. When the muskrat emerged it had mud in its claws. The mud was spread on the back of the turtle. This became our earth. People say the earth rests on the back of a turtle. The Sky People then caught Sky Woman as she fell and safely placed her on this earth.

In the Finnish epic poem *Kalevala*, Vainamoinen, the oldest of the ancient wizards, was born of the virgin maiden of the air. The winds blew her pregnant and it took 700 years for this pregnancy to be born as the seas from which she fashioned the earth. Again, the winds blew her pregnant and for 30 years Vainamoinen was in her womb, and he was born into the sea and waves. (He rolled among the billows for eight years.)

Native Americans and the Hmong of Southeast Asia tell stories of man, with plants and animals, climbing out of a rock or opening in the ground to live on earth. Jewish and Christian beliefs hold that God made Adam from a little bit of dust—the earth.

Following these ideas of creation, it is thus appropriate that this book is divided into three sections.

Profiles of 15 animals are grouped within the parts according to the animal's usual habitat. Obviously, some creatures use more than one habitat, at least occasionally. Toads, for example, although grouped with the animals of the earth, use water for breeding.

Each profile has the following parts:

- A story and some of the folklore associated with the animal. The stories and folklore provide insights into how various cultures perceive these animals. They can serve as a foundation for the exploration of current attitudes about the animals.

- A description of the "animal as animal." We summarize the natural history of the animal, including a description of the animal and its life cycle, the range occupied by the animal, and interactions of the animal with other organisms, including humans. Our primary intention in writing about these animals is to celebrate the diversity that surrounds us. Sometimes this diversity is threatened. The accounts make note of animals or groups of animals that appear on U.S. Fish and Wildlife listings of threatened or endangered species.

- A variety of activities related to the animal. The activities can be done on an individual basis, as a class, or in small groups. The activities provide connection points to other areas of study: drama, language arts, mathematics, social studies, geography, and so on.

- Annotated resource lists for more information. The resources include books, magazine and journal articles, and tapes and compact discs.

Appendix A details some foods that may seem exotic and bizarre by North American standards. Appendix B provides information about the classification of the various organisms. Appendix C contains a summary of our survey on perceptions of animals. Appendix D contains the answers to some puzzles found in the activity sections. A glossary contains specialized terms used in the book. An index follows the glossary.

NOTES

1. Roger M. Knutson. *Furtive Fauna*. New York: Penguin Books, 1992, p. 118.

2. E. O. Wilson. *The Diversity of Life*. Cambridge, Mass.: Belknap Press of Harvard University Press, 1992, p. 349.

3. Desmond Morris. *The Naked Ape*. New York: Dell, 1967, p. 192.

4. Dan Bensimhon and Mary Brophy. "Man-Killer." *Men's Health* 7, no. 2 (1992): 78-79.

5. Mark J. Morgan and James H. Gramann. "Predicting Effectiveness of Wildlife Education Programs: A Study of Students' Attitudes and Knowledge of Snakes." *Wildlife Society Bulletin* 17, no. 4 (1989): 501-9.

6. Gary Gerhardt. "Imperiled, Slimy Critters Losing Funding Race." *Rocky Mountain News*, February 22, 1994, p. 2A.

7. Stephen R. Kellert. "Values and Perceptions of Invertebrates." *Conservation Biology* 7, no. 4 (1993): 845-55.

BIBLIOGRAPHY

Books

Charles, Donald. 1994. *Ugly Bug*. New York: Dial Book for Young Readers.
    Even the ugliest bug in the world can find another ugly bug to love.

Hanson, Jeanne K., and Deane Morrison. 1991. *Of Kinkajous, Capybaras, Horned Beetles, Seladangs, and the Oddest and Most Wonderful Mammals, Insects, Birds, and Plants of Our World*. New York: HarperCollins, 283 pp.
    Presents a miscellany of strange and interesting creatures.

Hoage, R. J., ed. 1989. *Perceptions of Animals in American Culture*. Washington, D.C.: Smithsonian Institution Press, 151 pp.
    Chapters by various authors explore the attitudes we have about different animals. A summary on wildlife attitudes by Stephen R. Kellert appears in chapter 2.

Morris, Ramona, and Desmond Morris. 1965. *Men and Snakes*. New York: McGraw-Hill, 224 pp.
    In chapter 9, the authors explore attitudes about snakes. They discuss their survey of approximately 80,000 British children, exploring which animals the children most like and dislike.

Robinson, Howard F., Victor H. Waldrop, Debby Anker, Elizabeth B. Blizard, et al. 1988. *The Unhuggables*. Washington, D.C.: National Wildlife Federation, 95 pp.
    This book, for juvenile readers, contains colorful photos with accounts of various unpopular creatures.

Rood, Ronald. 1971. *Animals Nobody Loves*. Brattleboro, Vt.: Stephen Greene Press, 215 pp.
    The author features chapters on a dozen "unlovable" animals.

Wilson, Edward O. 1992. *The Diversity of Life*. Cambridge, Mass.: Belknap Press of Harvard University Press, 424 pp.
    The author, well known for previous books such as *Biophilia* and *Sociobiology*, discusses both the resilience and fragility of life on our planet and how humans are affecting biodiversity.

Articles

Amato, Ivan. 1992. From 'Hunter Magic,' a Pharmacopeia? *Science* 258(5086):1306.
    Describes possible uses of chemicals found in secretions from a tropical frog.

Bang, Nils U. 1991. Leeches, Snakes, Ticks, and Vampire Bats in Today's Cardiovascular Drug Development. *Circulation* 84(1):436-38.
    Various chemicals with potential for treating circulatory disorders are found in animals.

Carbyn, Ludwig N. 1989. Coyote Attacks on Children in Western North America. *Wildlife Society Bulletin* 17(4):444-46.
    Describes and discusses coyote attacks on people.

Coursey, Don. 1994. The Revealed Demand for Public Goods: Evidence from Endangered and Threatened Species. Paper presented at annual meeting of the American Association for the Advancement of Science, San Francisco, February.
    A study and opinion poll compared the preference ranking of various endangered species with the funding levels used to recover the species.

Dial M for Movie. 1993. *People* 39(3):71. (January 25)
    Sharon Kissack's telephone review service warns moviegoers of potentially upsetting creepy-crawlies as well as more typical sex and violence content of movies.

Gerhardt, Gary. 1994. Imperiled, Slimy Critters Losing Funding Race. *Rocky Mountain News*, February 22, page 24A.
    Summarizes the results of a study and opinion poll conducted by Don Coursey. The study looked at how funding varied by endangered species; the opinion poll showed how people felt about the different funding levels for conserving endangered species.

Langreth, Robert. 1993. The Frog Treatment. *Popular Science* 243(2):58-59, 78. (August)
    Describes possible medical applications of chemicals from frogs.

McKean, Kevin. 1986. Pain. *Discover* 7(10):82-90, 92. (October)
    This article outlines a scientist's efforts to control pain, and mentions the potential use of snake venom for controlling blood pressure.

The Scud, the Bat and the Ugly. 1993. *Nature Conservancy* 43(4):16-23. (July-August)
    This article seeks to increase appreciation of "the buck-toothed, the slimy-skinned, the bug-eyed" as part of the diversity of life on earth.

Temple, Stanley A. 1992. Appreciating Our Cold-Blooded Nature. *Wisconsin Natural Resources* 16(1):4-11. (February)
    Makes a plea for greater appreciation of reptiles, amphibians, and invertebrates because of the important roles these animals play in ecosystems.

Tilton, Pamela S., and Edmund A. Richards. 1990. Fear of Snakes in Students and Establishing a Snake as a Classroom Pet. *Journal of the Colorado-Wyoming Academy of Science* 22(1):40-41.
    This abstract summarizes the results of a study to determine whether fear of snakes is instinctive or learned.

Of the Air

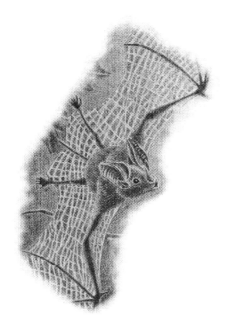

Chapter 1

BATS

Deep inside the cavern, Mexican free-tailed bats were hanging up by their toes, twenty million of them. They were the largest concentration of warm-blooded animals in the world. At dusk, all twenty million would fly out to feed, in a living volcano scientists call an emergence.

Diane Ackerman,
The Moon by Whale Light

FOLKLORE

Because bats are active at night, their lives can seem mysterious. Their faces, which sometimes have enlarged ears and bizarre noses, as well as their habit of hanging upside down, add to the eerie mystique associated with these mammals.

We use the expression "blind as a bat" when, in fact, bats have perfectly good eyesight. This misconception may have been reinforced by the fact that bats can maneuver in complete darkness by using echolocation. This ability (which, according to one superstition, is due to a special quality of the bat's blood) may have led to the belief that eating bats improves eyesight.

Bats flying into the house are sure to bring bedbugs with them, or even worse, bad luck. Or it may mean that you are going to move out. But catch a bat in your hat, and good luck will follow. A bat's blood brings luck at romance and cards, and an especially serious gambler might tie the heart of a bat to his sleeve.

Bats have been used in heraldry as the symbol of watchfulness in Spain. Legend has it that a bat once perched on the helmet of King James I, who included the bat in his standards.

Don't ever let a bat get into your hair. You won't be able to get it out unless your mother cuts all your hair off—or, according to another superstition, until it thunders. In the Middle Ages it was believed that if a bat became entangled in a woman's hair, only a man could extricate it. In a curious switch on bats giving us all this trouble with hair, if you eat an Old World fruit bat, it will cure baldness.

Bats are weather predictors, swooping low to the ground in the hours preceding a storm and fluttering about in your house, making a great racket, when rain is at hand. Bats are ghosts, their ghoulish images a must at Halloween. One bat was a god, ruling the underground of the Mayans. This terrifying creature had the body of a human and the head and wings of a bat. Bats are messengers, the connection between the traditional Navajos and the gods, and even money—a "bat-wing" in the Texas backwoods is a dollar bill that has become crumpled and limp from being in circulation for a long time.

In Chinese art five bats represent the blessings of health, long life, prosperity, love of virtue, and a peaceful death. Ancient Chinese scholars thought bats lived to old age because they "swallowed their breath" in the deep, dark caves. In many places in the Far East, the bat is the symbol of happiness and family unity. The bat is also a symbol of the union of light and darkness, denoting that some life-and-death struggle is at hand.

Perhaps the most troubling superstitions about bats—based, as they are on an element of truth—are that they carry rabies and drink blood. All mammals, including bats, can become ill with rabies. But most rabid bats probably die within a few days of becoming infected, and you are about 13 times more likely to get rabies from a dog or cat than from a bat. If you are one of the rare people bitten by a bat or other mammal, see your doctor for treatment.

Only three species of bats—out of more than 900 species worldwide—are vampire bats. In their habitat in Central and South America, vampire bats make small wounds in birds and mammals (rarely in people) and lap up the blood. No vampire bats live in the United States or Canada.

And as far as that pesky habit that bats supposedly have of getting into our hair, bats are not attracted to anybody's hair. Bats tend to be quite shy and make more of an effort to avoid people than approach them.

> ## *Bats*
>
> *Bat! Bat! Come under my hat,*
> *And I'll give you a slice of bacon,*
> *But don't bring none of your old bedbugs,*
> *If you don't want to get forsaken.*
>
> African-American rhyme

NATURAL HISTORY

Bats, the only mammals that can truly fly, are in the scientific order Chiroptera (debunking the belief that they are rodents, of the order Rodentia). This name means "hand-wing" and describes the bat's "finger bones," which are elongated and connected with membranes to form wings, the bat's most distinctive feature.

There are two main groups of bats: the Megachiroptera (the large Old World fruit bats and flying foxes found in the tropics) and the Microchiroptera (generally smaller bats found nearly worldwide). All the bats in the United States and Canada are in the group Microchiroptera.

> ## *The Bat*
>
> *By day the bat is cousin to the mouse.*
> *He likes the attic of an aging house.*
> *His fingers make a hat about his head.*
> *His pulse beat is so slow we think him dead.*
> *He loops in crazy figures half the night*
> *Among the trees that face the corner light.*
> *But when he brushes up against a screen,*
> *We are afraid of what our eyes have seen:*
> *For something is amiss or out of place*
> *When mice with wings can wear a human face.*
>
> Theodore Roethke, *Collected Poems*
> (Reprinted by permission of the publisher.)

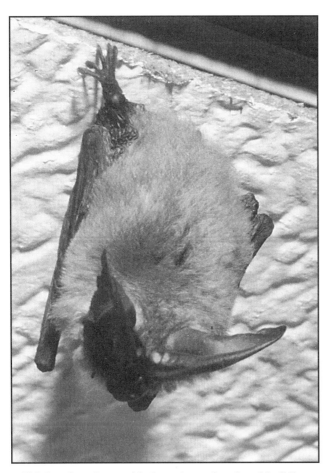

This bat, hanging upside down in an abandoned building, is one of the many bats in the genus *Myotis*.

Description

All bats possess wings. A few tropical species have wingspans of about 6 feet (1.8m), but most bats are on the small side. For example, the biggest bats in the United States weigh only about one-tenth of a pound (45g).

All the bats found in the United States and Canada use echolocation—a process of producing a high-pitched burst of sound and then analyzing the sound's echo—for activities such as avoiding objects and finding prey. Some of the strange facial features—elongated ears, "leaf" noses, and so on—are thought to be involved in echolocation.

Just before a hungry bat closes in on an insect or other prey, it increases the number of calls, allowing it to home in on its meal. Many insects, however, can hear the echolocation calls and take evasive action. A praying mantis in flight can hear ultrasonic bat calls. When the calls are far away, the mantis may ignore them. However, the closer the ultrasonic calls, the more vigorous the mantis's maneuvers to get out of range. Within a fraction of a second, a frightened mantis can go into a nearly vertical dive. Other insects, such as tiger moths, even make their own clicking sounds when they hear a bat's echolocation calls. At least some of these moths taste bad, so perhaps bats learn to avoid the moths (and their noise) because of their taste.

In the desert Southwest, lesser long-nosed bats seek other food: the nectar and fruits of saguaro, organ-pipe cactus, and agave. The organ-pipe cactus is particularly dependent on pollination by bats, since its flowers open at dusk and close in the morning. Later in the season, the bats feast on the ripe cactus fruits and disperse seeds in their droppings.

Although bats may mate in autumn or late winter, depending on the species, the females don't necessarily become pregnant immediately. Instead, the females of some species store the sperm for a time in a sort of suspended animation. Mexican free-tailed bats, for example, mate in late winter. After mating, the females migrate north, flying as high as 10,000 feet (3,050m) and traveling an average of 40 miles (65km) per hour until they reach their maternity colonies. Here, the sperm is activated and the four-month-long pregnancy begins. In other species, such as the California leaf-nosed bat, the egg is fertilized but develops very slowly at first.

Most female bats produce only a single pup each year, although in some species, such as the red bat, multiple births are typical. Relative to its mother's size, a baby bat can be *big*—up to 25 or 30 percent of the mother's weight. For humans, this would be like a 120-pound (54kg) woman having a 30- or 40-pound (13.6-18.1kg) baby.

Because bats are mammals, the mothers produce milk to nurse their young. A mother bat returning to nurse her pup can simply return to the area she left her baby if she belongs to a species of bat that roosts alone. In large maternity colonies, or crèches, however, where there can be thousands of baby bats per square yard (meter), the mother bat needs additional help to find *her* baby. Bat pups living in these situations make distinctive calls that their mothers recognize. Up close, the mother can detect her pup by its odor.

Baby bats grow quickly. Within three weeks, little brown bats begin flying; big brown bats require about a month. With luck, a bat may live many years. Several species live longer than 10 years; one little brown bat survived in the wild for more than 30 years.

Bats need protection from cold weather, so they often migrate with the seasons. For some species, migration is a simple exchange of a summer roosting site for a more protected hibernation site. North American bats have been recorded as migrating for distances up to about 300 miles (480km) to hibernation sites north, east, and west—as well as south—of their summer homes. Their destination is a suitable hibernation site rather than a direction. Possibly the longest bat migration is that of Brazilian free-tailed bats from a summer roosting site in the San Luis Valley of Colorado to Mexico, a distance of about 1,000 miles (1,600km). Details of migration for many species simply aren't known.

A hibernating bat allows its body temperature to drop, a strategy that saves energy over the long, cold winter. The heart that beats at a rate of 13,000 times per minute when in flight slows to perhaps 10 beats per minute during hibernation.

Hibernation can be dangerous. If a hibernation site is too warm, the bat uses up its stored fat too soon and dies. If a hibernation site is too cold, the bat may freeze to death. Up to 50 percent of young bats die during their first winter. The best hibernation sites in cold areas have high humidity and temperatures just above freezing. Even in areas as far north as Indiana, little brown bats, northern bats, and pipistrelles are sometimes active during winter, although they don't feed until spring.

Range

The tropics has the greatest number of bat species, but bats occur throughout the world, absent only from polar regions and very dry deserts. About 40 of the world's 900 bat species live in the United States and Canada. Hawaii, because of its remote location, has a single bat species, as does southwest Labrador, Canada. California is home to about 25 bat species.

Interactions

In southern Montana, the bat is the mascot for a local high school. The name of the town? Belfry.

Such examples of friendly feelings toward bats are rare in North America, where few other animals have the evil reputations associated with bats. This is unfortunate, both for bats and for us, since bats have an important role in controlling flying insects—including pests such as mosquitos. Bats, especially mothers with young, need to eat between 30 and 50 percent of their weight nightly. That's a lot of insects. If we add to this the value of guano—bat droppings—as a fertilizer, the bat might better be a symbol of health and prosperity, as it is in China.

Guano has also been used as an ingredient in gunpowder, and even bats themselves have been used for destructive purposes. A project during World War II investigated using bats as part of a secret weapon. A small group of people working on the "bat bomb" tested whether bats could be dropped from airplanes and dependably carry small fire-starting devices into enemy buildings. At one time, the plan involved dropping as many as a million bats—all carrying napalm with a time-controlled ignition system—over cities in Japan. The bat bomb project was discontinued in 1944. The next year, another type of bomb, this one based on atoms, was dropped on the Japanese cities of Hiroshima and Nagasaki.

In many parts of the world, such as Thailand, the Mariana Islands in the West Pacific, and along Africa's Ivory Coast, local people consider bats a delicacy—especially the fruit bats or "flying foxes"—and have caused the bat population to decline from overhunting. Throughout North America, bat populations have also declined. Some of the reasons for vanishing bats may include:

- Destroyed habitats, including deforestation and destruction or pollution of roosting sites. Clearing trees from land has obvious consequences for bat species that only forage or roost in forests. Quarrying or sealing caves can exclude bats from roost sites outright. Groundwater changes can alter cave temperature and humidity regimes, which can also make them useless as bat roost sites.

- Reduced insect populations from the use of pesticides, which in turn affect bat populations. Bats accumulate pesticides in their bodies after eating insects exposed to pesticides. Newly weaned, migrating, and hibernating bats are particularly susceptible to pesticide poisoning.

- Disturbed roosting sites, for example, explorers visit caves used by bats. Maternity colonies and hibernation sites are particularly sensitive to this kind of disturbance.

These problems have contributed to endangering several North American bat species, including the gray bat (*Myotis grisescens*), Hawaiian hoary bat (*Lasiurus cinereus semotus*), Indiana bat (*Myotis sodalis*), Mexican long-nosed bat (*Leptonycteris nivalis*), Ozark big-eared bat (*Plecotus townsendii ingens*), Virginia big-eared bat (*Plecotus townsendii virginianus*), and Sanborn's long-nosed bat (*Leptonycteris sanborni*).

Some bat populations continue to decline; others appear to be on the rise. For example, in West Virginia, bat grates and other ways of protecting bats have helped Virginia big-eared bat populations increase.

Bat biologists use a variety of techniques to study bats. One basic study technique is simply determining whether bats occur in an area, such as a cave or abandoned mine. By using a bat detector—a device that translates the bat's ultrasonic signal into a range that human ears can hear—people can listen for bats even if they are in situations where they can't see the bats.

Another basic technique involves counting bats in roost areas to determine their numbers. Biologists sometimes videotape bats leaving caves or other roost areas and use a computer program to count the bats. This method is very useful for counting large numbers—sometimes millions—of bats. Information from individual bats is useful too. When caught in fine nets called mist nets, bat species can be identified, the gender determined, and so on. Biologists also track individual bats with radio transmitters that give information about how far bats travel when they forage, the types of habitats they use, and other activities.

In a 1991 survey of human deaths caused by wildlife, bats didn't even make the list, which was headed by deer, bees, and dogs. Rather than fearing bats, we should admire them for their unique abilities and the role they play in ecosystems.

BAT ACTIVITIES

1. Look for bats in your neighborhood. During dusk and at night, you can often see bats fluttering around streetlights, where they go to catch the insects attracted to the light.

2. Learn more about bats by visiting places where they live. One famous place is Carlsbad Caverns National Park in New Mexico, where you can watch bats emerge from the mouth of the cavern at dusk. This park also schedules an annual breakfast for visitors to watch the bats returning to the cave in the morning. In Austin, Texas, an estimated one million bats live under the Congress Avenue bridge. And a new Texas park, the Kickapoo Cavern State Park, contains a cave used by migrating bats.

3. Contact a local museum or your state's wildlife department to see if they sponsor any bat conservation projects. For example, the Colorado Division of Wildlife organizes volunteers into teams to survey inactive mines for bats. Because inactive mines are hazards for people, they need to be sealed. However, these mines sometimes provide important habitats for bats. By sealing off mines that don't contain bats and using the more expensive bat grates for mines with bat populations, the Division of Wildlife and other agencies are able to protect both bats and people.

4. Consider installing a bat house in your yard. Although relatively few bats appear to use bat houses, perhaps over time more will. Bat Conservation International and several garden supply companies sell bat dwellings.

5. Make a contribution to Bat Conservation International, Inc., P.O. Box 162603, Austin, TX 78716.

6. When bats are causing problems by roosting in a home, wait until they are gone before "bat-proofing" the building. Watch to see where bats exit, then seal cracks or install netting. Do not use chemicals to try to kill the bats—effective chemicals would be dangerous to you, too.

7. We use many similes in the English language that involve animals, for example, wise as an owl, smart as a fox, hungry as a bear. We know that the "blind as a bat" simile doesn't reflect the truth because bats are not blind. Invent a better simile using the bat. Research similes that use animals in their comparisions; then find out enough about the natural history of the animals so that you can tell whether the simile is a good one.

8. Some bats eat enormous amounts of insects in comparision to their own body weight. A 45-gram bat may eat a third of its body weight in insects. If you were to eat the same amount of food relative to your body weight, calculate how many hot dogs, pizzas, or any other foods that would represent.

9. Of the over 900 species of bats in the world, only three are blood eaters—vampires—yet much of the traditional dislike that people seem to have for all bats stems from the literary and movie depiction of the myths concerning vampires (people who feed on human blood and turn into bats at night). Read about Count Dracula and catalog the movies that use this theme as their basis.

From *Of Bugs and Beasts*. © 1995. Teacher Ideas Press. (800) 237-6124.

10. Batman is a mythical superhero who began as a comic book character and was later portrayed on television and in the movies. Why did Bruce Wayne find bats so fascinating? Why do you think the creator of Batman chose the bat as the motif in the making of the superhero? What qualities of the bat make that a good choice? Try to determine whether the recent popularity of the Batman character has made bats more likable.

11. Pretend you are a journalist and interview a bat, a friend who has agreed to play the part. Both of you should do enough research to make the interview realistic. Ask questions you think reporters might ask, questions that the reading public might find interesting, and write your report as if it were a feature article for a newspaper.

12. Bats in the suborder Microchiroptera weigh only about 40 grams on the average. You can get an idea of how heavy that is by holding eight U.S. nickels in your hand (each nickel has a mass of about five grams). Find other things in your environment that have about the same mass. Make a list of them.

13. Bats in the suborder Microchiroptera have the ability to locate objects in their environment using echolocation. Echolocation is something like radar or sonar. High-frequency sounds are made by the bats; these sounds reflect off objects in the environment and return to the bats' ears so that bats get a "picture" of what lies ahead. People have some ability to echolocate, though certainly not as well as bats. Try your ability to echolocate. Go outside near a building, and have a friend blindfold you and turn you around several times so that you no longer know where the building is. Use a sound or whistle to see if you can locate the building by listening to the echo. If you are successful, try smaller targets. Do you think you could improve with practice?

14. Find a book on oriental paper folding and make an origami bat.

An origami bat.

From *Of Bugs and Beasts*. © 1995. Teacher Ideas Press. (800) 237-6124.

BIBLIOGRAPHY

Books

Ackerman, Diane. 1991. *The Moon by Whale Light*. New York: Random House, 249 pp.
   In the first chapter, "In Praise of Bats," we tag along with poet Diane Ackerman as she tags along with Merlin Tuttle, one of the world's foremost bat experts.

Cannon, Janell. 1993. *Stellaluna*. New York: Harcourt Brace Jovanovich.
   After she falls headfirst into a bird's nest, a baby bat is raised like a bird until she is reunited with her mother.

Couffer, Jack. 1992. *Bat Bomb: World War II's Other Secret Weapon*. Austin, Tex.: University of Texas Press, 252 pp.
   The author was among the participants researching the use of bats as a means of starting fires in enemy cities during World War II.

Dewey, Jennifer Owings. 1991. "Tent-Making Bats." In *Animal Architecture,* 52-53. New York: Orchard Books.
   Discusses the hanging tents made by a small white fruit-eating bat.

Fenton, M. Brock. 1992. *Bats*. New York: Facts on File, 207 pp.
   Summarizes current information on bat life.

Greenaway, Frank. 1991. *Amazing Bats*. New York: Knopf, Eyewitness Junior Books.
   A real-life look at the amazing but true behavior of bats. The photographs are outstanding.

Greer, Gery, and Bob Ruddick. 1993. *Jason and the Escape from Bat Planet*. Illustrated by Blanche L. Sims. New York: HarperCollins.
   The Intergalactic Troubleshooting Team is back heading toward the Bat Planet, which is the home of the Demon Bats of Bluggax.

Hall, Katy, and Lisa Eisenberg. 1993. *Batty Riddles*. Illustrated by Nicole Rubel. New York: Dial.
   "Which bat knows its ABC's? The alpha-bat!" This is a sample of the riddles found in this collection.

Horowitz, Ruth. 1991. *Bat Time*. Illustrations by Susan Avishai. New York: Four Winds Press.
   Before Leila goes to bed, she shares a special moment with her father, watching bats enjoying an insect feast in the backyard.

Lovett, Sarah. 1991. *Extremely Weird Bats*. Santa Fe, N.M.: John Muir Publications.
   Includes a detailed and entertaining description of the bat along with full-color photographs. Intended to instill a greater awareness of and respect for the wonderful variety of life on our planet.

Norman, Howard. 1990. "Ayas'e and the Origin of Bats." In *Northern Tales: Traditional Stories of Eskimo and Indian Peoples*, 86-87. New York: Pantheon.

An Ojibwa story about how two blind old women who were cannibals in the shape of monster bats were defeated by an Ayas'e man. He took their bodies and cut them up into small pieces and threw them into the air, and they sailed off. They were transformed into small bats as we see them today.

Pringle, Laurence. 1982. *Vampire Bats*. New York: Morrow Junior Books.

This book describes the behavior of three species of small blood-eating bats of the leaf-nose family found in Mexico, Central America, and South America.

Roethke, Theodore. 1966. *Collected Poems*. Garden City, N.Y.: Doubleday, 274pp.

Schlein, Miriam. 1982. *Millions of Bats*. Illustrated by Walter Kessell. New York: Lippincott.

Discusses several unusual varieties of the more than 800 different kinds of bats, such as the vampire bat, the flying fox, the tomb bat, and the sword-nosed bat.

Stuart, Dee. 1994. *Bats: Mysterious Flyers of the Night*. Minneapolis, Minn.: Carolrhoda Books.

Wonderful photos enhance the text in this natural history book.

Articles

Adams, Rick A., and Scott C. Pedersen. 1994. Wings on Their Fingers. *Natural History* 103(1):48-55. (January)

This article describes the growth and development of young bats.

Backhouse, Frances. 1992. Winged Victory. *Nature Canada* 21(3):44-48. (Summer)

The author describes the natural history of bats, with comments on Canadian species.

Ezzell, Carol. 1992. Cave Creatures. *Science News* 141(6):88-90.

The author describes the Mexican free-tailed bats of Bracken Cave, near San Antonio, Texas.

McCracken, Gary F. 1984. Communal Nursing in Mexican Free-Tailed Bat Maternity Colonies. *Science* 223(4640):1090-91.

A technical article describing how scientists determined that mother bats could find their own pups in crowded communal maternity colonies.

McCracken, Gary F., and Mary K. Gustin. 1987. Batmom's Daily Nightmare. *Natural History* 96(10):66-73. (October)

Includes photos showing the incredible densities reached by bats in maternity colonies of the Mexican free-tailed bat.

Suga, Nobuo. 1990. Biosonar and Neural Computation in Bats. *Scientific American* 262(6):60-66, 68. (June)

This article describes how bats create and interpret the signals they use for echolocation.

Tuttle, Merlin D. 1984. Harmless, Highly Beneficial, Bats Still Get a Bum Rap. *Smithsonian* 14(10):74-81. (January)
Tuttle, a world-renowned bat expert, describes poaching of bats in Thailand.

―――. 1991. Bats: The Cactus Connection. *National Geographic* 179(6):130 40.
Wonderful photographs and an interesting article show how saguaro and other cacti depend on bats for pollination and seed dispersal.

Whitaker, John O. Jr., and Leslie J. Rissler. 1992. Winter Activity of Bats at a Mine Entrance in Vermillion County, Indiana. *American Midland Naturalist* 127(1):52-59.
A technical article investigating activity of bats during winter.

Wilkinson, Gerald S. 1990. Food Sharing in Vampire Bats. *Scientific American* 262(2):76-82. (February)
This article describes how vampire bats feed (they greatly prefer horses and mules to humans) and how they share food to help one another survive.

Yager, D., and M. May. 1993. Coming in on a Wing and an Ear. *Natural History* 102(1):28-33. (January)
Discusses how a praying mantis can sense bats' ultrasonic calls and take evasive action.

Chapter 2

BUZZARDS

*What a lovely child of God it is, soarin' up
there. Of course, down on the ground it's a buzzard. Lots of things in the world seem like that.*

Bob Hines and Peter A. Anastasi
quoted in *Fifty Birds of Town and City*

FOLKLORE

The Buzzard and the Hawk

Buzzard has no sense at all. You watch him, you'll see. When the rain pours down he just sets on the fence and squinches himself up. He will draw in his neck and try to hide his head and look so pitiful that you really feel sorry for him. He half cries and says to himself. "Never mind, when this rain is over I'm going to build a house right off. I'm not going to let the rain lick me this way no more."

When the rain is gone and the wind blows and the sun shines, what does Buzzard do? He just sets on the top of the dead pine tree so the sun can warm him and he stretches out his wings and he turns around and round so the wind can dry his feathers and he laughs to himself, "The rain is over. It ain't going to rain no more. No use for me to build a house now."

Now one day Buzzard and Hawk were sitting up in the pine tree and the Hawk asks Buzzard, "How do you get your living, Brer Buzzard?"

Buzzard turned his head and found some feathers on his side to straighten. "I do pretty good, Brer Hawk. I just have to wait on the gifts of the Lord."

"Humph," sneered Hawk. "I don't wait for the mercy of anybody. I take mine."

"Well now, Brer Hawk," drawled Buzzard, "I'll live to pick your bones."

"No way, never, Brer Buzzard!" said Hawk. "Watch me get my living right now!" Hawk spied a sparrow sitting on a dead limb of a tree and he sailed off and dived straight down at that sparrow. The end of the limb was sticking out and he ran his breast right up on the sharp point and hung there. The sparrow flew right past him.

After a while Hawk got so weak he knew he was going to die. Buzzard flew past just so—flying slow you know, and said, "See here, Brer Hawk. I told you I was going to live to pick your bones. I wait for the gifts of the Lord."

And that's the way it is with some people!!

African-American folklore
Adapted and retold by Norma J. Livo

13

> *If you see a buzzard*
> *And don't see two,*
> *You'll soon see someone*
> *You're not expecting to.*
> —old folk rhyme

Buzzards are celebrated in modern folklore in Hinckley, Ohio, a small community between Cleveland and Akron. According to local legend, the buzzards began coming to Hinckley in 1818 after hunters killed "varmints"—bears, foxes, and wolves. The buzzards, attracted by the smell of the dead varmints, gathered for their natural work on the cleanup crew. Crowds are anticipated for the annual return of the buzzards in mid-March and the local Chamber of Commerce sponsors a Buzzard Day breakfast in honor of the event.

The Romans held that vultures were valued by the god of war, Mars. Perhaps they served him in their time-honored capacity as cleanup crew. A vulture was used by Apollo to punish Tityus, one of the race of giants who warred against the gods. Having assaulted a goddess, he was killed and sent to Tartarus, where his body covered nine acres. While his immense form stretches over these nine acres, a vulture preys upon his liver, which grows again as fast as it is devoured, thereby guaranteeing a punishment that will have no end.

A Hopi legend explains why the buzzard is bald. This story begins before the sun, before the moon, in the beginning of time. The sun was being raised in the sky and it became stuck before it had reached its proper height. Its heat was too intense and too great for the people to survive, and many desperate attempts were made to push it higher in the sky. They all ended in failure until the buzzard flew aloft. Instantly all the feathers on his head were burned away, but the buzzard refused to give up. Fighting the terrible pain and the sickening smell of his own feathers burning, he eased the sun slowly higher and higher until it was at last where it is today. Since then, buzzards have never been able to grow feathers on their heads.

The Russian writer Valery Carick (1869-1942) never tired of hearing folktales. As soon as he was old enough he made drawings of the story characters, and when he was 40 years old, he wrote down the tales he remembered. One such story explains why the jaguar always leaves a piece of whatever beast he kills for the buzzard. This story, "The Crab and the Jaguar," can be found in Valery Carick's *Picture Folk-Tales*, illustrated by the author.

Another buzzard story comes from African folklore. Nat "King" Cole first heard the story from his father, a Baptist minister in Montgomery, Alabama. In 1943 he wrote and recorded "Straighten Up and Fly Right," based on the story. Here is a part of that song:

> *A buzzard took a monkey for a ride in the air,*
> *The monkey thought that everything was on the square,*
> *The buzzard tried to throw the monkey off his back,*
> *But the monkey grabbed his neck and said, "Now listen Jack;"*
> *Straighten up and fly right,*
> *Straighten up and fly right,*
> *Straighten up and fly right,*
> *Cool down Poppa,*
> *Don't you blow your top!*
>
> "Straighten Up and Fly Right"
> Nat "King" Cole and Irving Mills
> ©1944. Reprinted by permission of CPP/Belwin, Inc.

NATURAL HISTORY

The term *buzzard* was brought from Europe, where it refers to a group of birds called buzzard hawks. However, American folk culture has adopted the word to mean our large carrion feeders—the widely distributed turkey vulture (*Cathartes aura*), the less common black vulture (*Cathartes atratus*), and the nearly extinct California condor (*Gymnogyps californianus*). *Cathartes*, the genus name for turkey and black vulture, comes from a Greek word for cleanser.

Description

With a wingspan of nearly 6 feet (1.8m), the turkey vulture approaches the size of an eagle. Black vultures are somewhat smaller. In comparison, the rare California condor has the greatest wingspan of any North American bird, up to 9.5 feet (2.9m).

Adult turkey vultures have bald red heads. In fact, they are called turkey vultures because the skin on their heads looks somewhat like that on a turkey. Black vultures and immature turkey vultures have black heads. California condors have yellow or orange heads. Buzzards' heads lack feathers— probably because their choice of meals makes bare skin easier to keep clean—so buzzard heads appear smaller than those of the hawks and eagles.

The turkey vulture has the largest range of North America's three "buzzards."

Buzzards often stretch their wings in the morning sun, warming themselves while they wait for thermals to develop. Thermals are bodies of warm air, and large thermals often develop near cliffs. Because warm air rises, buzzards can use thermals to help them get up into the sky more easily.

During the day, buzzards are commonly seen soaring high overhead, barely twitching a feather for hours at a time while they silently glide through the air. From below, turkey vultures have a two-toned wing with dark front parts and lighter rear margins. Black vultures have white patches near their wingtips. California condors have striking white markings on the underside of the wings.

When one buzzard locates food, other buzzards are likely to follow. Turkey vultures have keen eyesight but also use their sense of smell to detect the dead animals on which they feed. Our habits of driving at high speeds have ensured a ready supply of carrion on roads.

Buzzards lack the lyric vocalizations of other birds, restricting themselves to hissing and grunting when disturbed. When severely harassed, they resort to the truly nasty behavior of regurgitating their already aromatic food at the harasser—and they have good aim. During hot weather, vultures may defecate on their legs—the evaporation of the moisture helps them cool off.

Buzzards often roost together. Gettysburg, Pennsylvania, is famous among birders not only as a Civil War battlefield but also as a winter roosting area for black and turkey vultures. Between 500 and 900 buzzards use a roost area at Big Round Top, near the southern end of the battlefield. During the summer, both buzzard species also nest in the area.

Both turkey and black vultures nest on ledges, in hollow logs, or on the ground. Each summer the female lays one to three dull white eggs with chocolate-colored blotches. Males and females share the five or six weeks of incubation duty. Downy turkey vulture hatchlings are white; dark down covers black vulture hatchlings. By August the young buzzards molt and begin to fly. Young turkey vultures' dark heads don't develop the characteristic red coloring until the second year. Buzzards can live for 20 to 30 years.

Range

Turkey vultures are our most common buzzard and migrate as far north as Canada for the summer. Their distinctive soaring forms can be seen year-round in the southern United States. Less common than turkey vultures, black vultures occupy the southeastern United States and range as far west as southern Arizona.

The rare California condor has the most restricted range; at this time, only a few young condors soar in the skies of southern California. Their range used to be more extensive; condor fossils have been found as far away as New York and Florida.

Interactions

The American pioneers of aviation, Wilbur and Orville Wright, prepared for their historic flight at Kitty Hawk, North Carolina, by observing, among other birds, the buzzards. Rather than making a machine that would go flapping through the sky, the Wright brothers intended to build a machine that would allow them to soar. In November, 1900, Wilbur wrote: "Kitty Hawk is a splendid place to observe soaring flight. I think at least a hundred buzzards, eagles, ospreys, and hawks made their home within a half mile of our camp. We were enabled to make a number of observations and settle conclusively to our minds some points which have been much disputed among writers on the soaring problem."[1] By observing creatures designed to soar, the Wright brothers were able to construct the first successful heavier-than-air flying machine.

Although related to eagles, hawks, and falcons, buzzards are not held in the same high regard as their feathered relatives. In fact, Florida once attempted to pass a law to permit the destruction of buzzards on the unlikely grounds that they spread hog cholera.

Sometimes hunters set out carrion to attract bears or other animals to traps. However, buzzards and other carrion-feeding animals may be caught. The California condor, already in decline from habitat loss and being shot, has suffered from feeding on carrion contaminated by lead from bullets or poisoned as bait for coyotes. In order to protect the remaining birds, biologists captured all the wild California condors by 1987 to set up a captive breeding program. This program was successful enough that eight captive-bred condors were released into the wild in 1992. However, the captive-bred condors are curious about people and often land near them. Apparently the condors sometimes visited Castaic Lake near Los Angeles to watch water-skiers. On other occasions, the condors have been harassed by dogs or even shot at. Biologists recently moved the young condors to an even more remote location.

In the 1930s, engineers for natural gas companies pumped ethyl mercaptan into pipelines so that they could find leaks in the pipeline simply by looking for turkey vultures. These birds can detect the smelly chemical—the same chemical produced by rotting flesh—and would fly over to investigate the source.

Buzzards normally feed on dead animals. However, a flock of about 200 black vultures in northern Virginia has been acting much more aggressive than normal. An Associated Press report from February 20, 1994, claimed that these birds have been attacking ducks and domestic animals, including horses, dogs, and cats. Bird experts consider this very unusual behavior.

Because turkey vultures usually don't prey on living rodents or other small mammals, these animals may learn to ignore soaring birds that look like turkey vultures. The zone-tailed hawk, a raptor of Arizona, New Mexico, and western Texas, closely resembles the turkey vulture in appearance. By mimicking the turkey vulture, a zone-tailed hawk may have the opportunity to approach—and capture—a prairie dog or other animal that is used to turkey vultures.

Whether a solitary turkey vulture stands in the shimmering desert heat over a bullsnake killed by a passing car, or a crowd of a dozen or more flocks around a fallen, bloated steer, buzzards provide valuable ecosystem services by removing and recycling carrion. Just as a human community suffers when labor disputes result in cancellation of local garbage collection, our ecosystems might become overwhelmed by dead, rotting animals if buzzards didn't help with the cleanup.

BUZZARD ACTIVITIES

1. Go places where you can see buzzards:

    Visit a local museum or zoo and see if they have an exhibit on buzzards (turkey vultures, black vultures, or California condors). In Kansas, you can visit the Milford Conservation Education Center (near Junction City) to see a turkey vulture up close. Make a list of the features that you notice most on these birds: size, color, and so on. How are buzzards like their relatives, the eagles and hawks? How are they different?

    Take a pair of binoculars with you when you visit state parks or other natural areas that might have buzzards. Look for buzzards in the sky during the day. See if you can tell the difference between buzzards, with their smaller heads, and other soaring birds like hawks.

    Contact a bird-watching group, such as a local chapter of the Audubon Society, and go on a bird-watching field trip.

    Visit Hinckley, Ohio, for their Buzzard Day festival in mid-March. Contact the Hinckley Chamber of Commerce at P.O. Box 354, Hinckley, OH 44233.

2. For more information, contact the Vulture Study Group, c/o the Center for the Study of Tropical Birds, 218 Conway Drive, San Antonio, TX 78209-1716.

3. Buzzards serve a very useful function, helping to dispose of the decaying carcasses in our environment. Most people, however, find the very idea of eating putrid flesh to be repugnant and tend to hold that against the buzzard. A buzzard has died. It is your responsibility to deliver the eulogy for its funeral. Deliver this eulogy in the presence of all the "mourners" you can find.

4. Scavengers such as buzzards and microscopic decomposers provide a much-needed cleanup service. Without scavengers and—perhaps more important—decomposers, this cleanup would not take place. Imagine what the world would be like if there were no scavengers and no decomposers. Write an account of a day in such a world.

5. The Wright brothers learned how to build an airplane partly from watching buzzards soar. How are airplane wings like buzzard wings? How are they different?

6. Visit a zoo or a museum and study the leading (front) edge of the wing of a vulture. You will notice that the shape is very much like that of the leading edge of an airplane wing. The shape of that wing is essential to flight. Hold a sheet of notebook paper on the shorter edge between your thumbs and index fingers (thumbs on top of the paper); then rotate your hands toward you slightly so that the paper rolls a bit. Next, blow gently across the paper and you will notice that the paper lifts upward. This demonstrates the Bernoulli effect. The Bernoulli principle states that a fluid (in this case, air) passing over a surface produces a partial vacuum on that surface. This partial vacuum we call lift. Without it, neither vultures nor planes could fly.

7. The sport of parasailing relies on the lift provided by a combination of wing design and thermals. If the sport is practiced in your area, watch the fliers closely. Notice that once they become airborne they do not simply lose altitude and float to the earth. At some stages in flight they gain altitude. If possible, talk with parasail pilots and ask them how they maneuver to stay in the air as they do and find out what is the longest they have stayed aloft. What determines how long they can stay in the air?

From *Of Bugs and Beasts*. © 1995. Teacher Ideas Press. (800) 237-6124.

8. Pretend that you are a talk show host. Interview a turkey vulture (buzzard), played by a friend. The vulture feels undervalued and wants to get her story out. Videotape the interview for a critique by your friends.

9. Imagine you are a buzzard, soaring above your neighborhood. Draw a picture of what you see.

10. Turkey vultures are keenly aware of rising masses of air called thermals. These large birds depend on thermals for their livelihood. The sun heats the earth, warming the air above it. That warm air rises in small or large masses. As the air mass breaks away from the cooler air around it, the outer edges of the mass are slowed, making a donut-shaped mass of air in which the center portion rises faster than the outer portion.

   The faster-rising air is known as a thermal and represents considerable energy. Vultures use air masses for sustained soaring—an almost effortless way to patrol a large area for food.

   To get an idea of the energy that comes from heating an air mass, make a whirligig as shown to the right. Cut the spiral on the lines and attach thread to the + with a piece of tape. Hold the whirligig over an illuminated lamp. Even a little heat causes the whirligig to turn, showing that energy is available in a mass of rising air.

Thermal Energy

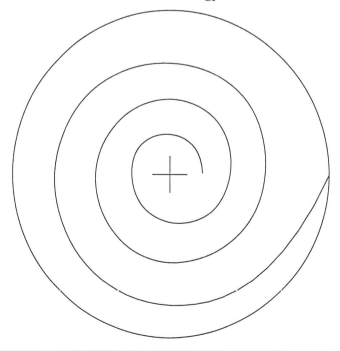

From *Of Bugs and Beasts*. © 1995. Teacher Ideas Press. (800) 237-6124.

READERS THEATRE
THE JAGUAR AND THE BUZZARD
(based upon Valery Carick's story, "The Crab and the Jaguar")

CHARACTERS:
Crab
Jaguar
Animale-Podole
Buzzard
Narrator

Narrator:
One day a crab sat on a stone playing a game with his eyes. He would say to them:

Crab:
Eyes, little eyes of mine! Fly away to the blue sea, quick-quick-quick-quick-quick!

Narrator:
And the eyes would leap from his head and fly off to the blue sea. There he would say:

Crab:
Eyes, little eyes of mine! Fly back to me from the blue sea, quick-quick-quick-quick-quick!

Narrator:
Then his eyes would come flying back and settle down again in their proper place. And in this way the crab used to play endless games and keep himself amused.

Narrator:
One day a jaguar came to that place and looked at the crab and was very much astonished and said:

Jaguar:
Whatever are you doing, my friend?

Crab:
What am I doing? I'm just having a game with my eyes. I tell them to fly away, and they fly away. Then I tell them to fly back, and they come back to their proper place.

Jaguar:
What a wonderful thing! Please do it again!

Crab:
All right! I will. Eyes, little eyes of mine! Fly away to the blue sea, quick-quick-quick-quick-quick!

Narrator:
And his eyes flew away.

Crab:

Eyes, little eyes of mine! Fly back from the blue sea, quick-quick-quick-quick-quick!

Narrator:

His eyes flew back and settled in their proper place.

Jaguar:

What a lovely game that is! Tell me, could you play it with my eyes?

Crab:

Well, yes, I could, but you know, just now, the terrible Animale-Podole, father of the Trahira-fish is swimming about in the blue sea, and I'm very much afraid he might eat your eyes!

Jaguar:

Oh, I don't suppose he will! There's not much chance of that. Anyway, I'll risk it! Come, now, do make my eyes fly away!

Crab:

Very well, I will. Eyes of Mr. Jaguar—fly away to the blue sea, quick-quick-quick-quick-quick!

Narrator:

The eyes of Jaguar leapt out of his head and flew off to the blue sea.

Jaguar:

Now tell them to come back again!

Crab:

Eyes of Mr. Jaguar! Fly back here from the blue sea, quick-quick-quick-quick-quick!

Narrator:

Jaguar's eyes came flying back and settled again in their proper place.

Jaguar:

Oh, that is really wonderfully funny! Please do it again!

Crab:

Make sure you remember I told you the terrible Animale-Podole, father of the Trahira-fish, is swimming around in the sea. If he does eat up your eyes you'll be left without any!

Jaguar:

Oh, never mind. Please do it again!

Crab:

Very well. Eyes of Mr. Jaguar! Fly away to the blue sea, quick-quick-quick-quick-quick!

From *Of Bugs and Beasts*. © 1995. Teacher Ideas Press. (800) 237-6124.

Narrator:

The Jaguar's eyes flew off again to the blue sea. It just so happened that just in that spot, and just at that time, the terrible Animale-Podole, father of the Trahira-fish, was swimming about and he saw the eyes of Jaguar.

Animale-Podole:

Look what I see. Two juicy eyes floating in the sea. What dainty morsels they will make! Slurp!

Narrator:

With that, the Animale-Podole swallowed Jaguar's eyes.

Crab:

Eyes of Mr. Jaguar! Fly back from the blue sea, quick-quick-quick-quick-quick!

Narrator:

But the eyes never flew back. The crab called to the eyes again and again but it was no good. The terrible Animale-Podole, father of the Trahira-fish, had eaten them!

Jaguar:

Where are my eyes? I am very angry with you, Crab! I think I will kill you.

Narrator:

Jaguar tried to find the crab to kill him but he couldn't. Crab crept under a stone. There was no help for the whole thing so the jaguar went off without his eyes. After he had been walking for a long time, he met buzzard.

Buzzard:

Where are you going my friend?

Jaguar:

I don't know where I'm going. That's my problem. The crab sent my eyes away to the blue sea, and there the terrible Animale-Podole, father of the Trahira-fish, swallowed them. Now I have to go about without eyes! Couldn't you make me some new ones?

Buzzard:

Yes I can but you must make a promise to me and keep it. The promise is that whatever beast you kill while hunting, always give me a share!

Jaguar:

I promise, I promise, I promise. Only make me some eyes and I promise!

Narrator:

So the buzzard made the jaguar some new eyes, even better than his old ones. Ever since then, whatever beast the jaguar kills while out hunting, he always leaves a piece for the buzzard.

—The End—

From *Of Bugs and Beasts.* © 1995. Teacher Ideas Press. (800) 237-6124.

READERS THEATRE
THE LAST DAYS OF THE CONDOR

CHARACTERS:

Narrator

Eight California Condors

Ivan	Pegasus
Bono	Doban
Sobon	Xol (the oldest)
Xonon (the youngest)	Albion

Narrator:

The scene is a high mountain ledge overlooking the San Joaquin Valley in southern California. The seven remaining condors in the wild have gathered to watch the convoy of trucks of their would-be captors snake along the valley floor. The convoy stops, people get out, and a flurry of activity begins with the workers erecting a huge net west of an open pasture. The condors speak.

Ivan:

Just look at that! See them work so hard? What do you think the uprights are doing today?

Bono:

They're up to no good. You can be sure of that.

All:

Yeah!

Sobon:

Just wait. More of us will disappear. It seems our numbers always get smaller after the uprights have worked like this.

Ivan:

So it seems. As I count, we're the only ones left. The last of a proud flock of condors that were here long before the uprights.

Xonon:

What happens to us—I mean, after we're captured by the uprights?

Ivan:

You're too young to remember much, Xonon. Your own mother was taken away by the uprights. She put up such a fight. All the screeching, clawing, and biting. I saw it all. You were still a chick then. They took Lorelei away in a big truck with a cage on the back. I soared as near as I dared, afraid that they might take me, too. I followed them to a large cage where I think I saw many of our flock. Who knows what happens after that?

From *Of Bugs and Beasts*. © 1995. Teacher Ideas Press. (800) 237-6124.

Pegasus:

Don't scare the child, Ivan. She's been through enough. At least we know her mother is alive and seems to be well-treated.

Sobon:

How can you say "well-treated" when they are taken from us never to soar again? If you are not free, can it be said that you are treated well?

Pegasus:

How well are we? We are almost to the point of starvation. We have to fly a couple of hundred miles to get any food at all and then we are lucky to find a small coyote that has died. Even then, we often get sick from the thing that killed the coyote. The days are gone when the meat supply was plentiful and we didn't have to compete so much for a meal.

Doban:

Are you saying, Pegasus, that you would trade places with your brothers and sisters captured by the uprights? Would you give up your freedom, as hard as it is to live, to the uprights?

Pegasus:

At least I could eat regularly. No, Doban, I cherish my freedom but I am beginning to see that our days are numbered, free or not.

Xol:

Don't despair, my friends. We might make a comeback yet.

Ivan:

You're senile, old man. What are you? Forty? Fortyfive? Don't you see what is happening? In your lifetime you have seen our number decrease from 40 or 50 to just the 7 of us, plus, of course, the captives in the cages. Do you really think we can make a comeback? Return to our former glory?

Xol:

Oh, we've been through a lot. We've been revered as gods, hunted as cattle killers, killed for our feathers. But, we're still here. We may not be many, but we're still here.

Doban:

For how long, old man? For how long?

Xol:

Who knows the answer to that? Maybe the uprights are helping us, taking us away to protect the precious few of us left.

Doban:

It sounds like you want to be captured like Pegasus. Why don't the two of you just fly down and right into the cages on their trucks?

Xol:

Just hold on, Doban. I'm not saying I want to be captured. I don't want to see our numbers dwindle even further, either. Look at the uprights. What are they doing now?

Ivan:

Are you also blind, old man? The uprights are taking that dead cow off their truck. They'll leave it in the field for us. Then when we land and eat some of it they'll swoop down with their nets. They don't think we know what is happening. See how they've put the carcass next to those trees? They know we'll glide in and land on the carcass. They know, too, that we'll have to take off the same way we came in. See the net they're setting up to trap us as we take off? I've seen this lots of times before.

Albion:

Oh, you're right, Ivan. That's what they're up to.

Xonon:

You mean if I fly down there the uprights will capture me and take me away? Maybe I'll get to see my mother.

Doban:

Don't even think about it, Xonon. You might get hurt. They might kill you. They might take you to a different place from your mother. You can't trust the uprights.

Pegasus:

We don't know about that, Doban. We've never seen the uprights kill any of us. They seem more concerned with our safety than our death.

Doban:

Think what you like, Pegasus. Whatever happens, I'll stay here and watch it all. You wouldn't catch me down there flying into their trap.

Narrator:

Most of the other condors seem to agree with the assessment by Doban and Ivan and are content to stay on their perches, preening themselves and considering their afternoon flight for food. Sobon agrees to soar first as a scout and to let the others know the distance and direction they will have to go for food today. Shortly after noon, Doban becomes airborne, riding the thermals to heights of over two miles.

Xonon:

I hope he finds something, enough for all of us. I am so hungry.

Bono:

Me, too. I haven't eaten for three days, at least nothing substantial. Even then, I could only find a small squirrel.

Ivan:

Just relax. Maybe today will be different. There's always that cow in the valley down there (chuckles).

Narrator:

Eventually Sobon returns. Faces fall as they refuse the bad news.

Sobon:

Nothing worth flying out for. Sorry. I saw some ravens and eagles circling to the north about 20 miles away. When I got close I could see that they were circling a small deer that already had dozens of birds on it. We'll just have to take our chances on whatever small game hasn't yet been spotted. Good luck.

Pegasus:

I'm not even going out. It takes more energy than the energy we'll get from the little bit of food we find.

Ivan:

If you keep this up, Pegasus, you'll just starve to death. Is that what you want?

Pegasus:

Is that what any of us want? We're so near the end now, I'm thinking of sampling the cow that the uprights brought.

Bono:

No, Pegasus. Our number will drop even lower. We love you and don't want to lose you.

Pegasus:

You'll lose me soon enough to starvation. Who knows? I might be able to eat some of the cow and escape too. I've sized up the situation down there. I see where their net is and I think I can gain altitude faster than they think I can. I'm going to try. Who's coming with me?

Xol:

I think I will, Pegasus. I don't really think your plan will work but I have nothing to lose.

Xonon:

Me, too. I think I'll see my mother if I'm captured. If I'm not captured at least I will have had a good meal.

Ivan:

You're all talking crazy. You don't have a chance.

Pegasus:

At least if we don't make it we won't be competing with you for food. You'll have more to eat after we're gone. But I think we'll make it.

Ivan:

Well, then, if your mind is made up, good luck!

Narrator:

The three birds take off and head straight for the carcass that has been brought by the researchers from the animal park in San Diego. As they glide in they see that only a few crows are clustered on the large body. After the long glide they land awkwardly near the carcass, scaring the crows away. They hop up on the mound of meat and begin to eat, taking in great beaks of food that begin to satisfy their great hunger. Eagerly they tear at flesh until there seems to be more bones than flesh. Warily they watch the researchers who stand about trying to hide and saying nothing. They eye the giant net that now lies on the ground but which they know will be lifted on great pulleys by the uprights when the condors start to fly away. At last, having eaten their fill, Pegasus speaks:

Pegasus:

Well, this is it. Let's make a run for it.

Narrator:

The giant wings of the three magnificent birds begin to beat furiously. Very slowly they begin to gain altitude as the researchers quickly lift the net. Just as the researchers had predicted and the condors had dreaded, it becomes obvious that the great birds are not going to clear the net. As the condors become entangled the net begins to lower. Gingerly the researchers approach the helpless birds and gently take them to the waiting trucks.

Xol:

It was worth a try. At least I'm full and I can see that the uprights mean us no harm.

Pegasus:

I have no regrets. We were doomed either way. Maybe our luck will change and we can make a comeback with the help of the uprights.

Xonon:

Maybe I'll get to see my mother again.

—The End—

—Glenn McGlathery and Norma J. Livo
Who's Endangered on Noah's Ark

From *Of Bugs and Beasts*. © 1995. Teacher Ideas Press. (800) 237-6124.

NOTES

1. John Alexander and James Lazell. *Ribbon of Sand*. Chapel Hill, N.C.: Algonquin Books, 1992, pp. 162-63.

BIBLIOGRAPHY

Books

Alexander, John, and James Lazell. 1992. *Ribbon of Sand*. Chapel Hill, N.C.: Algonquin Books, 238 pp.
    This book is about the Outer Banks of North Carolina. See the chapter "Flight" for a discussion of the Wright brothers and the development of the airplane at Kitty Hawk.

Burton, Philip. 1991. *American Nature Guides Birds of Prey*. New York: Gallery Books, 142 pp.
    This field guide gives descriptions and natural history information for raptors, including vultures.

Carick, Valery. 1967. *Picture Folk-Tales*. Illustrated by the author. New York: Dover Books.
    Included in this book is the story "Jaguar and Buzzard," pp. 72-80.

Ehrlich, P. R., D. S. Dobkin, and D. Wheye. 1992. *Birds in Jeopardy*. Stanford, Calif.: Stanford University Press, 259 pp.
    Contains an account of the California condor and other threatened and endangered birds.

McGlathery, Glenn, and Norma J. Livo. 1992. *Who's Endangered on Noah's Ark: Literary and Scientific Activities for Teachers and Parents*. Englewood, Colo.: Teacher Ideas Press.
    The readers theatre, "The Last Days of the Condor," is from pages 91-94 of this book.

Palmer, E. Laurence, and H. Seymour Fowler. 1975. *Fieldbook of Natural History*. 2d ed. New York: McGraw-Hill, 779 pp.
    This book gives brief natural histories for a wide range of plants and animals that amateur naturalists are likely to encounter.

Peterson, Roger Tory. 1980. *A Field Guide to the Birds*. Boston: Houghton Mifflin, 384 pp.
    A classic field guide to eastern and central birds.

———. 1990. *A Field Guide to Western Birds*. Boston: Houghton Mifflin, 432 pp.
    A complete field guide to western birds of the United States and Canada.

Robbins, Chandler S., Bertel Bruun, and Herbert S. Zim. 1966. *Birds of North America: A Guide to Field Identification*. New York: Golden Press, 340 pp.
    A well-organized and compact field guide to bird identification.

Stone, Lynn M. 1993. *Vultures*. Minneapolis, Minn.: Carolrhoda.
    Describes the life cycle, habitats, and reputation of both Old and New World vultures.

Wolkstein, Diane. 1973. *The Cool Ride in the Sky*. Illustrated by Paul Galdone. New York: Knopf.
    A sly buzzard is outwitted by a monkey who finds a way to protect his animal friends.

Articles

Ahrens, Carsten. 1991. The Good, the Bad, and the Ugly. *Birder's World* 5(2):20-23. (April)
Describes nesting and other aspects of buzzard life, including the annual Buzzard Day at Hinckley, Ohio.

Bonta, Marcia. 1990. The Vultures of Gettysburg. *WildBird* 4(2):47-50. (February)
The author describes the interactions between black vultures and turkey vultures at a famous winter roosting site.

Buzzards Terrorize Va. County. 1994. *The Denver Post*, Sunday, February 20, p. 2A.
Describes recent attacks on ducks, dogs, and other domestic animals by a flock of about 200 black vultures.

Caughlan, Rob, Kathryn Simon, and David Oke. 1992. Return of the Condor. *Outdoor California* 53(2):7-9. (March-April)
Discusses the captive-breeding program for the California condor.

Lampe, G. Michael. 1990. The Day Shift, The Night Shift and the Garbage Man. *Missouri Conservationist* 51(3):14-19. (March)
Even though hawks, owls, and vultures are raptors, they have very different adaptations.

Regional News. 1993. *Endangered Species Technical Bulletin* 17(12):2, 13.
The news from Region 1 describes the release of captive-bred California condors and the establishment of a new breeding facility.

Schneider, Dan. 1992. Guess Who's Coming to Dinner? *Nature Canada* 21(2):35-41. (Spring)
This article describes the natural history of the turkey vulture and reasons for its range expansion into Canada.

Silovsky, Pat. 1991. The Carrion Crew. *Kansas Wildlife & Parks* 48(4):36-40. (July-August)
This article provides information about the natural history of American vultures.

Thompson, William L., Richard H. Yahner, and Gerald Storm. 1990. Winter Use and Habitat Characteristics of Vulture Communal Roosts. *Journal of Wildlife Management* 54(1):77-83.
Examines the characteristics of roosts used in the winter by turkey vultures and black vultures in southern Pennsylvania.

Toops, Connie. 1991. Coming Home. *Birder's World* 5(6):12-16. (December)
Discusses efforts to save the California condor and reintroduce it into the wild.

Willis, E. O. 1963. Is the Zone-Tailed Hawk a Mimic of the Turkey Vulture? *Condor* 65:313-17.

Tapes and Compact Disks

"Straighten Up and Fly Right," from *The Nat King Cole Story*. Capitol compact discs or cassette tapes. Hollywood, Calif.: Capitol Records, #95129, 1991.
Nat King Cole sings the song he wrote in 1943 after his father told him the story of the buzzard and the monkey.

Chapter **3**

MOTHS

One night a moth flew into the candle, was caught, burnt dry, and held. . . . All that was left was the glowing horn shell of her abdomen and thorax—a fraying, partially collapsed gold tube jammed upright in the candle's round pool.

Annie Dillard, *Holy the Firm*

FOLKLORE

The Moth and the Star

A young and impressionable moth once set his heart on a certain star. He told his mother about this and she counseled him to set his heart on a bridge lamp instead. "Stars aren't the thing to hang around," she said; "Lamps are the thing to hang around." "You'll get somewhere that way," said the moth's father. "You don't get anywhere chasing stars." But the moth would not heed the words of either parent. Every evening at dusk when the star came out he would start flying toward it and every morning at dawn he would crawl back home worn out with his vain endeavor. One day his father said to him, "You haven't burned a wing in months, boy, and it looks to me as if you are never going to. All your brothers have been badly burned flying around street lamps and all your sisters have been terribly singed flying around house lamps. Come on, now, get out of here and get yourself scorched! A big strapping moth like you without a mark on him!"

The moth left his father's house, but he would not fly around street lamps and he would not fly around house lamps. He went right on trying to reach the star, which was four and one-third light years, or twenty-five-trillion miles, away. The moth thought it was just caught in the top branches of an elm. He never did reach the star, but he went right on trying, night after night, and when he was a very, very old moth he began to think that he really had reached the star and he went around saying so. This gave him a deep and lasting pleasure, and he lived to a great old age. His parents and his brothers and his sisters had all been burned to death when they were quite young.

Moral: Who flies afar from the sphere of our sorrow is here today and here tomorrow.

—James Thurber, *Fables for Our Time*
(©1940 James Thurber; ©1968 Helen Thurber.
Published by Harper & Row.)

31

Many people associate moths with death. In Colombia, for example, spirits of ancestors visit in the form of a large, white moth. In Europe, the large Death's-head moth has markings that resemble a skull and crossbones and is considered an omen of death.

In Navajo folklore, contact with moths can result in "moth madness"; symptoms are fainting, trembling, and seizures. According to the Mothway legend of the Navajo, a god named Begochidi acted as both male and female to the butterfly people. When Begochidi left them, the butterfly people began to commit incest, or "go wild." To this day, moths exhibit this wild behavior by flying into flames.

Some Asian moths feed on nothing but the eye liquids of cattle, deer, or elephants. Because of this, they are referred to as vampire moths.

A little bean moth lays its eggs inside the seeds of a shrub that grows in Mexico. The caterpillar, protected by the growing seed, uses it as food. The caterpillar eventually develops into a pupa, resulting in a "Mexican jumping bean" that twitches whenever the moth pupa inside the bean moves.

A group of strong flying moths has several names, including hummingbird moths, hawk moths, and sphinx moths. They received the name sphinx moth because the caterpillars rear up when disturbed and look a little like the Egyptian sphinx. According to the legends of a California Native American tribe, sphinx moths are baby hummingbirds. Others believe that they are crosses between hummingbirds and moths. These large moths, which can be active day or night, often hover like hummingbirds as they feed on the nectar of flowers.

The larvae of moths are referred to as caterpillars or worms, and they, too, figure in folklore. According to North American folklore, the woolly bear caterpillar can be used to predict how severe winter weather will be. If the reddish band in the middle of the black tipped caterpillar is narrow, a long, cold winter will follow; if the band is wide, winter will be mild. And the Chinese empress Si-Ling, credited with discovering how to make silk, was aided by a silkworm cocoon that, according to legend, she accidentally dropped into a cup of hot tea. This softened the cocoon enough to unwind, and Si-Ling used the resulting thread to make cloth. To ensure a successful hunt, South American medicine men would make cuts in the skin of hunters, then rub the cuts with the irritating hairs of caterpillars.

NATURAL HISTORY

Moths and butterflies belong to the order Lepidoptera, a term that means "scaly wings." Tiny scales coat the wings and bodies of these insects, like shingles on a roof. (Touch a moth wing and your fingers come away with a dusting of these scales.) Butterflies and moths form a large, diverse group containing about 165,000 species around the world. Of these, about 150,000 species are moths, and 15,000 species are butterflies.

Following are some of the differences between moths and butterflies. Moths tend to be active at night; butterflies usually are active during the day. Moths, although sometimes beautifully colored, tend to have less flashy and bright colors than butterflies. Moths have threadlike or featherlike antennae; butterflies have slender, clubbed antennae. Most moths hold their wings flat when at rest; butterflies usually hold theirs upright. Finally, most moths have a small hook or bristle on the front edge of each hind wing that attaches it to the front wing.

This moth has an interesting pattern on its wings.

Description

Moths are insects that undergo *complete metamorphosis*, with egg, larva, pupa, and adult stages. The contrast between a cylinder-shaped caterpillar and the airborne adult moth it becomes is so great that it is difficult to believe they are different stages in the life of the same creature. In general, female moths deposit their eggs on a plant or other food source. After hatching, the larvae—which are usually called caterpillars—become virtual eating machines, gnawing and growing. Caterpillars seem to contradict the rule that insects have six legs. Actually, the six true legs at the front of a caterpillar have a very different appearance than the 10 or fewer fleshy "prolegs" on the middle and rear portions of the body.

Many caterpillars have distinctive common names. For example, the caterpillars of geometer moths are sometimes called inchworms. Other common caterpillars include woolly bear caterpillars (because of their fuzzy hairs), hornworms, and cutworms.

Many animals eat caterpillars. Although most caterpillars are harmless, they have numerous ways to defend themselves. Some caterpillars blend into the background; they may look like twigs or dried leaves. In Costa Rica, one moth caterpillar mimics the head of a snake. Other caterpillars give off a bad smell when bothered. A few have stinging hairs or taste bad; these caterpillars often possess vivid patterns that serve as warning signs.

As a caterpillar grows, its skin gradually becomes too tight. So the caterpillar periodically molts, shedding the old skin and replacing it with a new, looser skin that was growing just beneath the surface. The time between molts is called an *instar*, and each different type of moth has a predictable number of instars and molts.

At the end of the last larval instar, the caterpillar becomes ready to change into a pupa, the next stage in its life cycle. The pupa, or resting stage, often takes place within a silken cocoon spun by the caterpillar. The caterpillar usually selects a sheltered place to spin its cocoon, because when it becomes a pupa, it cannot move around or protect itself. Depending on the type of moth, the pupal stage can last a relatively short time or can last for several months, especially for species that survive over the winter season as pupae.

Finally, the time comes for the adult moth to emerge from the cocoon. At first, its four wings appear crumpled and small. The newly emerged moth pumps fluid from its body into the wings, making them expand. The wingspans of moths vary greatly. In the United States and Canada, Cercopia moths reach the largest sizes, attaining wingspans of up to 6 inches (15cm). Moths in the group Microlepidoptera can have wingspans of only one-eighth of an inch (3mm).

Adult moths often closely match the backgrounds on which they rest. For example, moths that rest on trees often resemble bark. Further, if they have stripes, they frequently align themselves so that their stripes match the stripes in the bark.

Most adult moths have mouthparts like a rolled tube—called a proboscis—designed for sucking nectar, sap, or other liquids. A few moths don't eat anything as adults but simply breed and then die a short time later.

Some moths in the Arctic of North America have unusually long lives, which they spend mostly as fuzzy little caterpillars. Although the eggs of Arctic woolly bear caterpillars hatch a few days after the female moth lays them, the resulting caterpillars must spend the next 14 years or so growing and molting six times before becoming pupae and then reaching their brief adulthood as moths.

The caterpillars remain inactive during the long winters, and their short summer is further shortened by the need to avoid the wasps and bristle flys that parasitize the woolly bear larvae and pupae. Consequently, these caterpillars concentrate their activity in a short, three-week period of warmth before the summer solstice, then go into hiding. During the time they are active, the caterpillars' long orange-brown hairs help them retain the heat they gain by basking in the sun. They spend their winters frozen. To avoid being damaged by ice crystals, the caterpillars use a chemical called glycerol to control the way ice forms inside their bodies.

While Arctic woolly bears wait out winter as little frozen lumps, about 50 species of owlet moths use the season of cold to their advantage. These moths are active on winter nights, feeding on the sap of injured trees, mating, and laying their eggs. By spring, when most other moths become active, the winter moths are dead.

At rest, winter moths are about the same temperature as the air around them—something we would expect of cold-blooded creatures. They seek shelter in leaf litter when inactive because the leaves protect them from freezing. In order to fly, though, winter moths must somehow attain relatively high temperatures—at least 86 F (30 C)—in their thoraxes.

This might seem a difficult task for a small insect on a night when temperatures are just above freezing. A winter moth accomplishes this feat by shivering, an act that generates heat, just as shivering generates body heat for warm-blooded creatures. Additional features help the moth maintain the warmth it produces. The dense hairy coating serves as insulation, and adaptations in the circulatory system help keep heat concentrated in the thorax rather than dispersed throughout the moth.

Moths use chemical scents, or pheromones, to locate mates. For example, females of the moth family Saturniidae "call" males by releasing a specific blend of pheromones. Downwind, scent organs in the males' feathery antennae enable them to detect the pheromones. These scent organs are wonderfully acute, and the males fly upwind, tracing the route to the female. Each Saturniidae species also has a specific time period at which the females release the pheromones.

Occasionally, it is the male moth that releases pheromones to attract females. In the cabbage looper moth, for example, the male moth finds an appropriate host plant for the caterpillar and "calls" the females to the site.

Range

Moths occur throughout the world. In North America, some species range into the high Arctic of Canada and Alaska. Moths even occupy the remote Hawaiian Islands, where unique forms have developed. For example, caterpillars of several species in the genus *Eupithecia* attack small invertebrates such as spiders and insects, then consume the body fluids.

Interactions

Early each summer, miller moths migrate westward from the Great Plains into the Rocky Mountains. Most years see relatively small numbers of these moths passing through. However, during years that see large numbers of migrating miller moths, people call them a plague, invasion, or infestation—even though messy, the moths are completely harmless. A similar abundance of butterflies would probably be met with delight.

"Like a moth to a flame" is an expression we often use when we talk about someone irresistibly drawn to something (or someone) bad for them. We may find dead moths littering the ground beneath porch lights. Moths are attracted to light because they use it to navigate. Normally, they use very distant light sources, such as the moon, for navigational cues. Since the moon is so far away, a moth can fly in a straight line by keeping the moon's light at the same angle to its eyes. When a moth encounters *our* light sources, which are very close rather than very distant, keeping the light at the same angle to its eyes causes it to fly in a spiral pattern around the light—and sometimes to get burned.

Moths are important pollinators for flowers, including some that bloom only at night or late in the fall when few other insects remain active. Many flowers depend exclusively on moths to pollinate them. One of the most intricate pollination relationships occurs between yucca plants and little insects called yucca moths, which belong to the family Prodoxidae. About 30 yucca species grow throughout the Southwest, varying in size from relatively small Spanish bayonets to massive Joshua trees. In the spring and summer, the yuccas produce bundles of creamy white flowers. At about the same time, yucca moths emerge from their underground cocoons. The moths then fly to the yucca blossoms, where they mate.

The female yucca moth has specialized mouthparts. She uses them not for feeding but to collect a little ball of pollen from the yucca flower. She then carries the pollen to another freshly opened yucca flower. Here she lays some eggs into the ovary of the flower and deposits the pollen onto the flower's stigma. Because of the structure of the flower, this is the only way that yucca flowers are pollinated. As a consequence of the moth's actions, seeds develop in the flower. Some of these serve as food for the moth larvae.

The reliance of the yucca on the moth for pollination, and the moth on the yucca for food for its larvae, is known as *mutualism*. Some related moths, though, "cheat." They lay their eggs in the yucca but don't pollinate the flowers—the moths benefit, but at the cost of the yucca.

On a mountain near Flagstaff, Arizona, scarlet gilia blooms from July to September. In the early part of their blooming period, the flowers are a brilliant red color. Later in the season most flowers bloom pale pink or white. The plants shift the color of their flowers because hummingbirds, which prefer red flowers, pollinate the flowers early in the season. When the hummingbirds migrate from the area in late summer, the plants depend on a sphinx moth to pollinate their flowers. Unlike the hummingbirds, sphinx moths tend to visit light flowers, especially after dark.

This small yucca moth waits inside a yucca blossom for evening.

Another relationship—this one between a little geometrid moth and oak trees—exemplifies the saying "You are what you eat." In this case, moth caterpillars that hatch during the spring feed on oak catkins (flowers). Those that hatch later in the season eat oak leaves. Their diet directly affects their appearance: The catkin-eating caterpillars look almost exactly like catkins; the leaf-eating caterpillars resemble twigs. In addition, when catkinlike caterpillars find themselves on leaves or twigs, they seek out catkins; the twiglike caterpillars prefer to hide on twigs. The contrasts in shape and hiding behavior help both groups of caterpillars hide from potential predators.

Adult moths are seldom pests, but the caterpillars of some moths can ravage crops, make sweaters "motheaten," and set up extensive "tents" in foliage. Often the moths that cause problems were accidentally introduced to an area. For example, the gypsy moth, whose larvae continue to devastate millions of acres of forest in eastern North America, are invaders brought to the United States in 1869 from France.

Moths play important roles in ecosystems. Aside from their importance as pollinators, some moths and their larvae help keep plant pests under control. And caterpillars and adult moths are, of course, important foodsources for birds and other animals.

In 1993, U.S. Fish and Wildlife listed 18 butterflies as threatened or endangered species. At the same time, only one moth, the Kern primrose sphinx moth, occupied this list—despite the fact that there are about 10 times as many moth species as butterfly species. Several problems beset this threatened moth. First, the moth occupies a very small area. Its rarity made it a favorite of collectors, one of whom captured about 70 individuals shortly before the moth was given protection. In 1979, many female Kern primrose sphinx moths were observed laying eggs on an introduced weed instead of on the native food source for the caterpillars. For several years, no more moths of this threatened species were sighted. Finally, in 1990, a researcher observed a worn-looking female moth in the tiny area that is the moth's remaining habitat. In 1993, a stamp put out by the state of California featured the Kern primrose sphinx moth. Funds raised by the sale of these stamps go toward restoration and environmental education on lands owned by California Fish and Game.

The nocturnal habits of most moths probably prevent biologists from learning about them as readily as they learn about the day-flying butterflies. As a result, it is more difficult to discover when moth populations decline. Ecologist Paul Ehrlich estimated that fewer than 1 in 100,000 people collect or study butterflies. How many fewer the individuals who investigate the silent wings of night?

MOTH ACTIVITIES

1. Moths flying at night often land near porch lights. Some warm summer night, turn your porch light on. Over the course of the evening, see how many kinds of moths come to the light.

Watch for moths near lights at night.

2. Find a dead moth and look at its wings under a magnifying glass or microscope. (If you do this to a living moth, you might injure it.)

3. The Xerces Society is named after the Xerces Blue butterfly, a California butterfly that became extinct because of humans. The mission of this society is to protect rare and endangered invertebrates. As one of its activities since 1975, the society sponsors an annual July 4 butterfly count. For information, write The Xerces Society, 10 Southwest Ash Street, Portland, OR 97204.

From *Of Bugs and Beasts*. © 1995. Teacher Ideas Press. (800) 237-6124.

4. "Like a moth drawn to a flame" is an expression that is used to describe a relationship that is bad or even deadly for one. Write a short essay that begins with these words.

5. A haiku poem has three lines and follows a specific form: the first line contains five syllables; the second line, seven syllables; the third line, five syllables. Write a haiku poem that begins "Like a moth to flame."

6. As you have read in this chapter, moths are experts at camouflage. Play a game in which each player finds a different habitat (place where an animal lives) outside. Next, each player uses craft materials (paper, crayons, cotton balls, pipe cleaners, toothpicks, and so on) to design a moth to fit in the habitat chosen. After all "moths" have been placed, allow all players to search for each other's specimens. When all of the designed insects have been found, discuss the characteristics that made them hard or easy to find.

7. Metamorphosis is an almost unbelievable transformation during which insects change from egg to larva to pupa to adult. The appearances in each stage are dramatically different. Write, produce, and perform a play in which the theme is metamorphosis. Use all the props you can to inform the audience of the differences between stages of development.

8. Read *The Very Hungry Caterpillar* by Eric Carle (New York: Crowell, 1971). Pretend that you are the caterpillar described in the story. Write a page in a journal that describes one day in your life.

9. Science supply houses sell kits for butterfly and moth study. Try your hand at raising moths or butterflies. Such close interaction with these wondrous insects will enable you to make many observations that you could not otherwise enjoy. You can, of course, capture a caterpillar, feed it fresh leaves (use ones from the plant on which you captured it) until it spins a cocoon—then see what emerges. You will want to provide a branch or similar structure on which the caterpillar can spin and attach its cocoon. You can make a cage from cheese cloth stretched around a frame made from Tinker Toy pieces. Make sure the cage is big enough for the resulting butterfly or moth to spread out its wings when it emerges. Keep a laboratory book that chronicles the development of your insect. Use sketches, photographs, and pictures from other sources. Use a good insect book to identify your specimen.

10. If you are interested in the further study of metamorphosis, you might want to observe this process with other organisms. A good choice is the mealworm (*Tenebrio molitar*), for a number of reasons. First, mealworms are readily available from pet shops and are very inexpensive (a couple of cents each). Second, the mealworm is quite sturdy and undergoes complete metamorphosis, as do moths and butterflies. Third, the metamorphosis takes place over a relatively short period of time (three weeks to three months). Finally, caring for the mealworm is easy, just a little bit of cereal and a slice of apple or potato occasionally for moisture. All you need to do is observe the mealworms periodically. They can be kept in a plastic container with a top. Many salad bars have such containers. From the mealworm (larval stage), they become pupae. After a couple of weeks in this stage they undergo their final molt and become adults (darkling beetles). Adults mate, females lay up to 500 eggs, the eggs hatch into tiny larvae, and the process starts all over again. You can read more about mealworms in a variety of sources, such as the article by Glenn McGlathery listed in the following bibliography.

BIBLIOGRAPHY

Books

Borror, Donald J., and Richard E. White. 1970. *A Field Guide to the Insects of America North of Mexico.* (Peterson Field Guide Series.) Boston: Houghton Mifflin, 404 pp.
The accounts in this book help identify and describe insects, including moths.

Carle, Eric. *The Very Hungry Caterpillar.* New York: Crowell, 1971.
A book for young readers.

Clausen, Lucy W. 1954. *Insect Fact and Folklore.* New York: Macmillan.
A book full of charming myths and legends interspersed with explanations of the biology of insects. Although an older book, it remains available in many larger libraries.

Doris, Ellen. 1993. *Entomology.* Photographs by Len Rubenstein. New York: Thames and Hudson.
This book was produced in association with the Children's School of Science, Woods Hole, Massachusetts. This study of insects includes projects, field trips, ideas and suggestions. There is a whole section on raising caterpillars.

Heinrich, Bernd. 1989. "Thermoregulation in Winter Moths." In *Life at the Edge: Readings from Scientific American Magazine,* edited by James L. Gould and Carol Grant Gould, 73-83. New York: W. H. Freeman, 162 pp.
Describes the researcher's investigations into how winter moths can generate and maintain high enough body temperatures to fly.

Hopkins, Lee Bennett. 1992. *Flit, Flutter, Fly!* Illustrated by Peter Palagonia. New York: Doubleday.
A collection of poems by a variety of authors about bugs and other creatures that crawl.

Johnson, Edna, Evelyn R. Sickels, and Frances Clarke Sayers. 1970. "The Moth and the Star." In *Anthology of Children's Literature,* 112-13. Boston, Mass.: Houghton Mifflin.
A classic anthology of children's literature.

Kirk, David. 1994. *Miss Spider's Tea Party.* New York: Scholastic.
A damp moth befriends a spider in this counting book in verse.

Still, John. 1991. *Amazing Butterflies and Moths.* Photographs by Jerry Young. New York: Knopf.
Photographic guide illustrates the life cycles and characteristics of various kinds of moths, butterflies, and caterpillars.

Whalley, Paul. 1988. *Butterfly and Moth.* New York: Alfred A. Knopf.
This book, one of the Eyewitness Books series, is loaded with wonderful photographs of moths and butterflies.

Articles

Capinera, J. L. 1993. Insects in Art and Religion: The American Southwest. *American Entomologist* 39(4):221-29.

    This article describes the role insects played in the myths and legends of various Native American tribes.

Greene, Erick. 1989. A Diet-Induced Developmental Polymorphism in a Caterpillar. *Science* 243: 643-46.

    In this technical article, the researcher describes how diet affects the appearance of moth caterpillars. (The cover of this issue of the magazine shows a catkin-eating caterpillar next to some catkins.)

Heinrich, Bernd. 1994. Some Like It Cold. *Natural History* 103(2):42-49. (February)

    Photos illustrate some of the winter-flying moths that Bernd Heinrich has studied in New England.

Kukal, Olga. 1988. Caterpillars on Ice. *Natural History* 97(1):36-41. (January)

    Arctic woolly bear caterpillars spend the winters frozen, tolerating temperatures as low as -95° F (-70.6° C). They are protected by glycerol, a cryoprotectant.

McGlathery, Glenn. 1989. Mealworms in the Classroom. *Science and Children* 26(6):29-31. (March)

    Shows how to use mealworms to study metamorphosis.

Paige, Ken N., and Thomas G. Whitham. 1985. Individual and Population Shifts in Flower Color by Scarlet Gilia: A Mechanism for Pollinator Tracking. *Science* 227(4684):315-17.

    In this technical paper, scientists examine how a plant changes the color of its blossoms to attract sphinx moths.

Pond, Doris. 1992. Gypsy on the Move. *American Forests* 98(3-4):21-24, 65. (March-April)

    Describes efforts to control the gypsy moth in eastern North America.

Powell, Jerry A. 1992. Interrelationships of Yuccas and Yucca Moths. *Trends in Ecology and Evolution* 7(1):10-15.

    A technical article describing some of the variation in yucca moth pollination of different types of yuccas.

Wickelgren, I. 1989. Caterpillar Disguise: You Are What You Eat. *Science News* 135(5):70. (February 4)

    Summarizes how diet affects the appearance of moth caterpillars.

Of the
Water

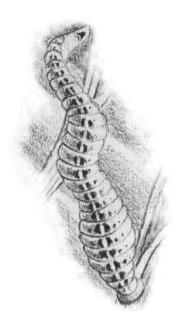

Chapter 4

LEECHES

If [there's] anything in the world I hate, it's leeches. The filthy little devils!

Humphrey Bogart
The African Queen

FOLKLORE

The Younger Brother

In the old days, there were three brothers. The oldest one was lazy but one of those kinds of people who knows everything. He told his brothers how to catch fish but when they came back with no fish he yelled at them and called them blind.

The youngest brother was angry with this outburst so he poked his oldest brother's eyes out. The younger brother regretted his short temper at once.

Again the two younger brothers went fishing with no luck at all. Then as they chopped banana leaves for lunch they ran into a bobcat. They captured it, killed it, and ate it for lunch. The youngest brother noticed that the oil from the meat had dripped on some wounds on his feet and healed them, so they saved the oil and took it home.

The youngest brother smeared some of the oil on his oldest brother's eyes and they were healed. But the lazy, nasty older brother began to berate and abuse the youngest boy. He said that he wanted to kill him.

The middle brother knew his brothers were going to do just that to each other some day, so he told his oldest brother that he would take the youngest one to the river and kill him.

On the day that the middle brother set off with the younger one, they each took a bamboo pipe along with them. As they were walking, leeches caught onto their legs and covered them. They let the leeches suck until they were full and then they picked them off and put them in their bamboo pipes. When they got to the river, they took the leeches and chopped them up. They smeared the blood on the knife, the knife sheath and the hands of the middle brother. The brothers separated and went in different directions. When the middle brother got home he told the oldest one that he had killed the brother and chopped him up.

Meanwhile the youngest brother traveled to a village where he found a poor widow with many children. They married. That night they heard people beating funeral drums and banging gongs in the village. The village leader's daughter had died.

The youngest brother went to the widow's home and got the rest of the bobcat's oil. He went to the village leader's home and asked to see his daughter. There he smeared the oil all over her body and mouth and she came back to life.

When the village leader offered to reward him, the widow told him not to accept the gold and silver but to ask for the rotting chicken nest. When he got home with it the widow told him to go back and ask for a little plot of land on the hill to build a house. The village leader gratefully gave him the land. The next morning, the boy and the widow took the rotting chicken nest to the plot of land. There they found three tree trunks. The widow told him to come back later with the chicken nest and put it on the top of the middle tree trunk. Then she told him to lie face down and close his eyes. He was to keep them closed even if tigers came, the dead came, the deer came, and even when it thundered and the wind blew.

He followed her instructions and after a great storm passed, he opened his eyes and saw a gleaming palace. He and the widow moved into the palace with all of her children. They became very wise and after the village leader died they became the head of the village where they ruled with wisdom and love.

—traditional story of the Iu-Mienh of Southeast Asia
Beard, Warrick, and Saefong, *Loz-Hnoi, Loz-Hnoi Uov*

Most people fear leeches with righteous revulsion. Maybe they have heard stories of giant leeches that enter a sleeping person's nose to feed on blood; they they become so fat that they can't get out and suffocate their victim! A most bizarre suicide was attempted in the late 1770s when a young woman swallowed 50 leeches.

But it is surely in the medical folklore that stories of leeches abound. Hippocrates is the dominant figure in modern accounts of Greek medicine, but the good doctor shared the stage in antiquity with Asclepius, who was elevated to the status of a god. The cult of Asclepius spread throughout the Greek world and established itself in Rome. Temples to Asclepius were places for hopeful pilgrimages and miraculous cures. The god supposedly cured a man who claimed to have swallowed leeches by cutting him open, removing the infestation, and stitching up the incision.

Early doctors were called leeches, from the Old English word *laece*, meaning " healer" or "one who relieves pain." It was applied early on to British physicians, with the practice of medicine itself being known as leechcraft. For centuries, practitioners of the healing arts believed that various human illnesses were caused by an imbalance in the body's "humors." They would often apply the animals we call leeches to patients to extract "excess blood" and restore the proper balance. Unfortunately, this treatment usually didn't help but instead simply made the patient weaker. However, the role of these animals in treatment is the reason they received the name *leech*.

By the late eighteenth century, the word *leech* began to acquire a darker meaning, referring to unpleasant people who "drain others dry" by their clinging and acquisitive behavior. Such people are said to "stick to someone like a leech."

During the nineteenth-century revival of interest in folklore, medical texts included a three-volume collection called *Leechdoms, Wortcunning and Starcraft of Early England, and Illustrating the History of Science in This Country Before the Norman Conquest*. These Anglo-Saxon leechbooks reflected the mingling of Greek, Roman, Teutonic, Celtic, and Christian concepts of medicine and magic.

NATURAL HISTORY

Leeches are members of the same phylum (Annelida, the segmented worms) as earthworms. Approximately 650 leech species exist worldwide. The smallest leeches are nearly microscopic; giant leeches from the Amazon in South America can attain lengths of 18 inches (45.7cm).

Description

The soft, somewhat flattened body of a leech appears to have numerous rings, or annuli, around it. A large, often circular, sucker is located at the rear end, and another sucker surrounds the mouth. Leeches use their suckers to attach themselves to a variety of objects, from rocks or vegetation to their prey. The suckers stick to these objects using two different mechanisms. First, the suckers can secrete sticky gluelike material from special adhesion glands. Second, the leech can create a vacuum with the sucker, helping it hold onto an object in the same way that suction cups adhere to flat surfaces.

Some leech species are uniformly gray and look very plain. Most leeches, though, have bright colors, with various leeches showing intricate black and orange patterns, others having yellowish spots on a green background, and still others possessing a combination of colorful stripes and spots.

Leech.

Depending on the species, leeches have one to five pairs of eyes located at the front of the body. Leeches are attracted to secretions of potential hosts, and some can detect temperature differences or movement of water that might indicate the presence of warm-blooded prey.

Leeches have some easily observed behaviors. They can move around by crawling (the two modes are crawling like earthworms and inching forward like inchworms) and swimming. Because they have no bones or other rigid structures, they can shorten their bodies. They attach their rear suckers to the substrate and move their heads or whole bodies as part of their search for prey. When a leech detects something, it may assume the alert posture, extending its full length and remaining motionless.

Most leeches that might use you for a meal make three small incisions in the skin with their jaws. The leech then releases substances with a variety of functions. At least one chemical acts as an anesthetic, so that you don't feel the incisions. Others prevent clots from forming in the blood and dilate the host's blood vessels so that the leech can continue to feed without interruption. A leech that feeds on blood might double or quadruple its weight during a large meal. Such a meal lasts the leech a long time, and some leeches have lived at least two years between feedings. If the leech gets a full meal, it usually drops off and swims away. Your only clue of its former presence might be a small, Y-shaped cut that may continue to bleed for a while.

Other leech species scavenge for dead animals or prey on snails, insects, and other small creatures. Still others live most of their lives attached to fish. Predaceous leeches feed frequently and grow a little at a time. Blood-sucking leeches feed infrequently and have large growth spurts after their occasional meals.

Leeches are hermaphroditic, each leech containing both male and female sex organs. A pair of mating leeches exchanges sperm. Later, the fertilized eggs develop in a cocoon formed from a structure called a clitellum.

Range

Of the approximately 650 leech species in the world, about 60 occur in North America. Leeches occupy lakes, ponds, marshes, and other quiet bodies of water and tend to be more common in northern states. Although some leeches take up nearly permanent residence on fish, most spend their days hiding under rocks or in aquatic vegetation. Most leech activity takes place at night. Consequently, an area may have a large leech population even though the leeches are seldom seen.

Leeches show some seasonal movements. During hot weather, for example, leeches sometimes migrate to shallow water, where more dissolved oxygen is available. When water evaporates in temporary ponds, some leeches burrow into the mud and can aestivate for a month or so until the pond again fills with water. Many leeches burrow beneath the frost line to survive cold winters.

Interactions

Sometimes ducks and other animals provide unwitting transportation for leeches from one place to another. Several leech species are known to have hitchhiked in this way. At least on occasion, leeches can invade a pond, remain a few years, and apparently disappear. A predaceous leech, for example, hadn't been found in an Indiana pond during 15 years of study prior to 1990. However, in 1990 and 1991, several leeches were found on tiger salamanders breeding in the pond. By 1992, the leeches had again disappeared.

Leeches can be important predators of amphibian eggs. Bullfrogs, for example, have several strategies to minimize egg loss to leeches. First, the clear jelly surrounding bullfrog eggs makes each egg a slippery, elusive target for a foraging leech. Second, although bullfrog eggs are deposited as a film on the surface of the water, after a few minutes the eggs drape onto the underwater vegetation. In areas with sparse vegetation, the individual eggs become even more difficult targets for leeches than eggs resting flat on dense vegetation. Finally, females choose as their mates male bullfrogs calling from high-quality sites. Male bullfrogs establish these territories, which they defend from other males. In general, the larger the male, the better his territory—and of the eggs deposited in his territory, fewer are lost to leech predation.

There is a growing industry supplying leeches for fish bait, especially for anglers seeking walleye and bass. In Minnesota, the Department of Natural Resources even cultures leeches in ponds so that anglers aren't faced with leech shortages.

Perhaps we would think more kindly toward leeches if they were still associated with healing. And actually, medicine is again turning its attention to leeches. Doctors usually use other more conventional methods to control blood flow in swollen tissues. Some plastic and reconstructive surgeons, however, are finding a new use for leeches: to help prevent blood clots following surgery to reattach severed fingers or ears. As it consumes blood, the leech secretes chemicals in its saliva that prevents clotting—ultimately reducing dangerous swelling in the reattached flesh.

Medical scientists look to leeches—and the biochemicals they produce—for a number of possible uses. Some of these chemicals and their effects include

- hirudin and decorsin—prevents blood from clotting

- hementin—dissolves mammalian blood clots; and

- antistasin—inhibits a blood-clotting protein called factor Xa.

Out of the 40 animals illustrated on our survey form, more people disliked leeches than any other animal. What causes this large outpouring of negative opinions? People prefer genuinely dangerous animals such as bears to the relatively innocuous leeches—many species of which won't even feed on the blood of mammals. And though leeches tend to be lumped together as blood-suckers, many leeches have lives as scavengers and active predators rather than as parasites.

Additional factors may play a role in the unpopularity of leeches. They lack backbones, which automatically distances them from animals people typically hold in affection. As part of their adaptation to aquatic habitats, leeches look slick and slimy—another characteristic that many people react to with disgust. Perhaps the ultimate response can be seen in the movie *Stand By Me*. A group of young boys travels through some muddy water, emerging on the other side festooned with leeches. One of the boys sees the leeches attached to his body and faints dead away.

Yet in their own way, leeches are active and interesting animals. Most leeches live in water, but some venture onto moist land. Many of them possess vivid patterns and display colors we would consider beautiful if the same colors were on, say, a bird. Finally, the sinuous movements and undulating swimming motions of leeches have their own grace if we can look at them with enough generosity to see.

LEECH ACTIVITIES

1. Make up songs about leeches. For instance, here is one to the tune of "Sweet Betsy From Pike":
    Another possibility is to use the folk song "There's a Hole in the Bucket" and transform the verses into "There's a leech in the bucket dear Liza, dear Liza . . ."

    > *Did you ever hear tell of the leeches at night,*
    > *Who sucked up the blood of swimmers at sight,*
    > *Doctors still use them with some patients' plights*
    > *And hungry birds call them tasty delights.*

2. Try leech-watching some summer evening along the shore of a pond. Bring insect repellent and a flashlight. You may see, as one of us has, leeches swimming near the shore with an undulating motion or attaching their rear suckers to plant stems or submerged objects and curling their foreparts around in the water.

3. If you have the opportunity to observe a leech, note any of the following behaviors you see: crawling, swimming, changing body length, searching, assuming the alert posture.

4. Leech suckers work partly by creating a vacuum to stick to objects. Get a suction cup, such as those used for hanging small objects on windows or on the ends of toy darts or arrows. Press the suction cups against various flat surfaces, such as glass, paper, cardboard, wood, tiles, metal, and fabric. What surfaces do the suction cups stick to best? What surfaces don't the suction cups stick to? Dip the suction cup in water and try sticking it to the same surfaces. Is there any difference in how well or poorly the suction cup sticks?

5. Some suction cups are strong enough that when stuck to a person's forehead, they can cause a red mark from where the blood is pulled to the surface (don't try this yourself, since the mark can last a day or more). How do you think this phenomenon affects a leech's ability to feed?

6. Leeches have value in medical research. In particular, they use an anesthetic and an anticoagulant as they draw blood from a victim. Pretend that a well-known leech, one used in research, has died. Write an obituary that praises the leech's efforts in furthering medical science.

7. The idea of leeches seems pretty bizarre and scary to most people. Design a Halloween leech costume. Have a partner dress as a "victim."

8. In the bibliography for this chapter is an article by Sawyer, "In Search of the Giant Amazon Leech." It is a serious account of a scientific expedition. But doesn't the title seem like a science fiction notion? Write your own sci-fi account of the giant Amazon leech. Invent its natural history in a story in which it terrorizes a Brazilian village.

9. A television series is entitled *In Search Of* . . . Watch an episode of the series so that you can get the general idea of the treatment given a story, then produce a videotape, "In Search of the Giant Amazon Leech." Use Sawyer's article as a starting place in your research.

10. Read the article "Leeches rescue youngster's ear" (*Rocky Mountain News*, Denver, Colorado, Saturday, May 14, 1994, 5A). The article tells the origin of the leeches used for the procedure.
    a. Why do you suppose they can say that the leeches are sterile? Why do you think so?
    b. What do you think they did with the leeches following the procedure? Why do you think so?
    c. Does this article make you feel more positive about leeches? Why is this? How do you think the patient, James Todisco, feels about leeches?

From *Of Bugs and Beasts*. © 1995. Teacher Ideas Press. (800) 237-6124.

Leeches rescue youngster's ear

Denver doctors reattach appendage that was nearly torn off in dog attack

By Bill Scanlon

Rocky Mountain News Staff Writer

After a dog bit off James Todisco's ear, doctors reattached it, watched it turn blue, then used six leeches to suck out the excess blood.

The leeches probably saved the 7-year-old's ear, James' doctor said Friday.

"His ear wasn't draining well, so we tried leeches to drain the blood," said Dr. James A. Harris, chief of otolaryngology at Denver General Hospital.

"It didn't scare me," said James, who lives in Cheraw near Lamar.

James says he was trying to push a friend's Rottweiler upstairs Saturday night when "it just turned around and bit me."

The ear was almost torn off, Harris said.

Twelve hours after doctors reattached the ear, they noticed that it was blue and swollen, Harris said. That meant that the red blood bringing oxygen to the ear couldn't do its job. The oxygen-spent blue blood wasn't draining and the wound was clogged.

So doctors telephoned Leeches U.S.A. in New York and asked for a rush delivery of 14 sterile leeches.

Doctors needed only six. The leeches weren't interested in biting a hole in the ear, so Harris made tiny incisions and brought the leeches' mouths to the cuts. The four-inch-long squirmers sucked the blood for 45 minutes before getting their fill and falling off.

Leeches have anticoagulants in their bodies, so after they fell off, the ear continued to drain for 18 more hours, Harris said.

James is ready to return to Cheraw. He'll be back in a week so doctors can make sure the ear is healing properly. Harris expects the ear to look normal and function normally in a short time.

Leeches never went completely out of fashion, and recently are making something of a comeback as anticoagulants useful to doctors who reattach severed fingers, ears or limbs, Harris said.

Saturday, May 14, 1994. *Rocky Mountain News*, p. 5A.

From *Of Bugs and Beasts.* © 1995. Teacher Ideas Press. (800) 237-6124.

ANIMAL PLACE-NAMES

We often give animal names to places. See if you can match the place-names in the list below with the numbers shown on the map of the United States. (Note: All the place-names can be found in recent editions of the *Rand McNally Universal World Atlas*.)

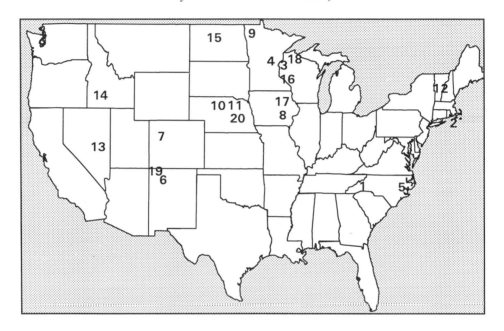

____A.	Snake River Plain, ID	____K.	Snake Range, NV
____B.	Coyote Basin, CO	____L.	Worms, NE
____C.	Spider Lake (island), WI	____M.	Clam Lake Island, WI
____D.	Leechville, NC	____N.	Turtle Lake, ND
____E.	Buzzard Roost, NC	____O.	Coyote, NM
____F.	Snake Falls, NE	____P.	Buzzards Bay, MA
____G.	Turtle River, MN	____Q.	Turtle Lake, WI
____H.	Toadlena, NM	____R.	Snake (stream), MN
____I.	Snake Mountain, VT	____S.	Snake Creek, NE
____J.	Skunk (stream), IA	____T.	Leech Lake Island, MN

Additional Activities

1. Find a detailed map of your state. Make a list of some of the communities, rivers, lakes, mountains, and other areas that use animal names.

2. Try to discover how these places got their names. If you can't find books about local place-names in your library, try contacting a regional historical society for information.

3. There may be many places close to your home that use animal names. Make a map of your community and show any streets or other features named after animals.

4. Make lists of athletic teams that use animal names or have an animal mascot. Show on a map where these teams are located.

From *Of Bugs and Beasts*. © 1995. Teacher Ideas Press. (800) 237-6124.

BIBLIOGRAPHY

Books

Beard, Tim, Betsey Warrick, and Kao Cho Saefong, eds. 1993. *Loz-Hnoi, Loz-Hnoi Uov, or In The Old, Old Days*. Berkeley, Calif.: Iu-Mienh Stories Project, Laotian Handcraft Center.
Traditional stories of the Iu-Mienh.

Ellfman, Eric. 1993. *The Very Scary Almanac*. Illustrations by Will Suckow. New York: Random House.
A collection of snippets of scary creatures and events.

Magner, Lois N. 1992. *A History of Medicine*. New York: Marcel Dekker.
A text that includes an up-to-date survey of medical history from paleopathology to the most recent theories and practices of modern medicine.

Pennak, Robert W. 1989. *Fresh-Water Invertebrates of the United States*. 3d ed. New York: John Wiley, 628 pp.
A thorough but technical account of leeches is in the chapter on Annelida.

Robinson, Howard F., Victor H. Waldrop, Debby Anker, Elizabeth B. Blizard, et al. 1988. *The Unhuggables*. Washington, D.C.: National Wildlife Federation, 95 pp.
Contains colorful photos in a brief account about leeches for juvenile readers.

Sawyer, Roy T. 1986. *Leech Biology and Behavior*. 3 vols. Oxford, England: Clarendon Press of Oxford University Press, 1,100 pp.
Although technical, these volumes are *the* recent books for anything you want to know about leeches.

Articles

Fackelmann, Kathy A. 1991. Bloodsuckers Reconsidered. *Science News* 139(11):172-73.
Discusses the research into the medical uses of hirudin, a substance produced in leech saliva.

Howard, Richard D. 1978. The Influence of Male-Defended Oviposition Sites on Early Embryo Mortality in Bullfrogs. *Ecology* 59(4):789-98.
A technical article that describes how male bullfrogs select calling sites with lower levels of leech infestation.

Pennuto, Christopher M., and Malcolm G. Butler. 1993. Distribution of the Ribbon Leech in North Dakota. *Prairie Naturalist* 25(2):109-18.
Researchers studied the habitat requirements of ribbon leeches to help biologists determine how these leeches should be harvested for bait.

Sawyer, Roy T. 1990. In Search of the Giant Amazon Leech. *Natural History* (December):66-67.
Recounts the author's experiences in finding the largest of the world's leeches and his establishment of a commercial leech farm for the development of new drugs.

Chapter **5**

CLAMS

The area lakes—and there are a number of them connected by the meandering branches of the Chippewa River—all have their bottoms pock-marked by fresh-water clams of no great size. They are unpalatable, according to the natives, and their shells are thin. The creature that inhabits them is vulnerable.

Edward Lueders, *The Clam Lake Papers*

FOLKLORE

Clamshell Boy

Back in the days when Basket Woman roamed the land searching for children who were out when they should have been home, she caught a group of children. She plopped them into her huge clam basket and set off for her home where she had a big pot of water boiling just in case she found some children. There wasn't anything she enjoyed more than a good meal of boiled children. She took the children out of her basket and put them in a small cage made of woven cedar bark and branches. She went down to the shore to wash up for dinner.

The mother of one of the children had found the trail of Basket Woman where the children had been playing. She started to cry and her tears fell on a clam shell on the beach. The clam shell opened and started to take the form of a boy. It was Clamshell Boy. He offered to help the mother.

Clamshell Boy found Basket Woman as she was washing her hands and face in the foamy water. Clamshell Boy tricked Basket Woman to lean over the edge of a cliff to see something amazing. He didn't need to push her over the bluff because the ground crumbled beneath her weight and over she went.

Clamshell Boy followed the trail to Basket Woman's house where he found the children. He released them and led them back home to their sorrowing village. When the people saw the children returning, they celebrated with a great feast and dances. Everyone gave gifts to each other to rejoice in the return of their children. That is how the first potlatch began.

56

Clams are mostly found in folklore as the main course of a clambake. The same goes for their relatives, the oysters. Here are three verses from Lewis Carroll's classic "The Walrus and the Carpenter":

This conversation must have taken place in a month with an "r" in the name because folklore tells us we must eat oysters only in those months.

Fables from the South Pacific tell of giant clams trapping divers and imprisoning them until their deaths. On the Chinese New Year clams provide more than food; they are customarily eaten for luck as well.

We often describe cold, damp, and unpleasant things as "clammy." Clams—at least their soft bodies—do indeed feel clammy to the touch. When you disturb a clam, it pulls its two shells together tightly. This behavior hints at other phrases we use, such as "clam up," or keep from talking. People who are "tight with their money" (stingy) are sometimes described as "close as a clam" for the same reason. Low tide is when clamdiggers seek clams, resulting in another phrase, "happy as a clam at high tide."

> "The time has come," the Walrus said,
> "To talk of many things:
> Of shoes and ships and sealing wax
> Of cabbages and kings
> And why the sea is boiling hot
> And whether pigs have wings."
>
> * * *
>
> "O Oysters, come and walk with us!"
> The Walrus did beseech.
> "A pleasant walk, a pleasant talk,
> Along the briny beach."
>
> * * *
>
> But answer came there none
> And this was scarcely odd, because
> They'd eaten every one.
>
> —Lewis Carroll
> *Through the Looking-Glass*

NATURAL HISTORY

Clams are among the many types of mollusks, a large group of animals that includes such diverse creatures as snails, octopuses, and squid. Clams come in many sizes and shapes, and all live in water.

The smallest clams are the tiny freshwater pea clams, which can be smaller than a split pea or lentil. At the other extreme, giant tropical clams living in the coral reefs of the Pacific Ocean can grow to lengths of about 3 feet (0.9m).

Clams often have colorful common names: anglewings, heelsplitter, pigtoe, washboard, spiny, elephant's ear, lady finger, penshell, razor, monkey face, and pocketbook. Usually the common names come from shell characteristics, since the shell is what we usually see first—and often is the only thing we see. Many edible clams, such as quahogs or hard clams (a species found along the Atlantic coast) and large freshwater clams (in the family Unionidae) are frequently called *mussels*. Biologists call the shells of clams valves; since clams have two shells, another term for them is bivalves. Altogether, there are more than 8,000 species of clams in the world.

Description

Whereas the outside of a clamshell might be a dull color, the inner surface often has a beautiful luster. A special organ, called the mantle, produces shell that contains mother-of-pearl, or nacre. When an irritant occurs between the mantle and the inner surface of the clamshell, the clam often covers it with mother-of-pearl, forming a pearl. Pearls can be perfectly round, have odd shapes, or even be attached to the clam's shell.

Clams that burrow use a muscular foot to dig into the substrate. Some small clam species, such as pea clams and fingernail clams, can drag themselves around by extending and then contracting the foot. Scallops, one of the few bivalves that swims, can move quickly using a sort of jet propulsion as they open and close their shells.

This tiny pea clam has its muscular foot extended.

Still other clams attach themselves to a rock or other hard surface and never move from that position. Rock oysters, for example, often fuse one of their shells to a rock. Some mussels and oysters anchor themselves with byssal threads, gluelike strands that the animal maneuvers with its foot to attach to hard surfaces. The internal structure of a byssal thread contains numerous tiny bubbles. In addition, the end of the thread near the shell is more elastic than the end anchoring the thread to the substrate. These properties allow the thread to withstand compression and tugging from waves, thus protecting the clam from injury. Other bivalves, such as shipworms, actually bore into hard materials such as soft stone and wood by scraping a hole with their shells.

Most clams feed by drawing water into elaborate internal chambers and filtering out small food particles, a type of feeding called suspension feeding. The parts of the body that take in and let out water are called siphons.

Along the Pacific coast, some California mussels (*Mytilus californianus*) have a coating of a red algae called *Endocladia muricata*. This algae helps protect the mussels from extremes in heat and cold. However, a coating of algae also makes it more likely that a mussel will be ripped away from its rocky home by strong waves. Perhaps because of this trade-off, about half the California mussels permit the algae to coat them while the other mussels keep their shells clear.

In general, clams release eggs and sperm into the water, where the eggs become fertilized and develop into larvae. The offspring of freshwater pea and fingernail clams, however, develop within the gills of the adult. When the young clams are released, they look like smaller versions of the adults.

Freshwater mussels have another interesting reproductive adaptation. The females keep their eggs in an area near the gills, where sperm drawn in from the surrounding water fertilizes the eggs. The fertilized eggs—which can number from several thousand to more than three million depending on the species—develop into larvae that have to attach to a fish to continue development. The larvae often have specialized hooks and threads that help them connect themselves to the fish, where they live for several weeks before dropping off and settling into the substrate. Some adult clams even have special "fish lures" that they use to entice a fish close enough that the clam can release a spray of the larvae on it.

Range

Because clams live in the water and often bury themselves in the substrate, people don't see some types of clams unless they look for them. Other species occupy rocky tidepools and other shallow saltwater habitats where they are easy to observe. Beachcombing often reveals the shells of dead bivalves that wash onto the shore during high tide.

Many more clams live at great depths in oceans and are only rarely seen. For example, scientists only recently discovered deep-sea communities near seafloor vents, where great sections of the earth's crust are spreading apart. These specialized habitats are also homes to other organisms such as crabs and tube worms.

Freshwater mussels live in rivers, streams, and lakes. As mentioned earlier, they depend on fish for part of their life cycle so are found only in bodies of water containing the appropriate fish hosts. The Mississippi River and its major tributaries contain hundreds of native clam species. Sometimes you can see clams half-buried in the shallow water of lakes or find their shells on the shores of rivers. Altogether, about 300 freshwater mussel species occupy North America.

Some pea and fingernail clams have broad distributions. In fact, a little bivalve called the ubiquitous pea clam can be found nearly worldwide, from North America and South America to Eurasia, Africa, and Australia. These small clams can sometimes hitchhike considerable distances on insects, birds, and even frogs. Because of their small size, almost nobody sees these clams unless they are looking for them.

Low tide often reveals numerous bivalves, such as these along the coast of California.

Interactions

Native Americans used clams as food, a practice that we continue today. Modern archaeologists often examine the midden piles created by ancient people and find enormous numbers of clamshells. Native Americans also used the shells to make jewelry, buttons, and beads. When they traded these items, they also produced evidence that archaeologists use to learn about early trading routes. The Hopewell Indians of Ohio made necklaces of freshwater pearls, and some of these necklaces were found in burial mounds.

Native Americans weren't the only people interested in clams. Vikings probably brought the edible soft-shell clams from North America to Denmark as early as 1245—well before Columbus arrived.

Although now most buttons are made of plastic, buttons and jewelry used to be made with the mother-of-pearl from freshwater mussels. Beginning about 1891, freshwater mussels were harvested in great numbers in the United States for this industry. Even today, commercial harvesters collect clams for their shells, and North American mussels are commonly used in the cultured-pearl industry as material to start pearl development. Scientists have become very interested in the "glue" that clams use to attach themselves, because a clam's natural adhesive performs better in aquatic conditions than any artificial glue yet developed.

Because clams feed by filtering water, they also draw in any pollutants that enter the bodies of water in which the clams live. Sometimes the pollutants kill the clams outright; even when the clams survive, they may carry toxic amounts of these pollutants and be harmful for people—and wildlife—to eat.

Clams face other challenges as well. People have changed the character of their river homes by building dams and channelizing the rivers. Some types of fish move between freshwater and ocean habitats during their life cycle. Because dams often prevent this type of migration, they often result in the disappearance of those fish from the river. Types of clams that depended on those migrating fish species may also disappear.

Our farming practices and other activities wash great amounts of soil into watersheds, resulting in what is called siltation. Siltation can smother clams. Gravel mining from rivers also can hurt clam populations. In the Buttahatchee River in Mississippi, for example, clam numbers plummeted in the areas where gravel mines were located.

In California, sea otters extend their range southward. Although this was good for the sea otter, it was bad for the Pismo clams that occupied the shoreline near the city of Pismo Beach. A single 50-pound (22.7kg) otter could eat 12 pounds (5.4kg) of clams per day. By 1981, few Pismo clams remained. Recently, populations of Pismo clams rebounded because of a combination of sea otters switching to other foods and a few good clam-spawning seasons.

Sometimes native clams are crowded out. Asian clams (*Corbicula fluminea*) were introduced in the late 1800s on the West Coast. Since that time, this species has spread throughout the United States, often taking over sections of streams and rivers that native clam species used to inhabit.

More recently, in 1986 zebra mussels were accidentally introduced into the Great Lakes region. Since then, zebra mussels have spread to all of the Great Lakes and several river systems. Groups of thousands of zebra mussels have been found covering—and killing—native clams. In addition to affecting native clams, the zebra mussels are causing expensive problems with water-intake pipes for cities and factories.

In Detroit, Michigan, police department scuba divers, community volunteers, Boy Scouts, and biologists collected northern riffleshells (an endangered clam) from the Detroit River in an area infested by zebra mussels. They removed the zebra mussels from the riffleshells and transplanted most of the riffleshells to the St. Clair River, where zebra mussels do not yet occur.

Because of pollution, dams, channelization, siltation, and the invasion of exotic clam species, our native freshwater clams are among our most endangered groups of animals. They are helping to remind us to take better care of our precious water resources.

CLAM ACTIVITIES

1. Go to a museum or an antique shop and look at the buttons on old clothing. Pearl buttons may be made from freshwater clams.

2. Water pollution hurts clams. List ways you can avoid using chemicals and fertilizers in places where they may contaminate streams and rivers.

3. If you live near the ocean, buy a field guide to the seashore and learn to identify the clams and other animals living near your home.

4. Boaters and anglers can help prevent the spread of zebra mussels: Inspect and clean boats and fishing equipment when moving from one body of water to another. Make sure mud and plants are cleaned off the boat, then let the boat air-dry for two or more days. Use hot water to flush bilge, cooling, and other water from the boat. Don't transport bait from one area to another. Make sure bait buckets are washed and dried thoroughly.

5. Contact your local state wildlife agency and see if you can help with local efforts to conserve native clams.

6. If you have access to a beach, do a population study of squirting clams. These clams will be found at low tide in bays and estuaries. They are burrowed in the mud with siphon tubes reaching up. If disturbed, they pump water out, revealing their little water jets. Mark off an area with flags so that the study area is about 33 feet (10 meters) square. Bend a clothes hanger so it forms a square. Toss the bent clothes hanger into the study area. Go to your hanger and jump up and down several times to make the clams squirt their water. Count the number of jets you see in the space defined by your hanger. Repeat this several times, then make an estimate of the number of clams in the entire study area.

7. The Lawrence Hall of Science at the University of California at Berkeley developed a program called Outdoor Biology Instructional Strategies. Delta Education markets this program (Box M, Nashua, NH 03061, 603-889-8899). If you are near a beach, get the folio called "Clam Hopping" and do some of the neat activities described. The previous activity was adapted from that folio.

8. Seashells have been found at ancient sites used by inland Native Americans. The reason? The shells were used as trade items as coastal and inland tribes met and exchanged goods. Probably seashells served very much as money does today among many peoples. Have you ever heard *clams* used in the place of *dollars*, as in "This suit cost me 50 clams?" The characters in the comic strip *B.C.* use clams as currency. Design your own monetary system using clams as the base unit. Devise other currencies and give them names. Estimate the exchange rate in U.S. dollars.

From *Of Bugs and Beasts*. © 1995. Teacher Ideas Press. (800) 237-6124.

BIBLIOGRAPHY

Books

Abbot, R. Tucker. 1985. *Seashells of the World: A Guide to the Better-Known Species*. New York: Golden Press, 160 pp.
An identification guide with advice on collecting shells.

Carroll, Lewis. 1984. "The Walrus and the Carpenter." In *The Scott Foresman Anthology of Children's Literature,* edited by Zena Sutherland and Myra Cohn Livingston, 79-80. Glenview, Ill.: Scott, Foresman.
Lewis Carroll's poem is included in this classic anthology of children's literature.

Clark, A. H. 1981. *The Freshwater Molluscs of Canada*. Ottawa: National Museum of Natural Sciences, National Museums of Canada, 446 pp.
Field guide with life-history information about the clams and aquatic snails in Canada.

Cohlene, Terri. 1990. *Clamshell Boy*. Illustrated by Charles Reasoner. Mahwah, N.J.: Watermill Press.
A retelling of the legend of Clamshell Boy, who rescues a captured group of children from the dreaded Basket Woman. The story is from the Makah tribe, and the book includes information on this group of people.

Gould, Stephen J. 1977. *Ever Since Darwin: Reflections in Natural History*. New York: W. W. Norton, 285 pp.
The chapter "The Problem of Perfection, or How Can a Clam Mount a Fish on Its Rear End?" discusses the fish lure used by some *Lampsilis* species to aid larvae in attaching to fish hosts.

Gryski, Camilla. 1985. *Many Stars and More String Games*. Illustrated by Tom Sankey. New York: Morrow.
Included in this book of string figures is one called the giant clam, found on pages 28-29.

McConnaughey, B. H., and E. McConnaughey. 1985. *The Audubon Society Nature Guides: Pacific Coast*. 2d ed. New York: Alfred A. Knopf, 633 pp.
Contains photographs and distribution information for bivalves and other plants and animals along the Pacific Coast.

Morris, Percy A. 1973. *A Field Guide to Shells of the Atlantic and Gulf Coasts and the West Indies*. 3d ed. (Peterson Field Guide Series). Boston: Houghton Mifflin, 330 pp.
Contains descriptions of seashells along the eastern coasts.

———. 1974. *A Field Guide to Pacific Coast Shells, Including Shells of Hawaii and the Gulf of California*. (Peterson Field Guide Series). Boston: Houghton Mifflin, 297 pp.
Contains descriptions of seashells along the western coasts.

Office of Technology Assessment. 1993. *Harmful Non-Indigenous Species in the United States.* Washington, D.C.: U.S. Congress, 57 pp.

This summary report discusses the presence and effects of introduced species in the United States, including the Asian clam and zebra mussel.

Pennak, Robert W. 1989. *Fresh-Water Invertebrates of the United States.* 3d ed. New York: John Wiley, 628 pp.

Pennak discusses clams and mussels in the final chapter of this book, which is a good introduction to many of the mysterious little creatures that you might find in freshwater habitats.

Articles

Brosnan, Deborah M. 1993. A Mussel Wears an Expensive Seaweed Scarf. *Natural History* (August): 51.

A biologist examines the costs and benefits of a coating of algae for mussels along the Pacific coast.

French, John R. P. III. 1990. The Exotic Zebra Mussel—A New Threat to Endangered Freshwater Mussels. *Endangered Species Technical Bulletin* 15(11):3-4.

This author reports on the problems caused by zebra mussels in the Great Lakes region.

Hartfield, P. 1992. Surface Mining Threatens Wildlife of the Buttahatchee River. *Endangered Species Technical Bulletin* 17(9-11):3.

This short article reports on the effects of gravel mining on clam populations in a Mississippi river.

Holloway, Marguerite. 1992. Musseling In. *Scientific American* 267(4):22-23.

Describes the spread of zebra mussels and other exotic species.

Kuznik, Frank. 1993. America's Aching Mussel. *National Wildlife* 31(6):34-39.

Describes the plight of America's clams and some of the conservation efforts that are being made.

Livo, L. J. 1993. Colorado's Miniscule Mollusks. *Colorado Outdoors.* 42(4):25-27.

Discusses the life cycles of the small pea clams in the Rocky Mountains.

Mackie, G. L. 1979. Dispersal Mechanisms in Sphaeriidae (Mollusca: Bivalvia). *Bulletin of the American Malacological Union* 45:1721.

Describes how fingernail and pea clams sometimes hitchhike on birds, insects, and other organisms.

Ogawa, Roann E., and Don W. Schloesser. 1993. Community Action Called to "Rescue the Riffleshell." *Endangered Species UPDATE* 10(5):5.

Describes how community volunteers and other individuals worked to save the endangered northern riffleshell mussel.

Owens, Sandy. 1992. Pismo Clams Rebound After Decade of Decline. *Outdoor California* 53(4):1-4. (July-August)
    Describes reasons for population fluctuations of Pismo clams in California. A sidebar shows the correct way for sport clammers to rebury clams smaller than legal size.

Simon, Cheryl. 1982. Deep-Sea Oasis. *Science News* 121(25):410-13.
    Describes how scientists are studying the newly discovered deep-sea vent habitats.

Ward, F. 1985. The Pearl. *National Geographic* 168(2):192-223.
    Describes both the cultured-pearl industries of Asia and the developing freshwater pearl industry in the United States.

Chapter 6

RAZORBACK SUCKERS

When the razorback sucker, Colorado squaw-fish, bonytail chub and humpback chub swam the Colorado's upper basin in more bountiful numbers, anglers considered them "trash fish" to be hurled on the stream bank.

Mark Obmascik
The Denver Post, May 14, 1989

FOLKLORE

Razorback Sucker

One lovely summer day I was enjoying a hike along the Colorado River. There was a section of the river with some rocks in the middle. As I came around a corner in the trail I saw an extremely agitated squirrel scampering along the shore. He would scoot for a ways, then turn around and run back. After watching him do this several times, I looked out in the river to see what he seemed to be paying attention to.

There on top of a big rock was a peanut. That was it! The squirrel wanted that nut! Then he changed his route and started back away from the river. He turned around and dug his feet in furiously and raced to the river. He took a mighty leap and darned if he didn't land on top of the rock. I felt so happy for his success but decided to stay and watch because I wanted to see how he got off the rock.

He sat out there in the sun on the rock and carefully broke the peanut open and took out the nuts. He stuffed them in the sides of his mouth because you could see the lumps there. Then he explored his rock. It was a good size rock but nothing special. I could see that he was now trying to figure out how he could get back to shore. He finally tried to do a short-field take off but I could see he wasn't going to make it to the shore. I was prepared to watch him get dunked.

Then a big fish flashed out of the water and snatched the squirrel in midair. It was a big sucker. I could see his large thick lips with the lower lip lobes. He disappeared back into the river. As I stood there stunned, I was even more stunned when I saw that sucker's head come out of the water and carefully place a peanut on the rock.

—old tall tale
Adapted and retold by Norma J. Livo

Many superstitions relating to fish originated, of course, with fishermen. In Europe, fishermen towed the fiddle fish behind their board in the hope that it would ensure a rich catch. British fishermen, after a meal of herring, never threw away the bones. They bundled them in a paper wrapping and tossed them into the sea, where the bones would magically reassemble themselves into a new herring that would then call his fellow fish from the deep and into the fishing nets. Scottish fishermen would throw a friend into the lake and then, pretending he was a fish, pull him in to shore. This was to let the fish in the lake know they were supposed to imitate the human.

Many western Europeans recommend spitting on the hook for good luck. Other fishermen's advice for a good catch:

> *Fish bite the least,*
> *With wind in the east.*
> *Near the surface, quick to bite,*
> *Catch your fish when rain's in sight.*

The mackerel is a fish that is easily caught by deception during the spring. In France, the person who was the butt of the day's foolery on All Fool's Day became known as the "April Fish," the nickname given to the mackerel.

The fish has flourished in religious symbology. The Syrians regarded fish as holy and not to be eaten. Early Christians took the fish as their symbol, representing Christ feeding the multitude with five loaves and two fishes; he also made his disciples "fishers of men." In Egypt, the god of darkness, Set, murdered his hated sun-and-moon-god brother, Osiris. He hacked his brother's body into 14 pieces and scattered them. Osiris's reproductive organ was thrown in the Nile River, where it was swallowed by a fish. Thereafter, the fish was associated with both gods. As Osiris, it represented fecundity and rebirth. It stood for evil, crime, and darkness when connected with Set. And the Greeks linked fish to their love deities. Aphrodite was born in the sea from an egg brooded by a dove. A fish shepherded her to land.

"He who eats no fish" referred to Catholics. "Neither fish nor fowl" is a phrase traceable to England's King Henry when he broke from the Catholic Church.

Fish represented many of the conflicting elements in life. In some cultures they stood for knowledge and wisdom. This belief began when someone noticed that fish was the staple food of monks. Their intelligence and learning was assumed to be a product of their diet, hence the fish as "brain food."

For many societies, the fish represented fertility. The Carib Indians of the Caribbean and South America thought of the fish as always being young and believed that anyone who lived on a fish diet would remain forever young and sexually powerful. In Greenland it was believed that eating a special fish could produce pregnancy in both men and women. In Java the husband of a childless wife would take a fish from the "childless sea" and eat it. Then he would be able to sire children. And in medieval Europe, people often burned fish during their fertility rites to drive off the evil spirits. Today, it is still the custom in Samoa, India, and Brazil to give fish as gifts to virgins to induce pregnancy.

Certain fish are able to produce their young without mating. In some societies, the expression "cold fish" means a person of little sexual ardor.

Fish take their place in the world of the supernatural as mermaids and even shape-shifters, who have sometimes given amazing gifts to fishermen for seting them free. The Ottawa Indians believed that fish contained the souls of their dead. In India, fish are the favorite food of ghosts; in Wales, they are used as oracles; and in Cornwall, England, the fairies hate their smell.

And finally, some philosophical fish folklore:

> *On being content—better a small fish than an empty dish.*
>
> *It is better to be a big fish in a small pond than a small fish in a big pond.*
>
> *In a great river, great fish are found,*
> *But take heed lest you be drowned.*
>
> *It is a silly fish that is caught twice.*
>
> *Don't bargain for fish that are still in the water.*
>
> *Gut no fish till you get them.*
>
> *No one cries over stinking fish.*

NATURAL HISTORY

Suckers belong to the Catostomidae family. Razorback suckers (*Xyrauchen texanus*), like many in this family, often reach large sizes. They are called razorbacks because of the sharp edged ridge in back of the head. This ridge is an adaptation to life in the large rivers of the West, where it helps stabilize the fish as they face strong currents.

Razorback sucker.

The razorback sucker is one of the handful of fish native to the Colorado River Basin in the western United States. And, like other large native fish, such as the Colorado squawfish, humpback chub, and bonytail, the razorback sucker is now listed as endangered by the U.S. Fish and Wildlife Service.

Description

The adult razorback sucker has three distinctive features that distinguish it from all other fish:

- a sharp-edged ridge behind its head (juvenile fish lack the sharp ridge but develop it as they mature);

- large, thick lips (a feature common to all "suckers" and the basis for the name), with two lobes on the lower lip; and

- large size—most adults are about 20 inches (51cm) long and weigh 2 or 3 pounds (0.9-1.4kg). The largest individuals are up to 3 feet (0.9m) long and weigh up to 14 pounds (6.3kg).

Razorback suckers consume invertebrates, such as small crustaceans, and some algae. Males tend to be smaller and slimmer than females. Razorback suckers tend to be rather drab in color, with olive or dark brown predominating above and grading into a white belly. Breeding males, however, develop yellow or orange color below, sometimes with rose-colored fins.

Razorbacks, like other fish, have lateral lines. These are a row of slightly lighter scales extending along the side of the fish from in back of the gills to near the tail. These specialized scales serve as sense organs that help the fish orient itself in the water.

Range

The Colorado River and its large tributaries once were the habitat for razorback suckers. Formerly widespread from Wyoming to Mexico in this basin, razorback suckers are now found in scattered and much-diminished populations. The largest concentration of razorbacks is in Lake Mohave, along the Arizona-Nevada border. In addition to the razorback sucker, another 62 species of suckers occur in the United States and Canada.

Interactions

Native Americans living along the Colorado River used razorback suckers as food and constructed V-shaped traps along the shorelines to catch razorback suckers and other fish. The Yumans called this fish *tsa'xnap;* Cocopahs named it *suxyex.*

However, after American settlement of this area, razorback suckers, as well as many other fish native to the Colorado River, were often considered "rough" or "trash" fish. In fact, people even disputed the edibility of the razorback sucker, with some people claiming that its flesh was "soft and unpalatable." This fish was common enough that it was harvested for food and fertilizer into the 1940s.

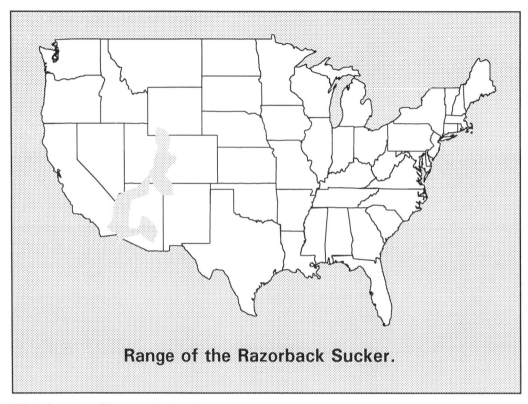

Range of the Razorback Sucker.

Historic range of the razorback sucker.

Being called a sucker probably doesn't help the popularity of the razorback. Even fishery biologists use words like *bizarre* and *prehistoric* when describing this large fish, so it isn't surprising that other people react to razorback suckers with words like *ugly* and *hideous*. Although the lips of razorbacks are formed for feeding on small aquatic invertebrates, we sometimes have the lingering—but erroneous—impression that they are the same type of blood-sucking arrangement found on leeches.

As the Colorado River goes, so goes the razorback sucker and other native fish. Since American settlement of the western United States, rivers in the Colorado River Basin have undergone fundamental changes. In many places, the water is now restrained behind large dams. Layers of different temperatures develop in the stilled waters; when water reenters the river below the dam, it is often several degrees cooler than normal. The dams also limit the amount of seasonal flooding that previously scoured the river bottoms and channels.

Farmers divert water from rivers to irrigate their crops. The water, bearing salts and agricultural chemicals, is then returned to the river. Portions of the rivers have been channelized (dredged and straightened), decreasing the variety and abundance of aquatic habitats. The surrounding land often has been altered so that increasing amounts of soil erode, entering the rivers as a smothering blanket of silt that suffocates eggs as well as the invertebrate life used as food by the adult fish.

We have also permitted—even encouraged—the introduction of sport fish that compete with native fish or prey on their young. Fifty nonnative fish species now occupy the Colorado River Basin, and many of them are abundant.

These alterations of native habitats have had catastrophic effects on many fish. Within the previous century, about 40 of North America's freshwater fish have become extinct, and about 80 percent of the fish in the arid Southwest are endangered.

The razorback sucker wasn't listed as endangered by the U.S. Fish and Wildlife Service until 1991. The continued presence of large fish in reservoirs such as Lake Mohave seemed to indicate that razorbacks remained in healthy, if diminished, numbers. However, when ages were determined for 70 of the razorbacks in this reservoir, all were at least 24 years old and the oldest individual was 44. For more than 20 years, these razorbacks had produced no surviving young. In other parts of the razorback's range, a similar lack of young was also observed.

The razorbacks *try* to produce young. Each year razorback suckers join in spawning aggregations in shallow water. During spawning, a ripe female settles to an area of gravel with males beside her. As she sheds her eggs, the males simultaneously fertilize them. The breeding season peaks between January and March in Lake Mohave and from mid-April to mid-June in upper-basin populations.

Although a single female may produce 2,000 or more eggs during the breeding season, few if any of the resulting young survive. The problem seems to be that nonnative fish gobble up larval razorback suckers. Now fishery biologists are protecting razorback suckers in refuge ponds and hatcheries.

Sometimes the razorbacks find such refuges on their own. In one area, gravel mining along the Colorado River produced a 20-acre pond. Apparently some razorback suckers entered the pond during a flood and got trapped there. A thriving population of about 600 individuals now occupies the pond. Young razorbacks were able to survive because there weren't other fish to consume them.

Birds also prey on razorback suckers occasionally. Cormorants—a type of fish-eating bird— consumed about 70 percent of the young razorbacks in a Utah hatchery one year. This type of predation probably isn't a big problem in the rivers and streams that constitute native razorback habitat, because birds would have a more difficult time seeing their prey in turbid waters.

Biologists are also reintroducing razorback suckers into rivers and streams where they once occurred. Some of the reintroduced fish are equipped with radio telemetry devices so that biologists can track movements and learn more about the requirements of razorback suckers. The long lives possible for razorback suckers may give biologists enough time to learn about and correct the problems facing this species.

One of the greatest problems facing razorback suckers and other large Colorado River fish is that, for the most part, we simply don't think about them. We don't observe them as we water ski and fish in the reservoirs taming the rivers of the Colorado River Basin. They are far from our thoughts when we bite into peaches or oranges grown with water taken from the razorback's native habitat. They are invisible, and without our efforts, they may disappear.

RAZORBACK SUCKER
ACTIVITIES

1. If you live in one of the western states, your local fish and game division might have razorback suckers that you can view in hatcheries or refuge ponds. For example, endangered fish such as the razorback sucker live in refuge ponds at the Horsethief Canyon State Wildlife Area near Fruita in western Colorado.

2. Do your part to help native fish by keeping alien fish out of streams, rivers, and lakes. Never release fish (including bait fish) into waters unless you got the fish from the same location. If you have aquarium fish but find you can no longer keep your fish, find other people to give them a new home. In some states, it is illegal to release nonnative fish.

3. Learn about the fish in your area, especially if you are an angler. A field guide, such as *Freshwater Fishes* by Lawrence Page and Brooks Burr (number 42 in the Peterson Field Guide Series), can help you identify fish you encounter.

4. Razorback suckers suffer from a public relations problem. Even though the fish is endangered and its loss would inevitably be felt ecologically, it seems hard to drum up support for the fish with the unappealing name. You head up a public relations firm and have just been hired to rename the razorback sucker. Study the natural history extensively and come up with three or four alternative names that might help the image of the fish.

5. In reference to the previous activity, now that you have an appealing name for the razorback sucker, plan a public relations campaign that will show the value of the fish so that people will want to join in efforts to save the species from extinction.

6. Using papier-mâché, make a full-scale model of the razorback sucker.

7. Organize a razorback sucker fan club. Publish a newsletter about the fish.

From *Of Bugs and Beasts*. © 1995. Teacher Ideas Press. (800) 237-6124.

BIBLIOGRAPHY

Books

Bestgen, Kevin R. 1990. Status Review of the Razorback Sucker, *Xyrauchen texanus*. Colorado State University Larval Fish Laboratory, Contribution 44, 92 pp.
This technical report summarizes the natural history of the razorback sucker and discusses research and management to aid this endangered species.

Lane, Margaret. 1994. *The Fish: The Story of the Stickleback*. Art by John Butler. New York: Dial.
Introduces the life cycle and mating habits of some small fishes found in freshwater and saltwater in northern countries.

Minckley, W. L., and J. E. Deacon, eds. 1991. *Battle Against Extinction: Native Fish Management in the American West*. Tucson: University of Arizona Press, 517 pp.
This book provides the most complete account of the history, endangerment, and current management of the razorback sucker and other fish native to the western United States.

Articles

Tyus, Harold M. 1992. Razorback Sucker Listed as Endangered: A Further Decline in the Colorado River System. *Endangered Species UPDATE* 9(5-6):1-3.
Summarizes why the razorback sucker was added to the endangered species list and describes the tremendous alterations humans have made to western rivers.

Young, Connie. 1992. Out of Harm's Way. *Colorado Outdoors* 41(6):27-29.
Describes recovery programs for the razorback sucker and other endangered fish.

Chapter 7

JELLYFISH

If the moon jellies are symbols of the coastal waters, seldom straying more than a few miles offshore, it is otherwise with the great red jellyfish, Cyanea, which in its periodic invasions of bays and harbors links the shallow green waters with the bright distances of the open sea.

Rachel Carson, *The Edge of the Sea*

FOLKLORE

There just aren't too many stories being written about jellyfish. However, some of the names of jellyfish are rooted in mythology. For example, the *Cassiopeia* jellyfish was named after the mother of Andromeda. She also became a constellation after her death, together with her husband, her daughter, her throne, and the sea monster sent by Poseidon to ravage the shores of her country. Scientists use the word *medusa* when they talk about a mature jellyfish. In Greek mythology, Medusa was the youngest of the Gorgons, a monstrous woman with snakes for hair and a gaze that turned people to stone. Dangling tentacles on a jellyfish reminded scientists of snakes.

NATURAL HISTORY

Jellyfish are not fish, and although they do contain a jellylike material, you probably wouldn't want to spread it on your morning toast. Jellyfish and related animals are members of the phylum Cnidaria (pronounced *nigh-dear-ee-ah*), a group that includes corals, sea anemones, and hydras. The term Cnidaria comes from a Greek word meaning "nettle." Contact with a Cnidarian's stinging cells—even after the animal is dead—can cause rashes or welts on the skin. As you may know if you have brushed against a nettle, contact with these plants also can cause a stinging rash. Because of their irritating stings, some jellyfish are called sea nettles and sea wasps.

Scientists divide the phylum Cnidaria into at least three classes or groups: Hydrozoa (animals such as hydras and fire corals), Anthozoa (sea anemones and corals), and Scyphozoa (true jellyfish). Some biologists place the box jellyfish in a fourth class, the Cubozoa. About 200 species of true jellyfish belong to the group Scyphozoa.

These anemones, like jellyfish, are in the phylum Cnidaria.

Other animals sometimes called jellyfish belong to the group Hydrozoa. One is a little freshwater jellyfish with the scientific name *Craspedacusta sowerbyi*. This small animal inhabits scattered reservoirs and lakes in North America. Two other interesting Hydrozoans often referred to as jellyfish are the Portuguese man-of-war and the by-the-wind sailor. Both of these animals are actually colonies of medusae and polyps. Like true jellyfish, the Portuguese man-of-war and the by-the-wind sailor contain stinging cells in their tentacles. The Portuguese man-of-war can produce a dangerous sting. In addition, animals called comb jellies belong to the phylum Ctenophora.

Technically, the only animals that should be called jellyfish are those in the group Scyphozoa. But since many other animals have similar characteristics, even scientists sometimes informally call these creatures jellyfish. You can also use the terms "jellies" or "sea jellies" to describe all these animals.

Description

Jellyfish have an entirely different body plan than more familiar animals like mammals, birds, reptiles, amphibians, and fish. Mathematicians often speak of an "axis of symmetry." On a graph, this is where points on opposite sides of a line balance one another. Animals also show symmetry. As vertebrates, we are most familiar with *bilateral* symmetry, that is, the left side of the body is the mirror image of the right side.

In comparison, jellyfish show *radial* symmetry. You can see the difference in these two types of symmetry in the figure below. Place a mirror on the lines. Only one line works to reconstitute an image of the face. In contrast, any line through the center works for the bell of the jellyfish.

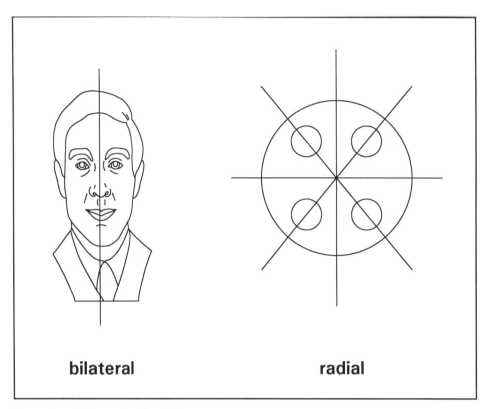

bilateral   **radial**

Examples of bilateral and radial symmetry.

The rounded bell of a jellyfish can be the size of a quarter in the thimble jellyfish or 12 feet (3.7m) across in the lion's mane jellyfish. A thick layer of jelly, which contains few living cells, fills the space between the upper and lower surface of the bell. A fringe of tentacles grows around the outer edge of the bell. Oral or feeding arms extend away from the body on the underside with the jellyfish's mouth located in the center. The mouth opens into the single body cavity.

Since water supports its body, a jellyfish doesn't need bones or other hard parts. It moves by a form of "jet propulsion": When the jellyfish contracts its muscles, it forces water out from under its body, allowing it to move in the opposite direction. A moving jellyfish looks a little like an umbrella opening and closing.

Jellyfish often form swarms. At least one little jellyfish has a special swimming pattern—swimming upward in clockwise circles while rotating counterclockwise—that helps individuals stay with others of their kind. According to James Lipton, the author of a book about collective terms, a group of jellyfish is called a smack.

In some ways, jellyfish can be described by what they don't have: no eyes, no ears, no tongue, no nose, and no brain to interpret sensory signals. The cells in a jellyfish can get oxygen directly from the water, removing the need for blood, heart, and gills or lungs. Yet a jellyfish can "smell" and "taste" with specialized cells scattered on its surface. Light-sensitive organs allow it to tell light from dark. The mouth and tentacles contain touch receptors that help the jellyfish capture food.

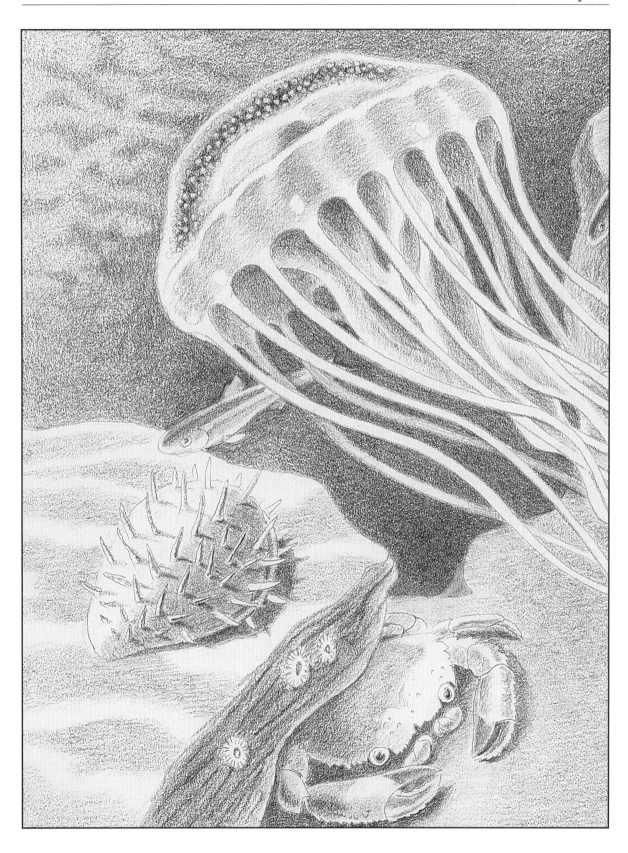

Jellyfish have stinging cells called nematocysts that help in defending themselves and capturing food. Each nematocyst contains a tube coiled like a spring. Depending on the type of jellyfish, the tubes are armed with a variety of spines, barbs, and venoms. Contact activates the nematocyst, and the tube shoots out, injecting any venom into the victim, whether fish or swimmer. The firing of a nematocyst happens *very* quickly—within 0.5 milliseconds—one of the fastest movements ever recorded for a living organism.

Touching a jellyfish can make your skin merely tingle or can result in serious stings. The most toxic venoms belong to box jellyfish called sea wasps. Sea wasps in Australia have caused many human deaths. Australian lifeguards used to wear pantyhose to protect themselves against sea wasps; now they wear bodysuits made of Lycra. A less toxic sea wasp occurs in the Gulf of Mexico and off the southeastern shores of the United States.

Although the body of a jellyfish seems very simple, its life cycle can be very complicated. In the typical jellyfish life cycle, male adults, or medusae, release sperm into the water. The sperm fertilizes the female medusa's eggs, and each fertilized egg begins to develop into a larva. After being released by the female jellyfish, the larva attaches itself to the ocean bottom and develops into a polyp.

The polyp grows for months or even for years. During this time, some polyps make buds and divide into two or more individual polyps, a form of asexual reproduction. When mature, the polyp begins to look like a stack of tiny, eight-armed snowflakes. Each of the snowflakes is a baby jellyfish that eventually breaks off the top of the polyp and floats away to grow and mature into a medusa. In this way, a single fertilized egg can result in many identical jellyfish. Both the moon jellyfish and cannonball jellyfish have this type of life cycle.

All true jellyfish have the medusa stage. However, jellyfish that live in the open ocean sometimes skip the polyp stage. Instead, they release eggs that develop directly into young medusae.

Range

Jellyfish occur throughout the oceans of the world, from tropical seas to Arctic waters. About 200 species of true jellyfish belong to the group Scyphozoa. Some of these jellyfish live at great depths in the ocean. Others occupy shallow water. For example, along the coast of New England lives a little jellyfish that attaches itself to plants and rocks in shallow water. In the mangrove swamps of Florida, a jellyfish called *Cassiopeia* rests upside-down on the shallow, muddy bottom.

Stinging jellyfish commonly encountered in American waters include the lion's mane, sea nettle, and sea blubber. Although not a true jellyfish, the Portuguese man-of-war is also responsible for serious stings. The tentacles of this animal can trail 50 feet (15m) behind its float. Lifeguards make swimmers leave the water when they spot this stinging sea creature.

Another animal often called a jellyfish is the freshwater medusa, or *Craspedacusta sowerbyi*, which occasionally is seen in reservoirs and lakes in North America. Big ones grow as large as three-quarters of an inch (1.9cm) across.

Interactions

The tide goes out along the seashore, revealing crumpled lumps washed up on the beach. Perhaps these blobs look a little greasy or remind us of slimy plastic bags draped on the sand. These are the only views some of us have of jellyfish. However, these dead or dying heaps bear little resemblance to the shimmering creatures in their native element, the water. Here delicate, umbrella-shaped animals pulsate above a tangle of tentacles that contain specialized stinging cells.

People who catch shrimp often catch jellyfish in their nets too. They refer to the jellyfish as "hot jelly" because the nematocysts (stinging cells) can sting even after the jellyfish has died. In fact, some animals, such as sea slugs, can "recycle" nematocysts. After the sea slug eats tentacles containing nematocysts, the nematocysts migrate to the slug's skin, where they help defend it.

Jellyfish are the favored food of the leatherback sea turtle, the largest turtle in the world. Because discarded plastic bags can mimic the appearance of jellyfish, sometimes leatherbacks eat plastic bags by mistake. Other animals, including starfish, fish, and humans, also consume jellyfish.

Sometimes jellyfish seem like pulsating communities. Little crabs and other crustaceans may hitch rides on their bodies while fish nibble at dangling tentacles. Algae can add color to some jellyfish, living symbiotically within the jellyfish's tissues. The jellyfish obtains food from the algae and provides nitrogen and other wastes that the algae can use.

Jellyfish are paradoxical and full of contrasts. They are predators that wait for their prey to come to them. The medusa drifting with ocean currents appear far removed from small polyps anchored on the sea floor. Their ability to sting contrasts with their faintly ridiculous delicacy. Jellyfish are 95 percent water and lack hard parts, but traces of them remain in fossils 500 million years old and the living creatures themselves shimmer today in the waters of our world.

JELLYFISH ACTIVITIES

1. Make a model of a jellyfish. To make a jellyfish like the one illustrated, you need three 12-inch (30cm) pipe cleaners, a square of plastic wrap approximately 12 inches (30cm) on a side, decorative (Easter basket) grass or Christmas tree icicles, and white glue.

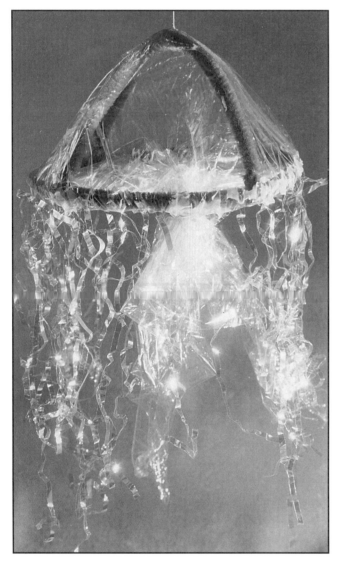

This "jellyfish mobile" uses pipe cleaners, plastic wrap, and transparent decorative grass.

a. Cut about 4 inches (10cm) from two of the pipe cleaners; counting the uncut pipe cleaner, you have one full-size, two medium, and two small lengths of pipe cleaner.

b. Make a frame for the body by bending the full-size pipe cleaner into a ring and twisting the ends together. Attach the two medium pipe cleaners in arches above the first ring to make the frame like an inverted bowl shape. The arches should be at right angles to one another.

c. Center a large square of plastic wrap where the arches cross one another. Gently wrap the plastic around the outside of the pipe cleaners, gathering it under the frame. Secure the gathered plastic with one of the short pipe cleaners. The hanging ends of the plastic represent the jellyfish's oral arms.

d. Squeeze a short, thin line of white glue onto the plastic wrap along the edge of the frame and attach the ends of decorative grass or icicles so they dangle. If desired, you can use a toothpick to help press individual strands of grass onto the glue. Continue working around the edge until the entire circumference contains "tentacles."

e. To make a quick and easy hook for hanging the jellyfish, pass the remaining short length of pipe cleaner through the plastic wrap under the point where the arches join. For a more delicate way to hang the jellyfish, use a needle and guide thread under the point where the arches join.

From *Of Bugs and Beasts.* © 1995. Teacher Ideas Press. (800) 237-6124.

2. Flowers show different kinds of symmetry just as jellyfish and people do. From the list of common flowers below, indicate the type of symmetry that each flower has. Cut pictures of flowers from magazines or seed catalogs. Paste flowers that have bilateral symmetry on one page and paste flowers with radial symmetry on another page.

Flower	Bilateral	Radial
tulips		
snapdragons		
irises		
daisies		
dandelions		
violets		
lilies		
roses		
marigolds		
lilacs		

3. Invent a recipe for a peanut butter and "jellyfish" sandwich.

4. Hydra belong to the same phylum, Cnidaria, as jellyfish. You can purchase hydras from biological supply houses. If you can obtain a few, spend some time observing them—how they look, how they move, and so on. Hydra are very interesting to watch on the screen or television monitor if your school has a projection microscope or a video attachment.

5. Because there aren't many stories written about jellyfish—either fact or fancy—this is the perfect subject to use in creating new stories. Start with a main character, a setting, and a problem that the main character has to solve.

   The main character usually tries three times (in Western cultures) to solve the problem. The story then has a solution to the problem and an ending. Sometimes heroes have to leave home to solve the problem and when they return, they have been transformed by their adventures. In Native American cultures, the hero has four tries to solve the problem. With these suggestions in mind, create a jellyfish story to add to the much-needed literature of jellyfish.

   Some activities to warm up for creating this story might be helpful. For example, working in pairs, one person can tell a story to a partner. The partner can then retell the story, varying the emotion, the language, the culture, the setting, and the time of the story. Or one person can start a selected story and then at a signal, the next person continues the story until the next signal is given. Another idea is to make up new verses to well-known folksongs using the jellyfish. The stories can then be illustrated and placed in class books or other media productions.

6. You learned in this chapter that several jellyfish together are known as a "smack of jellyfish." There are many interesting names for collections of animals. Using James Lipton's book (listed in the bibliography) as a resource, develop a quiz game based on the names of collections of animals.

From *Of Bugs and Beasts.* © 1995. Teacher Ideas Press. (800) 237-6124.

JELLYFISH MUST BE JELLY 'CAUSE JAM DON'T SHAKE LIKE THAT!—CLUES

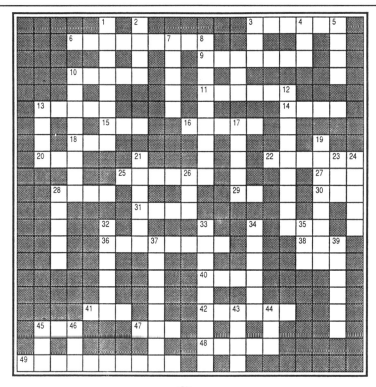

Clues

ACROSS

3 Middle-Eastern language
6 Jellyfish appendages
9 Class containing box jellyfish
10 Key member of Hydrozoa class
11 Group of related plants or animals
13 Type of evergreen
14 Mysterious snowman
15 Place to stay
16 Hard-shelled animal that often forms reefs
18 Roman breakfast
20 La _____, S.A. capital
22 Immature jellyfish form
25 Mythical woman with snake hair
27 Sound of a cat
28 Stinging insect
29 Former
30 Boston Transit Co.
31 Ms. Turner
36 Sea creatures
38 Attempt
40 King of the jungle
41 TV sitcom alien
42 Mineralized remains or imprint in rock
45 Fruit concoction to put on toast
47 Reverential wonder
48 Use chewing gum in a rude way
49 Comb jellies phylum

DOWN

1 Jellyfish phylum
2 Spanish for "cow"
3 Commotion
4 Constricting snake
5 Basic unit of life form
7 Stretchable material
8 Jellyfish group
10 Another jellyfish group
12 Unfactual folklore
13 Poker money unit
17 Primitive plant form
19 Both sides identical
21 Stinging bush
23 Dog, cat, etc.
24 A group of bees
26 Liquid home to jellyfish and others
28 Chief ingredient in 26 down
32 A type of symmetry
33 Subject of this puzzle
34 Pain-producing structures
35 Airport abbreviation
37 Well-known dangerous jellyfish
39 Banana color
43 Hospital command
44 Kind
45 Propulsion system
46 Male humans

From *Of Bugs and Beasts.* © 1995. Teacher Ideas Press. (800) 237-6124.

BIBLIOGRAPHY

Books

Carson, Rachel. 1955. *The Edge of the Sea*. Boston: Houghton Mifflin, 276 pp.
The author, who later wrote *Silent Spring*, discusses the living forms, including jellyfish, found along the Atlantic coast.

Coldrey, Jennifer. 1982. *Jellyfish and Other Sea Creatures*. Photographs by Peter Parks. New York: G. P. Putnam.
Examines in text and photographs the physical characteristics and life cycles of the jellyfish and related sea creatures. An Oxford Scientific Film project.

Freedman, Russell. 1982. *Killer Fish*. New York: Holiday House.
The author describes jellyfish on pages 38 and 39. This book introduces readers to some dangerous sea creatures.

Gould, Stephen J. 1985. *The Flamingo's Smile*. New York: W. W. Norton, 476 pp.
Chapter 5, "A Most Ingenious Paradox," discusses the Portuguese man-of-war and how naturalists have viewed this colonial animal.

Gowell, Elizabeth Tayntor. 1993. *Sea Jellies*. A New England Aquarium Book. New York: Franklin Watts.
A thorough and wonderfully illustrated book about jellyfish and their relatives for younger readers.

Kite, Patricia. 1993. *Down in the Sea: The Jellyfish*. Morton Grove, Ill.: Albert Whitman.
A simple introduction to the jellyfish, describing its physical characteristics, life cycle, and eating habits.

Lipton, James. 1991. *An Exaltation of Larks: The Ultimate Edition*. New York: Viking.
This book lists collective terms for both animals and humans.

Livo, Norma J., and Sandra Rietz. 1987. *Storytelling Activities*. Englewood, Colo.: Libraries Unlimited.
A collection of ideas and activities to develop storytelling in a variety of social settings.

Articles

DeVries, Dennis R. 1991. The Freshwater Jellyfish, *Craspedacusta sowerbyi*: A Summary of Its Life History, Ecology, and Distribution. *Journal of Freshwater Ecology* 7(1):7-16.
Summarizes the geographic distribution of a freshwater medusa in North America.

Dybas, Cheryl Lyn. 1992. Space Age Jewels. *National Wildlife*. 30(5):18-24. (August-September)
Describes jellyfish research, including a trip to space by 2,700 moon jellyfish aboard the space shuttle.

Hall, Howard. 1992. High Seas' Drifter. *Natural History* (December):26-29.
    Filmmakers discover a 20-foot-long (6m) jellyfish and the community of small animals that use the jellyfish for a home.

Kingsmill, Suzanne. 1992. Medusa on the Move. *Nature Canada* 21(4): 12-13.
    The author describes recent sightings of the freshwater medusa in Canada.

Larson, Ron. 1991. Why Jellyfish Stick Together. *Natural History* (October): 66-71.
    A researcher describes the swimming patterns of thimble jellyfish.

Rudloe, Jack, and Anne Rudloe. 1991. Jellyfish Do More with Less Than Almost Anything. *Smithsonian* 21(11):100-4, 106, 108-11. (February)
    Some beautiful color photographs grace this article about jellyfish and other sea jellies.

Of the
Earth

Chapter **8**

SNAKES

People are both repelled and fascinated by snakes, even when they have never seen one in nature. In most cultures the serpent is the dominant wild animal of mythical and religious symbolism. Manhattanites dream of them with the same frequency as Zulus.

E. O. Wilson, *The Diversity of Life*

FOLKLORE

A Snake in the Road

One cold, frosty morning, a man was walking down the road to town. He came to a deep hole along the side of the road and from inside it he heard a voice saying, "Help me, help me." He walked over to the hole and looked down and there in the middle of the hole was a snake looking back up at him. "Help me, help me."

The man answered, "What kind of help do you want?"

"Get me out of here. I am too cold to do it myself," whined the snake.

"Why should I help you get out of there? You would only bite me," demanded the man.

"Oh no, I promise you if you help me I won't do that," hissed the snake.

So against his better judgment, the man went underneath a tree and snapped off a long branch. He went over to the hole and said, "Remember your promise." Then he carefully put the branch under the belly of the snake and flipped it out into the nearby field. He started walking on the road again. Then over in the field he heard, "Help me, help me."

"What is it this time, snake?" he asked.

"I am so cold I can't move. Please put me in your pocket and take me along with you. That way I can warm up," wheedled the snake.

"How do I know you won't bite me?" said the man.

"I promise you I won't," sneezed the snake.

Once more, the man took pity on the snake. He went over to the snake and told it to wrap itself up into a circle like a rag rug coil. He carefully, very carefully picked it up and put it in his coat pocket. He started back down the road and for about a mile he almost forgot about the snake because it never moved. But then he started to feel some movement in his pocket and then he saw the head of the snake come slowly, ever so slowly out of his pocket. Fast as a flash the snake lunged at his hand and bit him. Just before he dropped dead to the ground the man roared, "But you promised."

"You knew I was a snake when you picked me up."

—African-American folklore
Adapted and retold by Norma J. Livo

Some gods were combinations of two or more species. The feathered serpent, a blend of bird and snake, was worshipped under assorted names by the Mayans of Central America, the Aztecs of Mexico, and some tribes in the southwestern United States. The story goes that this plumed serpent, called Quetzalcoatl by the Aztecs, traveled to the underworld and came upon the bones of people who had lived in previous worlds. He took the bones back to the surface and mixed them with his own blood, thus creating human beings.

In the eastern and southeastern United States, native tribes believed that a great underwater serpent with one red and one green horn could be lured to land and to his death by the shamans. When the body of the snake was burned, his heart refused to burn and was cut up and used as witch medicine. In the Pueblos, the Hopi hold the Great Horned or Plumed Serpent prominently in sun ceremonies and hold snake dances largely as a prayer for rain. The Mojave of southern California believed in the gigantic Sky-Rattlesnake, who was killed and from whose blood came Rattlesnake, a supernatural being who lives at Three Mountains. The Yokut shamans of central California lure snakes out of their dens in early spring and use them in curing ceremonies. Another southwestern tribe tells of how the snake turned into the rainbow.

In Greek mythology, snakes were viewed both as evil creatures, such as Medusa with her hair of writhing snakes, and as a symbol of renewal. One story of Heracles combines both ideas.

Heracles (or Hercules, as the Romans called him) was born out of wedlock to Zeus and the mortal Alcmene. Hera, the goddess wife of Zeus, sent two serpents to destroy the infant when he was just a few minutes old. Tiny Heracles strangled them both in his crib. The second labor of Heracles was to slay the poisonous nine-headed water snake, Typhon. Every time he attacked the creature's heads and hacked one off, it immediately sprouted two in its place. He got his nephew Iolaus to burn the stump and seal it to keep new heads from growing. When Heracles severed the middle head, which was believed to be immortal, the monster was finally killed. He buried that head beneath a giant boulder so that it couldn't escape.

The snake was viewed as a symbol of renewal by the Greeks because of the snake's ability to shed its skin without dying, which was perceived as a process of shedding old age and returning to youth. Because this compared to a patient's shedding illness and starting a healthy life again, the snake-entwined staff, the caduceus, was adopted as a medical symbol (it is believed that the caduceus came from Egypt to the Greeks). Mercury held a caduceus, enabling him to induce others to sleep. In fact, Mercury presented the caduceus to the god of healing, Asclepius, who later took the form of a snake.

In Babylonian legends, in the region between the Tigris and Euphrates rivers the waters came together and produced two giant serpents, Lakhmu and Lakhamu, who gave birth to Anshar and Kishar. These two offspring were the sky and the earth, and all of the great gods of the celestial world and the underworld came from them.

The snake got its bad reputation in the Christian and Jewish religions from its nefarious tempting of Adam and Eve in the Garden of Eden. And of course, St. Patrick drove the snakes from Ireland, thus earning his place in history.

In pre-Christian times, medical researchers sought toxins from poisonous animals that might have medicinal value. Mithridates VI (132-63 B.C.) reasoned that the meat of the snake or some form of its venom might provide people with immunity because it was felt that a snake was immune to its own bite. The subsequent concoction, theriac, became used as a general cure-all. "Snake oils" were touted by medicine show quacks and physicians as an elixir that would cure anything. *Theriac* eventually became *treacle*, which eventually became known to mean *molasses*. It wasn't too many years ago that a mixture of sulfur and molasses was routinely used for the traditional spring tonic. These beliefs were also found in nineteenth-century reports about "wizards" in central Africa who told visiting Europeans that they could protect people against snake bites with a potion containing snake heads and ant eggs.

In Britain people believed that dried snake skin, when nailed over the hearth, would bring good luck to the family and protect the home from fire.

Some folks in Kentucky learned to be upset by dreams of a snake because it meant that the dreamer had enemies nearby. A dream of killing the snake meant that the dreamer had defeated those enemies. If the snake in the dream escaped, that was a warning to be wary of others and take care in dealings with them. It was also believed by Kentuckians that one could prevent headaches by wearing a headband fashioned from the rattles of the rattlesnake.

Some British and American rural folk believe that rheumatism can be cured by wrapping a strip of dried snake skin around the painful body area. In Louisiana, some believe that rheumatic pain can be relieved with a coating of grease from the rattlesnake.

As weather predictors, snakes were an American superstition.

> *Bury a snake,*
> *Good weather will make.*
> *Hanging it high*
> *Brings storm clouds nigh.*

This belief was widespread among the country's slave population and was possibly connected to the idea that snakes come out of their hiding places just before a rain. During slave times the practice was to hang the dead snakes out to dry before getting rid of them. Probably the real reason snakes were buried was because of the odor of decay. At any rate, it was believed that if you buried a snake you kept the rain away.

Following are some other misperceptions about snakes—and the facts:

- *Snakes can sting with their tails or tongues.* No snake has a stinger on its tail. The tongue is also harmless.

- *Milk snakes are often found near barns because they steal milk from cows.* Snakes don't drink milk (and no self-respecting cow would let them). Milk snakes are sometimes found near farm buildings because of the rodents that live in the area.

- *"Joint snakes" can break into pieces and then grow back together.* This myth is probably based on snake-like lizards called glass lizards, which possess fracture planes in the tail. These fracture planes allow a lizard to break off part of its tail to help avoid a predator. Once the tail breaks off, it can't rejoin the lizard. The lizard, though, eventually grows a new tail.

- *Rattlesnakes always rattle (or coil) before striking.* Rattlesnakes can strike without rattling and without coiling.

- *A hoop snake escapes by swallowing its tail and rolling away.* The "hoop snake" is a myth; no snake escapes in this manner.

- *Baby snakes seek shelter in their mother's mouth.* No snake protects its young in this way.

- *Snakes don't die until sundown.* Snakes may twitch and manifest other reflex motions after they are dead. However, when they are dead, they're dead regardless of the time of day.

- *Snakes are slimy.* Snakes have dry, scaly skin.

- *Snakeweed, snakeroot, or liberal drinks of alcohol cure a snake bite.* This seems to work—so long as the snake was nonvenomous to begin with.

- *Snakes can't bite underwater.* They can.

NATURAL HISTORY

Snakes belong to the order Squamata, a group of reptiles that includes lizards and amphisbaenians (burrowing animals that live in tropical and subtropical regions). Approximately 2,400 species of snakes have been identified.

Description

Snakes come in a bewildering array of sizes, patterns, and habits. Their eyes can be large and conspicuous or mere dots hidden beneath scales. In North America, snakes vary in size from tiny 6-inch (15cm) long blind snakes to indigo snakes, black rat snakes, bullsnakes, and coachwhip snakes reaching lengths of 100 inches (254cm). The largest snakes in the world are the reticulated pythons of Asia and the anacondas of South America, which can grow to lengths of 33 feet (10m) and weigh as much as 550 pounds (250kg). Yet for all their variety, snakes, with their elongated, legless, scale-covered bodies, are instantly recognizable.

Snakes look as though they are nearly all tail. Most of a snake's length consists of its tubular body. A relatively short tail lies behind the vent, or cloaca, the opening for waste products and reproduction.

Various legless lizards closely resemble snakes. All the legless lizards in North America, though, have eyelids that close. The glass lizards of the southeastern United States also have external ear openings. Snakes, in contrast, have unblinking eyes protected by transparent caps and lack external ear openings, eardrums, and middle-ear cavities. However, they can detect ground and waterborne vibrations, and at least some can hear low-frequency airborne sounds.

Snakes have an especially well-developed sense of smell. To smell, a snake flicks its tongue in the air, then inserts the forked tips into its Jacobson's organ, located in the roof of the mouth. Snakes use their sense of smell to find potential mates, detect prey, and generally investigate their world. A snake trying to find prey, for example, flicks its tongue at a much faster rate than when at rest.

Pit vipers (rattlesnakes, cottonmouths, and copperheads), and some boas and pythons have an additional sense: the ability to detect small differences in temperature. In pit vipers the heat receptors are located in a pair of pits near the nostrils. Boas and pythons have their heat receptors in pits on the lip scales.

Snakes have numerous internal adaptations. Their elongated bodies contain hundreds of vertebrae, resulting in extreme flexibility. (In contrast, our spinal columns contain 32 vertebrae.) Various internal organs have shifted position or have been eliminated. Most snakes, for example, have only one lung.

Many harmless snakes mimic the appearance or behavior of venomous snakes. Milk snakes and scarlet king snakes have a banded yellow, black, and red pattern that resembles that of coral snakes. Snake fanciers have a saying to help distinguish the venomous coral snakes from their harmless mimics: "Red to yellow, kill a fellow. Red to black, friend to Jack." The red and yellow bands are next to one another in coral snakes. In milk snakes and scarlet king snakes, the red bands are next to black bands.

Bullsnakes have a pattern of blotches that resembles the pattern on rattlesnakes, and an agitated bullsnake puts on a particularly convincing display that mimics the rattlesnake. It spreads its jaw, coils up, hisses, and vibrates its tail. If the bullsnake's tail should happen to be in dried grass or leaves, its display even sounds authentic.

Hognose snakes also look like rattlesnakes. If bothered, a hognose snake first tries to crawl away. Next, it tucks its head beneath its coils. When further annoyed, it flattens its neck, hisses loudly, and may "strike," but with a closed mouth. As the final act in this drama, the hognose snake writhes, then rolls onto its back and plays dead.

A hognose snake goes "belly up" when playing dead.

As anyone knows who has handled garter snakes and water snakes, many snakes smear predators (or people) with a smelly discharge from their cloaca. This odor is difficult to wash off, although it isn't nearly as bad (or long lasting) as skunk spray.

The garter snake was named because of its resemblance to the fancy garters people used to hold up stockings.

Snakes with brightly colored bellies often expose these colors when disturbed. Agitated ringneck snakes, for example, coil the bright tail into a corkscrew.

All snakes are carnivorous. They swallow their prey whole and usually start with the head. The type of prey a snake can handle depends partly on the snake's size; larger snakes are able to consume larger prey. However, to handle many prey—especially those larger than the snake's head—requires very flexible jaws. Snakes can "unhinge" their jaws, greatly expanding the mouth. Because snakes don't generate body heat like mammals, they sometimes go for weeks between large meals.

Although most people consider snakes and other reptiles to be cold-blooded, a better term is *ectothermic*. Ectothermic animals depend on the external environment for their body temperature. By basking or seeking warm microhabitats, ectothermic animals like snakes can often maintain relatively constant—and warm—body temperatures.

In temperate and cold climates, snakes escape cold winter weather by crawling into rodent burrows, deep crevices in the ground, or other hibernation sites. Sometimes great numbers of snakes den together over the winter. One person excavated an anthill in the fall and found 8 plains garter snakes, 101 redbelly snakes, and 148 smooth green snakes—257 snakes in all.

The largest gathering of snakes in the world takes place every fall in Manitoba, Canada, where 10,000 common garter snakes may hibernate together in a single den. Some of the snakes migrate ten miles (16km) between their summer feeding grounds and the dens, which are in underground limestone chambers.

Male garter snakes leave their dens as soon as it is warm enough. They court the females as they emerge, sometimes forming "mating balls" of several males trying to mate with a single female. Reproduction involves internal fertilization. Male snakes have paired sex organs, called hemipenes, which normally lie within the base of the tail. During mating, the hemipenes come out of the male's cloaca. The male snake uses one of the hemipenes to transfer sperm into the cloaca of the female.

Most female snakes lay eggs, seeking protected locations for their clutches. Snakes exhibit little if any parental care for their offspring. A few snakes, such as the Texas blind snake, may remain with their eggs for a time. However, most female snakes lay their eggs and then leave them to their fate.

Some snakes, including garter snakes and rattlesnakes, don't lay eggs. Instead, the females retain the developing eggs and give birth to live young. This mode of reproduction occurs especially often in cooler parts of the world. Whether the young snakes hatch from leathery eggs or are born live, they must immediately fend for themselves.

This newly hatched milk snake is ready to fend for itself. Some of its brothers and sisters are getting ready to hatch.

Snakes periodically shed their skins. A short time before shedding, a snake's eyes become cloudy looking and its skin looks dull. This change in appearance is from the secretion of fluid under the old skin. The snake begins the shedding process by rubbing its head against a rock or other object. This loosens the skin around the mouth and head. The snake gradually crawls out of the old skin. The discarded skin, usually inside-out, shows the imprint of each scale.

The shed skin of a bullsnake is in one large piece.

Range

Snakes are absent from polar regions and some isolated islands. Elsewhere, they occupy a variety of habitats from tropical jungles to suburban backyards, barren deserts to the open ocean. Of approximately 2,400 species of snakes in the world, 127 species live in the United States and the southern portions of Canada.

On most continents, harmless snakes outnumber dangerous snakes. The exception is Australia, where about 80 percent of the snakes are venomous. Following are the ranges of some of the approximately 19 species in North America that are dangerously venomous:

- Copperhead: one species ranging from Texas to Massachusetts

- Cottonmouth (water moccasin): one species ranging from Virginia and the Carolinas west to Texas

- Rattlesnakes: 15 species found throughout the United States, including two species that range into southern Canada

- Coral snakes: two species occupying Arizona, Texas, and southeastern states

- Yellowbelly sea snake: one species, occasionally seen in the Pacific Ocean off southern California.

Numerous field guides can help you learn about the dangerous snakes in your area. If in doubt about the identity of a snake, *always treat it as though it were venomous*. This means keeping your distance from the snake and leaving it alone.

Interactions

Few animals have the power to alarm us as much as snakes. We may be startled when we turn a stone and find a snake curled up beneath it, or frightened when we take a walk and see a serpent stretched across the trail. The phrase "snake in the grass" provides an image of hidden danger lurking in an otherwise peaceful scene. This phrase originated with the poet Virgil, who warned us to beware of someone who is a hidden enemy or who pretends friendship.

Part of our dread of snakes may be instinctive. After all, as one writer noted, early humans didn't have field guides to local snakes, so it was best to treat all snakes as potentially dangerous. However, we derive many, if not most, of our attitudes about snakes from the people around us. Seeing older individuals react to snakes with fear or disgust reinforces any negative feelings children might already have. Learning about these remarkable animals may be the best way to overcome a fear of snakes. Some studies show that schoolchildren given various types of positive information about snakes (including the opportunity to see someone handle a harmless snake) were less fearful than children without this knowledge and experience.

Despite the fact that many snakes are beneficial, they are the objects of endless persecution. Not only do some people kill any snake they happen to encounter, others search out dens to destroy. Our growing network of highways causes even more problems for snakes. Many are attracted to the warmth of the pavement, and vehicles take a tremendous toll, especially of the longer species. Snake populations tend to decline as highway traffic increases.

Loss of habitat threatens other snakes, such as the endangered San Francisco garter snake. This colorful garter snake occupies a very small area in California and is listed as endangered by the U.S. Fish and Wildlife Service. Home building also is destroying the habitat of the eastern indigo snake of the southeastern United States. These large snakes often live in the burrows made by gopher tortoises, another threatened species.

Because it is so well camouflaged, this smooth green snake is a difficult "snake in the grass" to see.

SNAKE ACTIVITIES

1. Two examples of the way snakes stir the imagination can be seen at Serpent Mound, Ohio, and Snake Path on the University of California-San Diego campus. Serpent Mound, an ancient quarter-mile-long (0.4 km) mound representing a serpent, is located near Hillsboro, Ohio. Adena Indians built Serpent Mound sometime between 800 B.C. and A.D. 1, but the significance of the mound is unknown. Artist Alexis Smith built a modern "Snake Path" on the San Diego campus of the University of California. Hexagonal slate tiles, arranged like scales, cover the 560-foot-long (170m) path. This serpent even has a pink granite tongue.

   One of these snake representations is very old and the other, very modern. What reasons can you think of that inspired the Adena Indians to make the giant Serpent Mound? What may have inspired modern artist Alexis Smith to create the Snake Path? How do you think the reasons for these two creations are similar? How are they different?

A view of Serpent Mound, in Ohio.

2. Get a field guide to reptiles and learn which snakes live in your state or province. How many species are harmless? How many species are venomous? How can you tell the harmless species from the venomous species?

3. Astronomers divide the night sky into various constellations. The constellation Serpens (the serpent) depicts a large snake. An associated constellation, Ophiuchus, is that of a man who holds the snake's head with his left hand and the tail with his right hand. Serpens contains the stars Alpha Serpentis and Theta Serpentis and the star cluster M16. Get a field guide to the night sky and locate Serpens and Ophiuchus. Observers in the Northern Hemisphere have a good view of these constellations in July.

4. There are many regional societies interested in snakes and other reptiles and amphibians. Contact the Society for the Study of Amphibians and Reptiles (SSAR) for information about societies in your area: SSAR Regional Societies, Eric M. Rundquist, Sedgwick County Zoo, 5555 Zoo Boulevard, Wichita, KS 67212.

5. We tend to think of snakes as dangerous, even as killers. And, in fact, a very small minority are. An article in *Men's Health* magazine gives the statistics of deaths in the United States by encounters with animals for 1991. The following table gives the number of human deaths caused by the various wild animals.

From *Of Bugs and Beasts*. © 1995. Teacher Ideas Press. (800) 237-6124.

Animal	Number of Deaths Caused
Deer	131
Bees	43
Dogs	14
Rattlesnakes	10
Spiders	4

The remaining deaths due to animals were caused by sharks, captive elephants, scorpions, rats, goats, captive leopards, jellyfish, coral snakes, alligators, grizzly bears, mountain lions, captive monkeys, stingrays, vultures, and killer whales. Deer, of course, we do not think of as being dangerous. They do, however, tend to run into or in front of cars and cause fatal accidents. Make a graph of this table. Instead of the words representing the animals, make drawings or collect pictures.

6. Poisonous snakes in the United States do not pose a great problem so far as human mortality is concerned, but other countries are not so lucky. It is estimated, for example, that the cobra kills about 10,000 people in India each year. Pretend that you are planning to visit India. Do research to determine what precautions you would need to make to keep from being a statistic.

7. Many snakes are beautifully decorated. Look in a good field guide that has photographs or drawings of snakes in color. Copy a pattern that you like and use it in designing a book cover.

8. Snakes are probably the first things we made when we started to work with clay. The basic technique of rolling clay under one's hand to form a cylindrical shape is easily learned. Go a step further. Fashion a snake from clay that is as realistic looking as you can make it. People interested in origami can try folding a paper snake.

9. Snakes vary greatly in length, from about 6 inches (15cm) to 33 feet (10m). Make a chart that compares the length of snakes. Research the speed of various snakes and make a chart of this information.

10. Almost without exception, snakes are, by human standards, poor parents. Young snakes have to fend for themselves from birth. Pretend that you are a crusader determined to make better parents of snakes. Write a parents' manual for snakes. Illustrate it with drawings.

11. Write an essay that has as its theme, "how to appreciate snakes."

12. Choral readings about snakes can be fun. For effect, exaggerate every sibilant "s" in the reading so that the hiss of the snake is a dominant feature. In this little reading, the narrator reads the first and third lines and the chorus reads the second and fourth lines. The last chorus line should be read with a slight trembling in the voice.

> ### S-S-S-S-Serpent
>
> I am S-S-S-S-Serpent.
> S-S-S-S-So pretty is your s-s-s-s-skin.
> S-S-S-S-Say you are not s-s-s-s-scared of me.
> Who's s-s-s-s-s-s-s-s-s-s-s-s-s-s-s-scared?

13. Create your own choral reading and perform it for an audience.

From *Of Bugs and Beasts.* © 1995. Teacher Ideas Press. (800) 237-6124.

BIBLIOGRAPHY

Books

Baker, Lucy. 1990. *Snakes*. New York: Penguin Books.
    This book is a mixture of facts and activities about snake habitats, hunting, babies, and daily life.

Bruchac, Joseph. 1985. "Battle with the Snakes" and "The Two-Headed Snake." In *Iroquois Stories: Heroes and Heroines, Monsters and Magic*, 92-103. Illustrated by Daniel Burgevin. Freedom, Calif.: Crossing Press.
    Bruchac includes two stories featuring snakes in his collection of Iroquois stories.

Carter, Anne. 1991. *Birds, Beasts and Fishes*. Illustrated by Reg Cartwright. New York: Macmillan.
    A selection of animal poems.

Cogger, Harold G., and Richard G. Zweifel, eds. 1992. *Reptiles and Amphibians*. New York: Smithmark, 240 pp.
    Provides information about reptiles and amphibians throughout the world.

Freedman, Russell. 1982. *Killer Snakes*. New York: Holiday House.
    Photographs and text introduce some deadly snakes and describe the ways they kill.

Greenaway, Frank, and Barbara Taylor. 1992. *Desert Life*. New York: Dorling Kindersley.
    Examines the variety of life found in the desert.

Halliday, Tim R., and Kraig Alder, eds. 1986. *The Encyclopedia of Reptiles and Amphibians*. New York: Facts on File, 143 pp.
    Provides information about reptiles and amphibians throughout the world.

Lavies, Bianca. 1993. *A Gathering of Garter Snakes*. New York: Dutton.
    Text and photographs depict the physical characteristics, behavior, and life cycle of the red-sided, or common garter snake.

Marsh, James. 1991. *Bizarre Birds and Beasts*. New York: Dial.
    A collection of light verse about creatures both real and imaginary.

Maynard, Christopher. 1993. *Amazing Animal Facts*. New York: Knopf.
    Provides answers to questions about animals, such as What is a snake?

McNulty, Faith. 1994. *A Snake in the House*. Art by Ted Rand. New York: Scholastic.
    An escaped snake finds many clever places to hide throughout the house while the boy who brought him home continues to search for him.

Polisar, Barry Louis. 1993. *Snakes and the Boy Who Was Afraid of Them*. Illustrated by David Clark. Silver Spring, Md.: Rainbow Morning Music.
    This book about fears says there's nothing wrong with having them.

————. 1993. *The Snake Who Was Afraid of People*. Silver Spring, Md.: Rainbow Morning Music.
This book tells a story similar to *Snakes and the Boy Who Was Afraid of Them,* but from an opposing view.

Rauzon, Mark J. 1993. *Skin, Scales, Feathers and Fur*. New York: Lothrop, Lee & Shepard.
Describes how animals are protected by their skin, scales, feathers, and fur.

Tate, Lindsey. 1993. *Claire and the Friendly Snakes*. Illustrated by Jonathan Franklin. New York: Farrar, Straus & Giroux.
Join Claire on her friendly snake hunt.

Articles

Aleksiuk, Michael. 1975. Manitoba's Fantastic Snake Pits. *National Geographic* 148(5):714-23. (November)
The photographs accompanying this article help emphasize the vast numbers of common garter snakes that congregate at overwintering sites.

Crews, David, and William R. Garstka. 1982. The Ecological Physiology of a Garter Snake. *Scientific American* 247(2):158-64, 166, 168. (November)
Describes how the reproductive cycle and other behaviors allow the common garter snakes of Manitoba to thrive.

Livo, Lauren J. 1985. The Small Snakes. *Colorado Outdoors* 34(4):3639.
Introduces various little snakes and some of their behaviors.

Murrell, Marc A. 1993. Snakes Alive! *Kansas Wildlife and Parks* 50(3):18-21. (May)
Describes some of the adaptations and behaviors of snakes, with an emphasis on species found in Kansas.

Place, Charles B. III. 1992. Meet the Rubber Boa. *Montana Outdoors* 23(5):35-37. (September-October)
Describes the author's encounters with rubber boas.

Snake Charmer's Quiz. 1993. *Kansas Wildlife and Parks* 50(3):17. (May)
A dozen true-false questions and answers (only one question is specific to Kansas) to rate your knowledge of snakes. Following this one-page quiz is an article about snakes by Marc A. Murrell.

Webber, Steve. 1992. Shake Hands with a Snake. *Outdoor Oklahoma* 48(4):28-35. (July-August)
Introduces a variety of snakes that live in Oklahoma.

Chapter 9

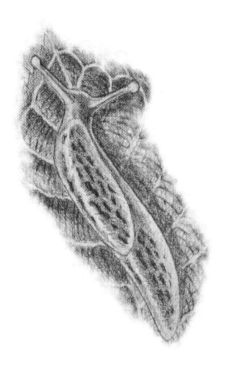

SLUGS

"Oh Yuck! What is that thing?" is a typical response [to slugs]. Because of such reaction, perhaps originating in the subconscious, many people think the banana slug unworthy of serious consideration. I tend to think of this as a human attitude problem, having little to do with the animal itself.

Alice Bryant Harper
(the "Banana Slug Lady")
The Banana Slug

FOLKLORE

Slug to the Rescue

This all happened a long time ago. Believe it or not, it is absolutely true. It happened in a rain forest on an island off the west coast of North America. In this lush rain forest lived many creatures including a careless woman.

She was walking along an animal trail and didn't pay attention to a particular rock which hid an evil spirit. She brushed past a bush whose branches snapped on the rock as she went by. The evil spirit was used to more respect than this so it decided to punish the woman and it did so. It swept her up from the ground and twirled her through the air and then let her go. She dropped, flopped and flipped until she hit a sharp branch of a cedar tree. She became impaled on the branch and was quite unable to get loose.

Drops of her blood began to fall. Surprisingly these drops formed into wild blackberries as they hit the ground. Forest animals stopped to eat the blackberries. There was the raven, deer, moose, elk, squirrels, bear, wolverines, coyotes, badger, otters, lynx, bobcats, mountain lions, weasels, raccoons, snakes, wolves, mosquitoes, butterflies, beetles, and skunks.

As they ate the blackberries each of them felt something dropping on their head. When they looked up they saw the wounded woman stuck on the tree branch. The animals of the forest held a meeting to decide how they should get the woman down. First the wolf said, "I can do it." He took a running leap at the tree but the branches wouldn't hold him and he tumbled down. The snake tried next. It wrapped itself around branches and made its way up to the woman but when it was there it couldn't figure out how to get her off the branch. A swarm of butterflies tried but only managed to get dust from their wings on the woman.

After all the animals had tried to release her, the slug, who was hiding under a fern leaf announced, "I'll see what I can do." He slowly crawled up the tree, leaving a trail of slime as he went. He found the branch where the woman was bouncing with the breeze and with agonizing slowness he made his way out to her. Then to the amazement of all the creatures below, he painstakingly and deliberately lifted her off the branch and inched his way back down the tree delivering the woman to safety. Slug was the hero.

The woman thanked the slug and got back on the trail. From this time on she was careful to not offend the evil trail spirits.

—A Lummi tale
A Native-American tribe from the Pacific Northwest

We use the term *slug* for a drink of liquor or other beverage. Slug also means to strike heavily, as in *slugged, slugging,* or *slugger.* A fistfight is sometimes called a *slugfest.*

The University of California at Santa Cruz campus has a slug mascot. The article "How the Banana Slug Became UCSC's Official Mascot" explains how the students forced the slug on the reluctant university administration.

HOW THE BANANA SLUG BECAME UCSC'S OFFICIAL MASCOT

Public Information Office

University of California, Santa Cruz

The banana slug, a bright yellow, slimy, shell-less mollusk found in the campus's redwood forest, has been—most of the time unofficially—the mascot for UC Santa Cruz's coed teams since the university opened in 1965. The students' adoption of such a lowly creature for a team mascot was their reaction to the fierce athletic competition fostered at most American universities. UCSC has always offered a wide-ranging physical education and recreation program designed to appeal to the greatest number of students, but it has based its approach on some unusual ideas: that athletics are for all students, not just team members of major sports; that the most important goal of a collegiate physical education department should be to introduce as many students as possible to lifelong physical activities; and that the joy of participating is more important than winning.

In 1981, when some campus teams wanted more organized yet still low-keyed participation in extramural competition, UCSC joined Division III of the NCAA in five sports. Since the application required an official team name, UCSC's then chancellor polled the student players, and out of this small group emerged a consensus for a new moniker—the sea lions. It was a choice that the chancellor considered more dignified and suitable to serious play than the banana slug.

But the new name did not find favor with the majority of students, who continued to root for the slugs even after a sea lion was painted in the middle of the basketball floor.

After five years of dealing with the two-mascot problem, an overwhelming proslug straw vote by students in 1986 convinced the chancellor to make the lowly but beloved banana slug UCSC's official mascot.

Popular emblem at the University of California at Santa Cruz. (Used with permission.)

By the time the chancellor had left office, he was won over to the proslug camp, even to the point of featuring the slug on his personal Christmas card.

A 1992 poll conducted by the *National Directory of College Athletics* ranked the banana slug No. 1 nationwide as a school mascot. The Slugs, who were honored in the silver anniversary edition of the directory, beat out Ogelthorpe University's Stormy Petrels, Arkansas Tech University's Wonderboys, UC Irvine's Anteaters, and Northern Montana College's Northern Lights, which ranked as the other top choices among the college officials and sportswriters who were polled.

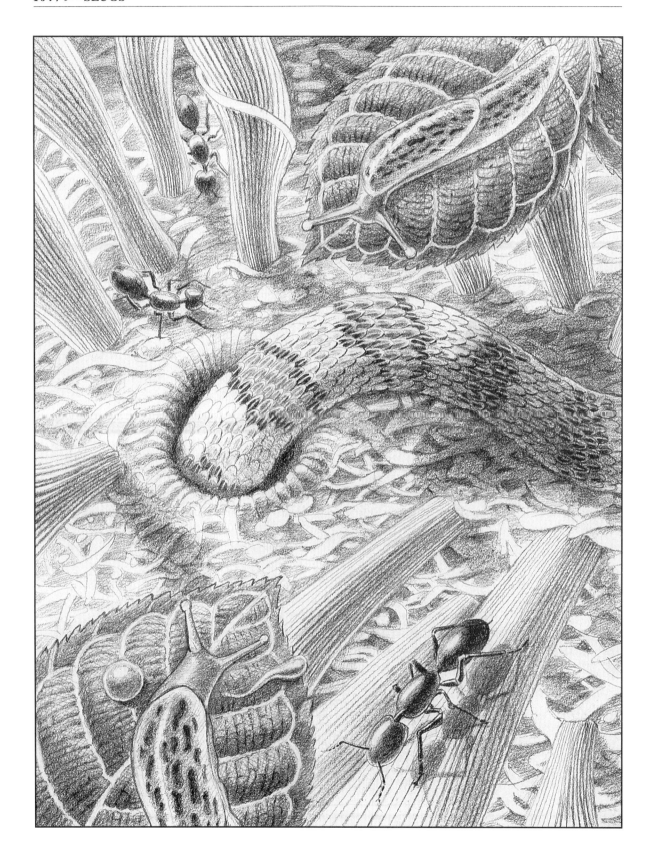

In September 1993 the nature center in Fairfax County, Virginia, held its third annual Slugfest. This Slugfest included a race with contestants such as Slippery (the winner), Dopey, Spike, Sluggy, and Speedy. Other Slugfest events were a slug face-painting and a slime toss. Elma, Washington, used to hold a Slug Festival but dropped it in favor of a wild blackberry festival. Prairie Creek Redwoods State Park, California, has also featured slug races.

Slugs and advertisments may seem an unusual mix, but a three-page spread by AT&T Bell Laboratories featured a slug, proclaiming "Slug as savant: Nature has shown us there are powerful computer designs very different from conventional machines."

Slugs have always been used for terrorizing others. Even Calvin in the cartoon strip Calvin and Hobbes (Monday, May 17, 1993) wants to lead Hobbes into finding slugs because they are gross and thus ideal for a game of daring each other to eat one.

The Slug Bug game is part of traveling-in-the car folklore and children's games. It is usually played by two or more people. The object is to make the first sighting of a Volkswagen Beetle and yell "Slug Bug." If you can add the color of the VW bug, so much the better. Originally the person calling out first would slug others on the shoulder, but keeping score with points is far more friendly.

NATURAL HISTORY

Terrestrial slugs are mollusks—a group that includes clams, squid, and octopuses. In contrast to the many mollusks that live in freshwater or marine habitats—including gaudily colored sea slugs—terrestrial slugs have abandoned water for a life on the land.

Description

The most striking difference between what we call slugs and what we call snails is the slug's apparent lack of a shell. Actually, slugs *are* snails, but ones without conspicuous shells. Various groups of snails contain animals with a slug-type body. Consequently, any one species of slug may be more closely related to snails than to other types of slugs.

Some types of slugs lack shells entirely; other types may retain reduced shells internally. Because of their streamlined and flexible shapes, slugs can squeeze into very small spaces. Scott McCredie described this ability as follows: "When necessary, a slug can stretch its body as much as 11 times its normal length, pouring itself like liquid plastic into improbably small openings." [1]

Four tentacles sprout from a slug's head. The upper pair of tentacles have eyes that can distinguish light from dark. The lower, shorter, pair of tentacles help the slug feel its way through the world and detect food. A slug scrapes at its food with its radula, a structure in the mouth that bears numerous—sometimes thousands—of tiny teeth.

Behind the head, a slug has a saddlelike organ called the mantle. This organ is a legacy from the slug's evolutionary past: In other mollusks the mantle is involved in building the shell. A slug can withdraw its head under the mantle. The genital opening and anus are also located under the mantle. Terrestrial slugs possess a type of lung. The opening to the lung, or pneumostome, appears as a hole in the mantle.

Like the sluggards, slugabeds, and sluggish among us, slugs move grudgingly, if at all. A fast racing slug was once clocked speeding along at 0.034 miles (0.05km) per hour. But, because predators are frequently attracted by movement, the slow movements of slugs help hide them.

Slugs grazing on vegetable scraps.

Slugs travel on self-made highways of slime. Muscular contractions in the "foot" propel the slug forward over this essential roadway. The lower surface of the foot is called the sole. A thirsty slug may seek out moist soil or litter, then soak up water through a specialized part of its foot.

We might not think of slime, or mucus, as being a very specialized material. However, in addition to the slime it travels on, a slug secretes many other types of slime.

Slime normally covers a slug's entire body. When a predator attacks a slug, the slug secretes an especially thick, sticky, cream-colored slime. Many predators seem repulsed by this secretion or get uncomfortably sticky from it.

Like a spider lowering itself on a strand of silk, many slugs can lower themselves from branches using a strong, thread-like, slime cord, which is produced by the mucus plug at the rear of the slug. In fact, some slugs, such as the great gray slug of Europe, mate while suspended on slime cords. Other slugs mate while resting on a generous blanket of mucus.

Slugs are hermaphrodites (containing both male and female organs) so they usually exchange sperm simultaneously when mating. Not all slugs need to mate to produce offspring. Many European slugs are self-fertilizing, so they can establish populations from just a single individual. European slugs that have to mate to produce offspring have been less successful in invading our country.

Range

Slugs occur throughout much of North America and are especially common in moist regions. Because slugs don't need to acquire calcium for shells, they sometimes live in a wider range of habitats than other terrestrial snails.

Many slugs remain small throughout their lives. In contrast, the banana slugs in the forests along the Pacific coast include spectacular creatures that can attain lengths of eight inches (20cm) or more. From their southern outposts in Ventura County, California, various species of these large slugs range north to Alaska. Some of the banana slugs are bright yellow, like bananas; others have a brown, spotted pattern.

Slugs lay their eggs in places with just enough moisture that the eggs don't dry out.

Interactions

For many people, there are only two types of slugs: live ones and dead ones. Most people seem to prefer the latter. This division, however, ignores the great variety in slugs—our "snails without shells"—that creep about our gardens, chomp our peas and lettuce, and leave silvery slime trails for us to find the next day.

Foreign slugs, with their appetite for cultivated plants, tend to cause much more crop damage than our native slugs. Some of these exotic species first appeared over a century ago in the large cities of the East Coast and have worked their way west. Sometimes slugs carry plant diseases or contaminate foods with their slime and droppings, causing even more problems for farmers.

Native slug species sometimes nibble on our gardens, but they often act as part of nature's cleanup crew; and many species prefer to eat decaying plants. A few slugs even have a carnivorous streak and eat earthworms and other slugs when they can. Slugs, in turn, may become meals for other animals. Salamanders, toads, some birds, and shrews are among the many animals that relish slugs.

Some scientists, in an effort to learn more about how nervous systems work, study slugs and other invertebrates with relatively simple nervous systems. In one experiment, researchers trained garden slugs to avoid foods slugs would normally prefer. For example, slugs usually relish instant potatoes. However, when the researchers added a drop of bitter chemical to the potatoes, the slugs learned to avoid this treat, even when offered potatoes without the bitter chemical added. The scientists say that this is an example of associative learning, because the trained slugs associated potatoes with an unpleasant experience.

SLUG ACTIVITIES

1. Try to observe slugs in your neighborhood. The best times to look for slugs are early in the morning and in the evening. Slugs are sometimes active on moist, overcast days. Look for slugs under stones, downed wood, and litter as well as around the base of plants. If you live in an urban or agricultural area, many of the slugs you encounter are likely to be some of the foreign slugs accidently introduced into North America.

2. If you live near Prairie Creek Redwoods State Park, California, you may want to visit their slug festivals. The festivals feature slug racing.

3. If you want to observe a small number of slugs for a while, consider setting up a small container for them. Pet stores often sell inexpensive plastic containers for small animals. 1) Put about an inch (2.5cm) of gravel or pebbles on the bottom of the container; 2) Top the gravel with about 2 inches (5cm) of soil; 3) Add some rocks or small pieces of wood; 4) To prevent escapes, put a piece of fabric across the opening of the container before putting the top on.

A combination of gravel, soil, rocks, and wood in a container makes a good environment in which to study slugs.

Your slugs will do best when you keep their container moist and place it in a cool area out of the sun. Put a small plastic lid on the soil and place food on this. Try feeding your slugs small bits of vegetables and a few flakes of fortified cereal. Finally, keep different species of slugs in different containers, as some slugs are aggressive toward other species.

From *Of Bugs and Beasts.* © 1995. Teacher Ideas Press. (800) 237-6124.

4. If you have a captive slug, try to do various experiments with it. Try to find out the following:

   • How fast is my slug?

   • What color does my slug prefer?

   • Is my slug attracted or repelled by light?

   • What are my slug's favorite foods?

   • Can my slug see?

   • Can my slug back up?

   • Does my slug like to be with other slugs?

   Make up other questions that you'd like to answer.

5. Try to determine the temperature that your slug likes best. Get a strip of aluminum about 1 inch (2.5cm) wide, 3 feet (90cm) long and 0.25 inch (6mm) thick. Use a felt marker to divide the length of the strip into 4-inch (10cm) segments. Prop the strip on a table. Put one end of the strip on a mound of ice. Put the other end of the strip on a hot-water bottle filled with hot water from a faucet. Careful! Don't burn yourself! After the apparatus has set for about five minutes, measure the temperature in the middle of each of the segments and record those values. Next, put your slug near the middle of the strip and see which segment it seems to prefer.

6. A relative of the slug, the edible snail, *Helix pomatia*, or escargot, is considered a delicacy. Talk with a restauranteur to find out how escargot are prepared, where they are obtained, and the relatively high price charged for these dishes.

SLIMED! GETTING TO KNOW SLUGS

Clues

ACROSS
3 Last name, Banana Slug Lady
5 Western college mascot
6 First name, Banana Slug Lady
8 Racing event in Virginia
10 Difference between slug and snail
13 Another word for slime
15 Slime _____ at rear of slug's body
16 Lower surface of the foot
17 Organ behind slug's head
18 To exchange sperm
21 Having both male and female sex organs
25 _____ Creek Redwoods State Park, CA, site of slug festival
26 Slug's head has four
27 _____ County, CA, southern locale for Banana Slug
28 Mammal that eats slugs

DOWN
1 Middle name, Banana Slug Lady
2 Group to which slugs belong
4 Slug relative
7 Santa _____, site of school with slug mascot
8 Secretion of slugs
9 Not a fast-moving person
11 What a terrestrial slug uses to breathe
12 Muscular organ that enables a slug to travel
14 Enables a slug to descend from a branch
19 Term for slugs that live on land
20 Western U.S. slug variety
21 Slug that eats plants
22 Slug that eats other slugs
23 Tooth-bearing organ
24 Genus name of the edible snail

From *Of Bugs and Beasts*. © 1995. Teacher Ideas Press. (800) 237-6124.

NOTES

1. Scott McCredie. They're Still Slimy, But Naked Snails Are Finding New Friends. *Smithsonian* 19(11):134-41.

BIBLIOGRAPHY

Books

Harper, Alice Bryant. 1991. *The Banana Slug*. Aptos, Calif.: Bay Leaves Press, 32 pp.
    This little book contains numerous photos showing all stages in the life cycle of banana slugs.

Monroe, Lucy. 1993. *Creepy Cuisine*. Illustrated by Dianne O'Quinn Burke. New York: Random House.
    A unique recipe book using traditional ingredients but combined to look disgusting and, according to the author, taste divine.

Puckett, Newbell Niles. 1969. *Folk Beliefs of the Southern Negro*. New York: Dover.
    Many of the folklore items in this collection involve the slug's relative, the snail.

Stadler, John. 1993. *The Adventures of Snail at School*. New York: HarperCollins.
    Snail goes on three errands for his teacher and has amazing adventures.

Articles

Dussart, Georges. 1989. Slugs and Snails and Scientists' Tales. *New Scientist* 123(1674):37-41.
    This scientist discusses research into controlling slug and snail populations.

Dykeman, Bob. 1990. An Extraordinarily Ordinary Common-Variety Garden Slug. *Flower and Garden* 34(5):11.
    A brief account of one man's encounter with a slug trying to cross a dry patio.

McCredie, Scott. 1989. They're Still Slimy, But Naked Snails Are Finding New Friends. *Smithsonian* 19(11):134-41. (February)
    Banana slugs feature prominently in this article.

Platts, Elizabeth. 1991. Out of the Slime. *BBC Wildlife* 9(6):420-23.
    The author describes the habits of slugs living in the United Kingdom.

Poolie, Robert. 1983. The Educated Nervous System. *Science News* 123(5):74-75.
    Describes how scientists are using slugs and other invertebrates to gain insights into how nervous systems work.

Chapter **10**

TARANTULAS

Living quietly in the ground or under rocks, they [tarantulas] cause no damage to the soil, or to plant life; they are in no way a source of annoyance. In fact, for anybody who has the good fortune of having one or more of them living in the backyard . . . tarantulas are good neighbors.

—William J. Baerg, *The Tarantula*

FOLKLORE

Minerva was the Roman goddess of wisdom and the daughter of Jupiter. She was said to have leaped forth—mature and in complete armor—from his brain. She was the goddess of agriculture, navigation, spinning, weaving, and needlework. It was in those latter arts that she competed with a presumptuous mortal, Arachne. This is that story.

Arachne

Arachne was a lovely maiden who was so skilled in the arts of weaving, needlework, and embroidery that the nymphs themselves would come to watch her work. Her stitchery was exquisite, and Arachne was delightful to watch as she was weaving. Arachne gracefully took the raw wool and separated it with her long fingers, carded it until it gleamed and seemed to float almost like a cloud. Even at the spindle she managed to make her work look like magic as she twirled the wool into yarn. Her weaving was enchanting to watch and touch. After she had woven the fabric, she proved to be a daring, inventive artist with the needle as she embroidered designs and decorations on it.

When others remarked that she must have learned her art from Minerva herself, Arachne stamped her feet, "I was not taught by anyone but myself! I taught myself everything I know. In fact, I would like to challenge Minerva to a contest. Let her try her skill with mine. I am so confident that if beaten I will pay the penalty."

When Minerva heard this audacious boast she transformed herself into an old woman. She was displeased with this upstart. In this form she went to Arachne to give her some friendly advice. "I have come to you to save you from some foolish actions. You could never best the goddess in either weaving or decorative sewing. Minerva has much more experience than you with weaving and needlework. I hope you will use your common sense and listen

112

to my words of wisdom. Do not deign to compete with a goddess. Challenge mortals as you will but I would suggest that you should ask the goddess for her forgiveness for all the shameful things you have said. In her merciful wisdom I feel that she might forgive you and pardon you your boldness."

Arachne stopped her spinning and tempestuously snorted, "Who are you to tell me this? Keep your advice to yourself! Better yet, give your silly counsel to your daughters or your serving maidens." Scowling, Arachne sneered, "I know what I believe. I know what I can do and I will stand behind it. Minerva doesn't frighten me. Let her try to beat me if she can and if she will. She has more to lose than I do!" Arachne chuckled to herself after the last comment.

Before Arachne's eyes, the old woman dropped her disguise and transformed herself back into Minerva. Everyone who had gathered to watch Arachne at work and listen to her bragging bowed low in reverence and respect to Minerva. Not Arachne! She had the grace to blush and then turn pale, but she was unrepentant.

Minerva decreed that the contest should begin at once. Each of the weavers took her place among the looms and threads. The shuttles flew and the contest was on. The threads were silken in form and the colors contrasted and deceived the eyes as they shaded off into one another. Colors seemed to blend into each other, forming shimmering sunbeam designs. The work seemed to be entirely different when viewed from a distance or up close.

Minerva wove the scene of her contest with Neptune—a competition to produce the gift that would be most useful to mortals. She also placed the 12 heavenly powers around Jupiter as they watched Neptune, the ruler of the sea. He seemed to flourish his trident as he had in their contest, and he appeared to create a horse that leaped from the earth. In the center of the circle Minerva wove herself in all of her glory. On the four corners she represented incidents illustrating the displeasure of the gods with presumptuous mortals who dared to be discourteous and arrogant. Obviously these scenes were intended as warnings to her rival to give up before it was too late.

Unimpressed, Arachne filled her weaving with depictions that showed the failings and errors of the gods. In one scene Leda was caressing the swan, which really was a transformed Jupiter, who had disguised himself. Another picture showed an imprisoned daughter and her father the god arriving in the form of a golden shower. Europa was depicted being tricked by Jupiter, who had disguised himself as a bull. Thinking the animal was tame, Europa mounted the bull and Jupiter then trotted out into the sea and swam with her on his back to Crete. Arachne's work showed the gleam in the eyes of the bull as well as the longing look of Europa as she called for help. There was terror on her face as well.

Minerva couldn't resist admiring the amazing creations of Arachne, yet at the same time she was indignant with her rebellious images. One of the scenes particularly insulted Minerva and she could not contain herself any longer. She struck Arachne's work with her shuttle and tore it to pieces. Minerva then touched the forehead of Arachne and made her feel guilt and shame. Arachne was filled with such remorse that she escaped and hung herself.

When Minerva saw her suspended and swinging from a rope she felt pity. "Live, guilty woman!" she said, "Keep the memory of this lesson. You and your descendants will continue to hang for all future times." Minerva sprinkled Arachne with the juices of aconite and immediately all of Arachne's lovely hair dropped off. Worse yet, her nose and ears dropped from her also. Arachne's body shrank and her head grew smaller and smaller. Her fingers turned into legs at her side and the rest of her body completed the transformation into a spider. There she hung, spinning her thread. Arachne had become a victim of her pride.

—Roman mythology
Adapted and retold by Norma J. Livo

> *"Will you walk into my parlour?"*
> *Said the spider to a fly.*
> *" 'Tis the prettiest little parlour*
> *That ever you did spy."*
>
> —Mary Howitt
> "The Spider and the Fly"

The word *spider* comes from Old English *spinnan*, which means "to spin," and much of spider folklore, as with the story of Arachne (arachnid), is related to this art. In South American native folklore, for example, Spider was the first weaver. In the myths of the plains, southwestern, and western Native American tribes, Spider, Spider Man, and Spider Woman are powerful characters, sometimes also weavers.

In Navajo mythology, Spider Man and Spider Woman taught the people how to weave. Blanket and basket weaving came from Spider Woman, through an unhappy Pueblo girl who wandered far from her hogan and discovered a small hole in the earth. At the bottom of the hole was an old woman spinning a web. Spider Woman invited the girl to enter. The girl stayed several days and learned weaving and passed this on to her adopted people. Spider Woman included in her teachings that a hole was to be left in the middle of each article to avoid bad luck. This is why a spider hole may still be found in the blankets and baskets of the Navajo.

The spider figures strongly in Native American myth as a helper. A Cherokee myth tells of the little spider in the beginning of the world when all was cold. Fire had come to earth in a hollow tree on an island as a result of thunder and lightning. The shivering animals took turns crossing the waters to secure the warmth of the fire. The raven was unsuccessful and returned with the blackened feathers it wears today. Other creatures tried, birds and snakes among them, but they all failed and returned with scars from the fire in the tree. Finally, the spider braved the trip. With a bowl of her spun silk fastened to her back, she skated across the surface of the water, crept through the grasses, and caught a little ember of fire in her bowl. She delivered this precious gift to the waiting animals.

For the Santee Dakota and other Dakota groups, Spider is the trickster. The Arapaho trickster's name, Nihansan, means spider.

The Zuni tell a story of how "old tarantula" tricks a handsome, richly dressed young man. The "old tarantula" talks the youth into letting him try on the youth's fine clothes so that the young man can see how handsome he is to all who see him. The spider moves away from the youth a little at a time as he asks him how he looks. The further away the spider is, the less repulsive he becomes to the youth, who acknowledges that there is an improvement. The spider is really moving closer to its burrow, where he dives into the earth, stealing all of the finery.

Some of the virtues attributed to spiders are industry, patience, and persistence. Scotland's Robert Bruce was said to have gained new courage by watching a spider reach its cobweb home after many unsuccessful attempts.

> *Daddy, daddy longlegs,*
> *Tell me where my cows are,*
> *Then I'll let you go.*
>
> —Traditional

Some rhymes indicate that the spider is really a friend of people. Spiders keep our surrounding insect world in check and are very positive helpers. The daddy longlegs verse includes dangling a daddy longlegs while you chant the verse; the spider will turn so that one of its legs points in the direction of the missing cows.

> *The spider taketh hold with her hands*
> *and is in kings' palaces.*
>
> —Proverbs 30:28

This verse indicates that seeing a black spider will bring sad news, a brown spider means good news, and the sight of a rare white spider predicts good luck.

> *Black, sad;*
> *Brown, glad;*
> *White, good luck be yours.*

> *Little Miss Muffet*
> *Sat on a tuffet,*
> *Eating some curds and whey.*
> *Along came a spider,*
> *And sat down beside her,*
> *And frightened Miss Muffet away.*
>
> —"Little Miss Muffet"

Little Miss Muffet was a real girl. Her father was an expert on spiders and, as was common two hundred years ago, believed that eating mashed spiders was a cure for the common cold. It has been said that Little Miss Muffet ate her share of mashed spiders.

Our ancestors looked around them for predictors of good or bad luck. The spider more often came out on the good side:

> *If you wish to live and thrive,*
> *Let the spider run alive.*

To the Irish, a spider on one's clothes was a sign of good luck. Find a spider in your pocket and you will always have, or soon receive, money. (The term "spider money" is not often heard anymore; it means that the amount of money coming soon will be small.) In Polynesia, a spider dropping down in front of you is a sign of a present, and in the Ozarks, if you find a spiderweb with your initials on it near the door, you will be lucky forever. (Could this be the seed of an idea that resulted in *Charlotte's Web*?) It is no wonder that you will have bad luck if you kill a spider, particularly one with long legs.

Spiders have a long history in folk medicine. An old European belief held that a fever could be cured by placing a spider in a nutshell and wearing it around one's neck. In England, the container was a silk bag, worn to avoid common contagion. Depending on the region, live spiders could be variously rolled in butter, molasses, or a cobweb and swallowed as medicine—or tied up and bound to the left arm to alleviate the ague.

Even spiderwebs were useful. They figure in stories in which Christ, Mohammed, and David were protected by freshly spun spiderwebs from being apprehended by their enemies. In some regions in the United States, they were thought to prevent bleeding and cure cankers. The Chippewa hung spiderwebs on the hoop of infant cradle boards to catch the harm in the air. Today, a Native American craft called a "dreamcatcher" represents the spiderweb.

Rain will not come when spiders abandon their webs, but if you kill a daddy longlegs, there will be rain the next day. Find a spiderweb spread on the ground or many cobwebs on the grass in the morning, and the weather will be fair.

The southern United States is rich with grisly lore about the use of spiders. In some parts of the South, a witch may be caught in a properly conjured bottle. If a spider is found in the bottle in the morning, it represents the witch. If this bottle is then hidden in the ashes under the fire, she will die in agony. In parts of Georgia, they say that if a person has not hung over hell on a spiderweb, that person has not been converted. In voodoo beliefs, if your husband desires another's wife, you can bake a spider, beat it into a powder, and slip it into his food. The concoction will cause him to go insane and he will have to be put away. New Orleans voodoo practices included pulverizing a dried spider and putting it into a person's food or drink. It would then grow to full size within that person.

NATURAL HISTORY

Spiders and their relatives are called arachnids, after the weaver Arachne. Some species, such as the infamous black widow and brown recluse spiders, have venom dangerous to people. However, the vast majority of spiders, including the tarantulas emphasized in this chapter, are harmless to humans.

In contrast to insects, which have three main body parts (head, thorax, and abdomen), spiders have two: the cephalothorax and abdomen. The eyes (usually eight), mouthparts, and appendages called pedipalps are arranged at the front of the cephalothorax, which also bears the eight legs. The pedipalps on tarantulas are often large enough that they look like an extra pair of legs. The silk producing organs, called spinnerets, are located near the back of the abdomen. Fossil spinnerets have been found in rocks 380 to 385 million years old, indicating that even the earliest spiders possessed this important adaptation.

Description

Size alone can distinguish tarantulas from other spiders. From the tip of the front legs to the back of the rear legs, tarantulas of the United States can measure up to 6 inches (15cm)—still small in comparison to South American giants of 10 inches (25cm)! In addition to size, though, tarantulas also have a generous coating of hair.

A tarantula from southeastern Colorado.

This fuzzy exterior plays a large role in tarantula self-defense. When threatened, a tarantula rears up into a defensive posture (some of them hiss!). If the threat continues, the spider brushes off some abdominal hairs, which predators find *very* irritating because of the numerous barbs on each hair.

Tarantulas of the United States make their homes in underground burrows, often located under rocks. They begin digging the burrows—which usually form their lifetime homes—as spiderlings. Most spiders have fairly short lives, living only a few months to a year. In contrast, tarantulas are virtual Methuselahs. Male tarantulas mature when eight or nine years old, then die a few months later. Females have even longer life spans. One female tarantula from Mexico was collected when about 10 or 12 years old and lived in the laboratory for another 16 years.

As young tarantulas grow, they molt, or shed their skin, several times to accommodate their increasing size. Molting seems to be quite an ordeal; the tarantula is immobile and vulnerable for much of the time. Tarantulas prepare for molting by spinning a soft "molting bed." They lie still on this silken sheet, belly up, for several hours once molting begins. As the old skin splits, the tarantula turns on its side and begins pulling its front parts out of the old skin, followed by the legs. When the abdomen comes free, the spider—glistening in its new, fresh skin complete with a new set of hairs—emerges. For males, the final molt produces dramatic changes, including longer legs, brighter colors, and the club-shaped pedipalps used during mating.

Tarantulas do not produce the elaborate webs that some spiders use to capture prey. Instead, they line the entrance of their burrows with silk and extend some strands onto the surrounding ground. When a grasshopper or other insect blunders against these silken lines, the tarantula detects the vibration and rushes out to capture a meal.

Most tarantula activity takes place after dark. These nocturnal animals return to their burrows before dawn. Because tarantulas weave some silk over the burrow opening upon their return, one biologist noted that such strands of silk were a sure indication that the resident tarantula was home.

When male tarantulas mature, they leave their burrows to wander about in search of a mate. When a male encounters the silk strands near a female's burrow, he jerks the silk and raps his pedipalps against the ground. The female rushes out, her predatory instincts aroused. To avoid becoming a meal (a fate that happens to unlucky male tarantulas), the male grapples with the female and inserts a sperm-bearing pedipalp into the female's genital pore. Mating accomplished, the male departs to live out the brief days or weeks that remain before he dies.

Although mating usually occurs during the summer or autumn, a female doesn't lay her eggs until the next spring. At this time, a female tarantula uses her silk to spin an egg case, which can contain anywhere from about 600 to more than 1,000 eggs, depending on the female's size. A mother tarantula takes tender care of her eggs during the several weeks of incubation, sometimes carrying the egg case to the mouth of her burrow to warm in the sun. When danger threatens, mother tarantulas vigorously protect their eggs.

Other spiders also care for their eggs. A female wolf spider, for example, carries the silk package containing her eggs. Later, the baby spiders will ride around on the mother spider's back.

Hatchlings of many spider species disperse by ballooning: The spiderling climbs to the tip of a weed or other object, extends silken threads into the air, then drifts off in air currents. These tiny balloonists have been found at altitudes as high as 10,000 feet (3,050m). Young tarantulas, however, are much too large even at hatching to balloon. Instead, they stay in their mother's burrow for several days or weeks before walking away to establish their own solitary burrows.

A female wolf spider with numerous tiny babies on her abdomen.

Range

About 30 species of tarantula occupy the United States. From the Mississippi River, they range west to California. The southwestern states are particularly rich tarantula territory, but these spiders range as far north as Missouri in the east and southeastern Oregon in the west. All of the species in the United States are terrestrial, living in burrows.

Many more tarantula species occur in Central and South America. Some of these make their homes in trees, nesting in such locations as bromeliads. Tarantulas also occupy parts of Africa, Madagascar, India, Sri Lanka, New Guinea, and Australia.

Interactions

Tarantulas look dangerous enough that at least one San Francisco jewelry store used a tarantula (named Henrietta) to discourage burglars. Despite their fearsome appearance, America's tarantulas possess neither an aggressive disposition nor a dangerous venom, although their bite can be painful. In fact, tarantulas become tame enough that many people keep them as pets. They greatly benefit humans because, like all spiders, they consume vast quantities of insects.

One of the most unusual animal associations occurs between a tarantula (*Dugesiella hentzi*) and a little amphibian called the Great Plains narrowmouth toad (*Gastrophryne olivacea*). Narrowmouth toads sometimes make their homes in tarantula burrows. Rather than evicting the toads, the resident tarantula tolerates them. When .predators such as garter snakes appear, the toads scurry under the body of the tarantula. Instead of getting a tasty toad, the garter snake gets a nasty surprise when the tarantula rears up in a defensive position and tries to bite the snake!

The narrowmouth toads are even permitted to remain in the burrow when a female tarantula has an egg case or young spiderlings. The toads don't try to eat the baby spiders. Instead, the narrowmouth toads eagerly consume ants and termites that might otherwise prey on baby tarantulas and bother the adult female. If a toad inadvertently picks up a spiderling, the toad immediately ejects the mouthful—because the spiderlings are already armed with irritating barbed hairs.

In spite of their defenses, tarantulas do have enemies. Skunks and other mammals dig out and eat tarantulas, and birds, reptiles, and amphibians sometimes eat the young.

The strangest foes are the tarantula-hawk wasps. The female wasps spend their days feeding on the nectar of flowers. Milkweeds are especially favored, although some tarantula-hawk wasps also feed on nectar from acacia flowers and sap from palo verde trees. By midafternoon, the wasps begin flying to the open areas favored by tarantulas. Here the wasp searches for a tarantula burrow. Once she finds one, she jerks the silken strands that the tarantula uses to detect prey and lures the tarantula out. Sometimes the tarantula flees from the wasp, abandoning the burrow that was home for so many years. Other times, the tarantula and wasp begin to fight.

It is a dangerous battle for both participants. The tarantula is fighting for its life, but if lucky, its fangs can rip and kill the wasp (the spider's venom isn't effective against the tarantula-hawk wasp). The wasp needs the tarantula to rear up in its typical defensive posture so that the wasp can twist its abdomen under the tarantula and deliver a paralyzing sting to a vulnerable spot where the spider's rear legs meet. If the wasp accomplishes this without being killed herself, the tarantula becomes immobile and the wasp then looks for a place to make her own burrow. The wasp checks on

the tarantula frequently because she needs to defend her prey against theft by another tarantula-hawk wasp. When the wasp makes a suitable burrow, she drags the tarantula into it.

Just before sealing the tarantula in the burrow, the wasp lays a single white egg on the spider's abdomen. The wasp larva that hatches from this egg begins consuming the still-living tarantula, carefully avoiding essential organs such as the heart. Finally, those organs are all that's left of the tarantula, and the larva eats them, too.

The next summer, a young tarantula-hawk wasp emerges from the shelter of the burrow. If female, the wasp mates and then spends her days feeding on nectar and her nights like her mother before her, searching for a tarantula for each of the 20 or so eggs she produces during her short life.

When defending itself, a tarantula raises the front of its body.

SPIDER ACTIVITIES

1. Learn more about spiders in your area by visiting museums or nature centers. Zoos sometimes have tarantulas or other spiders on display.

2. You can observe spiders wherever you live. If you live in the southwestern United States, you also may be able to observe tarantulas. Keep a nature diary about the spiders and other things you see.

3. Spiders make and use silk, but so do many insects. See how many different uses of silk you can observe. Some examples include

    *   an orb weaver spider's web

    *   the cocoon of a moth

    *   the webs of tent caterpillars

    *   the web of a funnel spider

    *   a spider egg case (which remains in the web of some spiders and is carried about by other spiders)

    *   a silk scarf or other clothing (made by the caterpillars of the silkworm moth)

    *   the case of a caddis fly larva (the aquatic larvae fasten sticks, tiny pebbles, or other material into a protective case bound together with silk)

    *   the silk a spider uses to bind insect prey

4. Spiders snare food in their sticky web, yet they do seem to maneuver around their webs without sticking to them. Do research to see how this is done. In this research observe a spider-web. Test it gently with a straw or weed to see if all strands of the web are sticky. Note which strands the spider uses for walking. Brainstorm possible human uses for a material that can be sticky for some things and not for others.

5. Locate several spiderwebs in the outdoors. Make comparisons to determine if webs were spun by the same spiders or spiders from the same species. Make sketches of the various webs.

A spider, viewed from beneath, sitting on its web.

From *Of Bugs and Beasts.* © 1995. Teacher Ideas Press. (800) 237-6124.

6. Make an art project using the spiderweb design as a model. Sketch a spiderweb on a piece of heavy cardboard. Put small nails at the intersections of the web strands. Next, use yarn or thread to duplicate the web design, wrapping the thread around the nails.

7. Locate a spiderweb during the day. At night, shine a flashlight on the web to entice flying insects to the web. Observe all the action as the spider becomes aware of a trapped insect.

8. Put a spider in a terrarium in your room. You will need to provide insects for it to eat until you release it. Observe the actions of the spider from spinning to the capture and eating of insects. Make a log that recounts your observations.

9. Try to observe a spider spinning. Try to measure how long a strand the spider can spin in a minute. Calculate how many spiders spinning at this rate (if they could all cooperate) it would take to spin a single strand of silk around the equator of the earth in one 24-hour day. (At the equator, the earth has a circumference of 24,901.55 miles (40,075.16km.)

10. Learn songs about spiders, for example, "The Itsy-Bitsy Spider." This song is fairly well known by most adults and children and has fun motions to accompany the words and music. Compose songs about spiders. Change songs about spiders into choral readings using percussion instruments such as sticks, cymbals, triangles, and drums for accompaniment.

11. Our eating habits are regulated by social customs involving fairly well-described manners. These customs vary among different cultures. Spiders do not use the same rules. Observe a spider eating, then write a book of etiquette that would apply to spiders. Use parts of human etiquette books such as *Ask Ms. Manners* for ideas on style.

12. Spiders are sometimes incorrectly referred to as insects. They, of course, are not insects at all but arachnids. Research the differences between the two classes. Show the similarities and differences with words and pictures.

13. Spider-Man is a cartoon hero. What characteristics of the spider are possessed by Spider-Man that help him in performing his duties as a superhero? If you are interested, try to find the first comic book written about Spider-Man and see if you can understand his origins.

14. Spider people are featured in the folklore of many Native American groups. Read about them. What are their functions in the cultures of these various tribes?

15. Many resources exist that feature activities involving spiders. *Science Through Children's Literature* by Carol Butzow and John Butzow and *Outdoor Biology Instructional Strategies* (OBIS), are two that have been used as references in this section. Check on these resources at school or public libraries to find more neat activities. The Butzows' book has a chapter on spiders (pages 78-81). OBIS has a couple of folios that pertain to spiders, namely, "Web It" and "Web Weavers."

BIBLIOGRAPHY

Books

Aardema, Verna. 1992. *Anansi Finds a Fool.* Illustrations by Bryna Waldman. New York: Dial Books.
  Lazy Anansi seeks to trick someone into doing the heavy work of laying his fish trap, but instead he is fooled into doing the job himself.

Baerg, William J. 1958. *The Tarantula.* Lawrence: University of Kansas Press, 85 pp.
  This slim volume describes the life history of tarantulas without becoming overly technical.

Brooks, Bruce. 1991. *Nature by Design.* New York: Farrar, Straus & Giroux.
  Includes information on spiders as well as on the construction of spiderwebs.

Bruchac, Joseph. 1992. *Native American Animal Stories from Keepers of the Animals.* Golden, Colo.: Fulcrum.
  This collection includes the Hopi story "How Grandmother Spider Named the Clans," pages 11-12, and the Osage story "How the Spider Symbol Came to the People," pages 13-15.

———. 1991. *Native American Animal Stories from Keepers of the Earth.* Golden, Colo.: Fulcrum.
  The Oklahoma Muskogee story "How Grandmother Spider Stole the Sun" is included, pages 27-29.

Butzow, Carol M., and John W. 1989. *Science Through Children's Literature.* Englewood, Colo.: Teacher Ideas Press, 240 pp.
  This book uses children's literature as an organizer for science themes and activities in an integrated fashion.

Climo, Shirley. 1985. *Someone Saw a Spider.* Illustrated by Dirk Zimmer. New York: T. Y. Crowell.
  A collection of myths, folklore, and superstitions about spiders from around the world with some facts about how they live.

Courlander, Harold, and Albert Kofi Prempeh. 1957. *The Hat-Shaking Dance and Other Ashanti Tales from Ghana.* Illustrated by Enrico Arno. New York: Harcourt Brace & World.
  A classic collection of Anansi spider stories.

Dewey, Jennifer Owings. 1991. *Animal Architecture.* New York: Orchard Books.
  Different kinds of spiders and their different webs are described. The final note is that without silk, a spider dies because it has no way to build traps and snares for insect prey.

———. 1993. *Spiders Near and Far.* New York: Dutton.
  The author identifies the two major types of spiders and describes their body parts, behavior, and habitats. The book begins with a Pima creation myth.

Dorson, Richard M. 1975. *Folktales Told Around the World.* Chicago: University of Chicago Press.
  This book contains a short story from Switzerland based on the legend in which the black plague is shown in the form of a spider. Two versions of the story are on pages 81-83.

Erdoes, Richard, and Alfonso Ortiz. 1984. *American Indian Myths and Legends*. New York: Pantheon.

    The Cherokee story "Grandmother Spider Steals the Sun," page 155, can be compared with the Bruchac version found in *Native American Animal Stories from Keepers of the Earth*.

Forsyth, Adrian. 1989. *The Architecture of Animals*. Camden East, Ontario: Camden House.

    More information on spiders as web builders.

Gertsch, Willis J. 1979. *American Spiders*. 2d ed. New York: Van Nostrand Reinhold, 274 pp.

    This book will help you get to know more about the lives and behaviors of spiders. It includes a section on tarantulas.

Gibbons, Gail. 1993. *Spiders*. New York: Holiday House.

    Examines the physical characteristics, behavior, habitats, and different kinds of spiders. The art in this book is very appealing.

Lane, Margaret. 1994. *The Spider*. Art by Barbara Firth. New York: Dial.

    In a brief introduction to several species of spider, the author discusses physiology, reproduction, and behavior, including the female's curious propensity to eat her mate.

McDermott, Gerald. 1972. *Anansi the Spider: A Tale From the Ashanti*. New York: Holt, Rinehart & Winston.

    A retelling of an African story of Anansi the spider that reveals how Nyame, the god of all things, comes to Anansi's aid and places the moon in the sky for all to see.

Milne, Lorus J., and Margery Milne. 1980. *Insect Worlds*. New York: Charles Scribner's Sons.

    This is a rather comprehensive guide for making the most of the environment, written by two biologists.

Mound, Laurence. 1993. *Amazing Insects*. Photographs by Frank Greenaway. New York: Alfred Knopf.

    This is one of the books in the Eyewitness Junior series. It introduces the reader to the world of insects.

——. 1990. *Insect*. New York: Knopf.

    Gives information on how spiders differ from insects, including a photograph of a Sri Lanka tarantula.

Norman, Howard, ed. 1990. *Northern Tales*. New York: Pantheon.

    The epic tradition of the Ainu, the original aboriginal race of Japan, includes "Song of the Spider Goddess," pages 191-93.

Outdoor Biology Instructional Strategies. 1981. Published by the University of California Board of Regents, Berkeley, California. Available from Delta Education, Box M, Nashua, NH 03061.

    A collection of 96 folios that feature activities in the outdoors involving many aspects of biology.

Radin, Paul, ed. 1983. *African Folktales*. New York: Shocken.

This collection includes two Ashanti stories, "How Spider Obtained the Sky-God's Stories," pages 25-27, and "How It Came About That the Hinder Part of Kwaku Ananse the Spider Became Big, at the Expense of His Head, Which Is Small," pages 139-40.

Royston, Angela. 1992. *Insects and Crawly Creatures*. New York: Aladdin Books.

You'll find a brief text along with photographs to introduce various creatures. This book is part of the Eye-Openers series.

White, E. B. 1952. *Charlotte's Web*. New York: Harper & Row.

The classic story of the doomed pig, Wilbur, and his helpful web-spinning friend, Charlotte.

Articles

Cook, John A. 1985. Of Sting and Fang. *Science 85* 6(1):64-69.

Tells how tarantula-hawk wasps capture and parasitize tarantulas.

Dollar, Tom. 1992. The Docile and Delicate Tarantula. *Arizona Highways* 68(7):24-25.

Depicts the author's encounters with tarantulas.

Hunt, R. Howard. 1980. Toad Sanctuary in a Tarantula Burrow. *Natural History* 89(3):45-53.

Details the relationship between tarantulas and narrowmouth toads.

Marshall, Samuel D. 1992. The Importance of Being Hairy. *Natural History* 101(9):40-47.

Describes how tarantulas rely on their hair as part of their defense.

Chapter **11**

COYOTES

Somehow [coyotes] always look distressed and miserable, and their whining howl at night seems to express all the hopeless despair of some wretched spirit of the blind 'viewless wind' that whirls away before a storm.

Witmer Stone and William Cram
American Animals (1914)

FOLKLORE

Coyote and the Lizards

Coyote was happiest when he was spying on someone or poking his nose into their business. It was that kind of a day. He was looking for somebody to spy on when he came upon a group of lizards on top of a big, flat rock with one sloping side. They were playing a game that was strange to him. They were taking turns sliding down the steep slope on small flat rocks. He decided to learn all about it so he joined them.

He saw that each time, the slider picked up his rock at the bottom of the slope and carried it up the hill on his back. Coyote trotted over to the rock and sat down. The lizards went on with their play and pretended they didn't see him.

Now Coyote didn't like to be ignored: the least the lizards could do was to notice him. He scooched over a little closer and began to talk to the lizards. "That looks like fun! What do you call this game?" he asked.

One of the lizards answered, "We just call it sliding," without even looking at him.

"It looks interesting. I'd like to join you in your sliding game," said Coyote as he scooted a little closer to them.

With this, all of the lizards turned and looked at him coldly through their lizard eyes. "Go play your own games. We are lizards and this is our game. You aren't a lizard and you don't know how to play our game."

Coyote wheedled, "But I can learn. Really your game looks like a very simple one. I can just stand on the rock and slide down too. Come on, let me try, I'll show you I can do it."

An old wrinkled lizard hissed, "This game is not as simple as you think. It is very dangerous and you could get killed. Maybe the first time you do it everything would be all right but the second time when you ride down the big rock you'd be smashed flat, flat, flat, flat."

125

Coyote was offended. None of the lizards had been smashed. Why should he? He didn't believe a word of what the old lizard said. He whined and wheedled for them to let him try it. He would show them.

The wrinkled old lizard got tired of his whimpering so he said, "Well, just once, cousin. You can ride the small flat rock but do not ask to ride the big one."

Really! thought Coyote. He intended to ride the big one too but he kept quiet. He slid down the little one just to show them how well he could do it. After that it would be easy to persuade them to let him try the big one.

Several of the lizards placed the small flat rock in position for Coyote. They looked at him with puckered faces. "I don't know why you want to play our games. I know you play games chasing rabbits and kangaroo rats and all sorts of other creatures. Running games are more to your taste. You are such a fast runner why don't play your own games?"

Arrogantly Coyote stepped on the flat rock, which tilted down the runway. With a scraping sound, he flashed down the hill. Before he reached the bottom of the slide, he jumped off. He picked up the rock and trotted back up the hill. "See," he panted, "I can do it. Let me use the big rock now!"

"We warned you. We don't want you to try the big rock. However, if you want to risk your life, it is your own problem if you get smashed flat, flat, flat, flat!" said the old lizard looking at him with a stern lizard look. "Get the big rock for him," the old lizard told the young lizards. They waddled away silently and came back with it. They placed the big rock on the very edge of the runway and then they slithered away.

Coyote was not at all afraid. He ran out to the rock, tipped it a little, and once again he was sliding down the runway with his tail flying behind him. The big rock caught on a smaller rock half way down the slide and flipped into the air. Coyote was frightened half out of his skin. His ears were flapping and his paws and claws were digging into the air. This wasn't nearly as much fun as the first ride. He hit the ground and rolled over in the dust. He saw the big rock right behind him coming down on top of him.

"Maybe I should have listened," he thought. "I am really going to be smashed flat, flat, flat, flat, just like old lizard told me." The big rock crashed into him and did indeed smash Coyote. The lizards were on top of the slide looking down at him.

"Even though he was no friend of mine, it still makes me sad to see poor foolish Coyote smashed so flat," observed the old lizard.

"The worst part is, that he is right in the middle of our runway," announced one of the young lizards. "It wouldn't be right to leave him there but he is so heavy, how are we going to move him?"

"It would be simpler to bring him back to life," wheezed a third lizard. "Then he could leave without us having to move him."

The oldest lizard stroked his scales and said, "You have a very good idea, young one. Let's do it."

They slid down to Coyote in a single file and made a tight circle around him so they could work their magic in private. Using their own lizard secrets they brought him back to life. "Now go along with you Coyote," the old lizard ordered him. "After this, don't try to play lizard games. We don't want to have to go through this again."

Coyote was glad to be alive again. He got up, dusted himself off, and dashed for home as fast as his four sore legs could go.

—Navajo

As the prince of chaos, Coyote is one of the most controversial characters among the Navajo. He is called Trickster or "Trotting Coyote," meaning that his behavior is socially unacceptable. Coyote is transformer, troublemaker, and deity, and his unruly behavior brings about change for the better, for example, he stole the stars laid out by First Man and scattered them throughout the sky. He is of the Great Basin, Plains, central California and some Plateau and Southwestern Native American groups. He is the court jester or wise fool, both sacred and profane, and as such is able to speak and act and create new ways of doing things that clarify human and animal conduct. Yes, he is a deceiver, but he also brings newness, makes changes through his good and bad actions, and reaffirms the eventual triumph of justice and morality. Coyote stories serve to strengthen and reinforce moral values, social harmony, and cultural norms by endowing them with the prestige and power of antiquity as well as with the sanction and affirmation of the supernatural.

Coyote stories are usually short, relating a single event and leading to a moral. Coyote is usually accompanied by a companion, Wolf, Wildcat, Fox, Rabbit, Porcupine, Badger, Lizard, or some other animal, and they belong to the mythical age when animals lived and talked as people. Coyote has the power of resurrection and has been translated into the popular cartoon character Wily E. Coyote.

In Arizona and Mexico, there is a ceremonial dance performed for the death of all soldiers, officials, and chiefs at specified fiestas. Three men dance to the accompaniment of a drum. Each wears a headband, crested with eagle, hawk, or buzzard feathers, that holds the head and hide of a coyote securely on the dancer's head. All of the dancers mime the coyote.

A number of plants grow in the Southwest that the Papago Indians call "coyote plants." According to legends, coyote plants, although apparently similar to domesticated varieties, have been altered in some way by the trickster Coyote so that they are useless to people.

Coyote melons, for example, taste awful because of substances called cucurbitacins. Domestic varieties lack these vile-tasting chemicals. Coyote cotton looks similar to the plant we use as a source for thread and cloth, but its bolls lack spinnable fibers. The Coyote tepary bean has pods that explode and scatter the ripe seeds on the ground—where they blend in and are difficult to find.

NATURAL HISTORY

The word *coyote* comes from the Aztec word, *coyotl.* Lewis and Clark were the first Americans to make note of the coyote (*Canis latrans*), or as they termed this animal, the "Prairie Wolff." According to one of their biographers, the "eery, discordant whines, yelps, and barks of the coyote accompanied Lewis and Clark to the Pacific and back."[1] These nocturnal calls have earned coyotes the nickname "song dogs."

Description

The coyote is a smaller cousin of the true wolf. Most coyotes are as big as a medium-size dog and weigh 18 to 30 pounds (8.2 to 13.6kg). Very large coyotes weigh 50 or more pounds (22.7kg). Although these wild dogs are primarily nocturnal, you may encounter them loping along a ridge or napping in the shade any hour of the day. At night, driving along country roads, you may catch a glimpse of the eyes shining greenish gold in the headlights of your car.

Coyotes hold their tails down between their hind legs when running. The larger wolves hold their tails high when running, and the smaller foxes hold their tails out straight. Coyotes can move fast; they have been clocked at speeds of 35 miles per hour (56km per hour).

A coyote pair mates sometime between January and March. About two months later, the litter is born, helpless and blind, in a den. At first the pups consume only their mother's milk. By the time the pups are three weeks old, they also eat food that both parents regurgitate for the young ones. As the pups grow older, they spend more time outside of the den, exploring, playing, and learning to find their own food.

Flexibility seems the key feature of coyote life. Adult coyotes catch and eat a variety of animals, preying on ground squirrels, jackrabbits, and other small animals. Sometimes they even eat fruit and insects. Coyotes hunt small game by themselves or sometimes in the company of badgers (see "Interactions" for more information about this unusual association). When coyotes hunt larger game such as deer or pronghorn, they usually hunt in packs.

Whether young coyotes stay with their parents after becoming mature depends on what the main foods are for the coyotes in that place. Young coyotes strike out on their own when they depend on small mammals but stay for a longer time with their parents when the family hunts large mammals. When several adult coyotes live together, only the dominant male and female breed.

Range

Coyotes used to live mostly in western North America. However, this adaptable wild dog has expanded its range and now occurs throughout the continent, often living even in suburban and urban areas.

Coyotes often move into areas previously occupied by wolves. For example, settlers exterminated wolves in New York State's Adirondacks by the late 1800s. Coyotes began to move in and are now fairly common in this area. The Adirondack coyotes have also begun to behave like wolves, running in packs and hunting deer.

Although coyotes once lived alongside wolves and cougars in Yellowstone National Park, eradication campaigns have since eliminated these other predators from the area. With the wolves gone, coyote populations increased. Now researchers are studying the Yellowstone coyotes to get an idea of how the park would change if wolves returned to this park.

Interactions

Coyotes sometimes travel and hunt with another predator, the badger. This association, which can be fleeting or can last for weeks, has earned badgers the Aztec name *talcoyote*, or "coyote of the earth." Coyote-badger pairs are most likely to hunt together when there are plenty of ground squirrels. While the badger digs belowground, the coyote is on the alert for ground squirrels attempting to escape from other exits to the rodents' extensive underground tunnels.

The ability of coyotes to hybridize with red wolves (a species native to the southeastern United States) has complicated the survival of this endangered wolf. As red wolf populations declined from habitat destruction and predator-control programs, coyotes moved into the wolves' habitat. After a time, red wolf populations dropped low enough that many red wolves couldn't find mates of the same species during the breeding season, so they mated with coyotes. Biologists testing the red wolves found more and more hybrids. In the late 1970s, the remaining pure red wolves were captured from Texas and Louisiana. Although the red wolf had become extinct in the wild, the captured individuals were used to establish a captive-breeding program.

From an initial captive population of 17, the number of red wolves increased to 65 in 1985 and 131 in 1990. Beginning in 1987, 29 red wolves were reintroduced into the Alligator River National Wildlife Refuge in North Carolina. This area was chosen because it has few, if any, coyotes.

Red wolves may be reintroduced to Great Smoky Mountains National Park, where coyotes do live. If the reintroduced red wolves cannot displace the coyotes here, biologists trying to promote the survival of the red wolf fear that red wolves may never be able to survive in the wild without continued help.

Nowadays, humans are the most important species interacting with the coyote. There are many opportunities for conflict in areas where coyotes live alongside large numbers of people. For example, many people have homes along the High Line Canal in metropolitan Denver. They and others enjoy this area for the recreational opportunities such as walking and bicycling or watching birds, butterflies, and other animals. Although the people living along the canal often want to feel close to nature, for many of them, coyotes are "too much nature."

Recently at least six coyotes lived along some portions of the canal and may have killed as many as 25 pet dogs. Although a few residents said that they enjoyed seeing the coyotes, most other inhabitants feared for the safety of their pets or even young children, and local officials had the coyotes removed from the area. Similar problems arise in many other communities where wild meets mild.

Sheepherders and ranchers often blame coyotes for killing valuable livestock. But poisoning campaigns and other attempts to eradicate coyotes often affect what are called "nontarget" species. In other words, cyanide, Compound 1080, or other poisons set out to kill coyotes may inadvertently kill hawks and eagles, bears, pet dogs, and other animals. In Wyoming's Thunder Basin National Grassland, someone illegally set out a tallow ball containing 1080 poison, probably to kill coyotes in an area where livestock grazed. However, two pet dogs and a great horned owl were among the accidental victims of this poison.

The U.S. government hires trappers to get rid of coyotes known to kill livestock. Some people charge that these trappers kill all the coyotes they find instead of just the ones causing trouble. In 1988, more than 76,000 coyotes were killed by the U.S. government's Animal Damage Control program. Traps also take their toll on other wildlife. Once an Animal Damage Control trapper found a bobcat, a golden eagle, a badger, a jackrabbit, and a magpie along his trap line. Ironically, the single coyote that he trapped "played dead" until the trap was released, then sprang to life and got away.

Eradicating coyotes causes other problems. Rodent populations such as ground squirrels, mice, and kangaroo rats can skyrocket when coyotes are removed, requiring even more intervention to bring the rodents into check. An outbreak of the deadly Hantavirus in New Mexico was tied to large deer mouse populations. Some people in New Mexico now want to provide additional protection to coyotes so that they can help keep rodent populations under control. In the Seedskadee National Wildlife Refuge in Wyoming, ducks had a nesting success rate of about 60 to 80 percent. After coyotes were removed, red foxes and racooons moved in, and the nesting success rate fell to 7 percent.

Ironically, coyotes reproduce faster in areas with predator control programs. In these places, females frequently have litters of eight or more, compared to the typical three in stable populations. Many biologists now believe that eradication efforts against the coyote may have helped this wild dog become what one biologist described as "a bigger, tougher, and smarter animal."

Guard dogs can protect sheep from coyotes and other predators, especially at night. Herding sheep into lighted pens at night can also reduce predation by coyotes. Sometimes a special bait—lamb meat laced with lithium chloride—is put out for coyotes. When a coyote eats this bait, the drug in the meat makes it sick to its stomach. This unpleasant reaction may discourage the coyote from trying lamb again. Many sheepherders are using these and other techniques in an effort to learn ways to live with coyotes.

COYOTE ACTIVITIES

1. Read chapter 5 in *Roughing It* by Mark Twain. This contains a simultaneously contemptuous and humorous account of coyotes. How have attitudes about coyotes changed since Twain's time? How have they stayed the same?

2. Sometimes National Parks are good places to see coyotes. Because they are protected in these areas, they often have little fear of people and can be observed closely. Park Service policy prohibits harassment of wildlife, so if you encounter coyotes (or any other wildlife), keep your distance while you observe it.

3. The words we use affect our feelings about things. Write a paragraph about coyotes using the words from the left column below. Rewrite the paragraph, but this time use the words from the right column.

"Good" or Neutral Words	"Bad" Words
inhabit	infest
hungry	bloodthirsty
shy	sly
single-minded	ruthless
hunt	stalk
prey	victim
wild animal	varmint
creep	slink
adaptable	indiscriminate

From *Of Bugs and Beasts*. © 1995. Teacher Ideas Press. (800) 237-6124.

COYOTE WORD SEARCH

E	C	F	H	Y	B	R	I	D	D	C	H	P
T	X	A	L	L	I	O	J	E	X	O	B	R
B	G	T	D	M	Q	K	R	F	L	Y	D	E
W	L	R	E	C	Q	E	E	O	D	O	O	D
O	K	I	M	R	G	A	Q	F	N	T	V	A
L	H	F	C	N	M	M	U	Y	J	E	B	T
V	C	F	A	F	L	I	F	N	E	F	A	O
E	Z	D	C	D	O	V	N	S	A	V	D	R
S	N	S	F	O	K	P	Q	A	B	X	G	H
E	O	L	R	O	D	E	N	T	T	D	E	X
D	H	N	B	B	O	U	N	T	Y	I	R	U
X	D	G	D	H	A	B	I	T	A	T	O	M
P	B	Q	V	D	O	M	E	S	T	I	C	N

BADGER   ENDANGERED   PREDATOR

BOUNTY   EXTERMINATION   RODENT

COYOTE   HABITAT   WOLVES

DOMESTIC   HYBRID

DIRECTIONS: Search for the words in the puzzle and circle them. Words can be found forward, backward, horizontally, vertically, or diagonally.

From *Of Bugs and Beasts*. © 1995. Teacher Ideas Press. (800) 237-6124.

NOTES

1. Paul Russell Cutright. *Lewis and Clark: Pioneering Naturalists*. Urbana, Ill.: University of Illinois Press, 1969, p. 85.

BIBLIOGRAPHY

Books

Baylor, Byrd. 1972. *Coyote Cry*. Illustrations by Symeon Shimin. New York: Lothrop, Lee & Shepard.

Antonio and his grandfather are sheepherders. After a long day of work they sit by the campfire, alert to the sounds of danger to their flock. Antonio is alarmed by the piercing cry of a coyote. In the morning there are coyote tracks leading to the collie dog's den. She has just had four pups and one of them is missing. Antonio tracks the coyote down and returns the pup, but he learns that the creatures he thought were his enemies have lives and needs of their own.

Bierhorst, John. 1987. *Doctor Coyote: A Native American Aesop's Fables*. Pictures by Wendy Watson. New York: Macmillan.

When Aztecs were introduced to Aesop's fables, they saw them as trickster tales and, in their retellings, made Coyote the chief character. The Aztec collection is preserved in a manuscript from 1628. This Bierhorst collection is an English retelling of 20 of the manuscript's 47 fables.

Bruchac, Joseph. 1991. *Native American Stories from Keepers of the Earth*. Golden, Colo.: Fulcrum.

This collection of stories includes "Old Man Coyote and the Rock," pages 33-36, and "How Coyote Was the Moon," pages 71-72.

———. 1992. *Native American Animal Stories from Keepers of the Animals*. Golden, Colo.: Fulcrum.

This story collection includes "Silver Fox and Coyote Create Earth," pages 3-4, and "Why Coyote Has Yellow Eyes," pages 73-76.

Burt, William H. 1976. *A Field Guide to the Mammals*. 3d ed. Illustrated by Richard P. Grossenheider. Boston: Houghton Mifflin, 289 pp.

Illustrations of the animals and range maps help you identify mammals you encounter in North America.

Erdoes, Richard, and Alfonso Ortiz. 1984. *American Indian Myths and Legends*. New York: Pantheon.

This anthology contains many Coyote stories. Part 7 in it is titled, "Coyote Laughs and Cries: Trickster Tales." Other Coyote stories can be found throughout this book.

Hillerman, Tony. 1990. *Coyote Waits*. New York: HarperCollins.

In this mystery, Hillerman captures the Navajo's ancient traditions. There are Coyote stories and folklore included. The book is actually a compelling cautionary tale about Coyote, the amoral opportunist that inhabits each soul. Hillerman has one of the characters say, "The children are told the funny stories about Coyote so they will not be afraid" (p. 233).

Leydet, Francois. 1988. *The Coyote, Defiant Songdog of the West.* Revised ed. Norman, Okla.: University of Oklahoma Press, 224 pp.

   Introduces some of the issues surrounding eradication campaigns and includes letters from both pro-coyote and anti-coyote people.

London, Jonathan. 1993. *Fire Race: A Karuk Coyote Tale.* Illustrated by Sylvia Long. San Francisco: Chronicle Books.

   With the help of other animals, Wise Old Coyote manages to acquire fire from the wicked Yellow Jacket sisters.

Mora, Francisco X. 1991. *The Coyote Rings the Wrong Bell.* Illustrated by the author. Chicago: Childrens Press.

   After being caught by a hungry coyote, a clever hare fools his captor into letting him go free. The book includes a list of storytelling activities for adults. There also is an accompanying cassette tape narrated by Anamarie Garcia.

Nabhan, Gary Paul. 1987. *The Desert Smells Like Rain: A Naturalist in Papago Indian Country.* San Fransisco: North Point Press, 148 pp.

   Chapter 6 discusses some of the "coyote" plants found in the desert southwest.

Norman, Howard. 1990. "Coyote and Fox." In *Northern Tales, Traditional Stories of Eskimo and Indian Peoples,* 158-59.New York: Pantheon.

   A story of how Fox out-tricks Coyote.

Nunes, Susan. 1988. *Coyote Dreams.* Illustrations by Ronald Himler. New York: Atheneum.

   A fantasy of a child who watches coyotes enter a suburban garden and bring the desert with them. His nights are transformed and populated with dreams of coyotes.

Reed, Evelyn Dahl. 1988. *Coyote Tales from the Indian Pueblos.* Santa Fe, N.M.: Sunstone Press.

   Reed collected these 15 stories from the southwestern Pueblos. Included is a lengthy bibliography of books and articles devoted to Coyote.

Roessel, Robert A. Jr., and Dillon Platero. 1974. *Coyote Stories of the Navajo People.* Illustrated by George Mitchell. Phoenix, Ariz.: Navajo Curriculum Center Press.

   This collection of 14 tales is part of the enormous mythological treasure of the Navajo people. The stories have great significance for the Navajo because they express, enhance, and enforce the morals and norms of their society. This collection is a representation of socially unacceptable behavior. Coyote's misfortunes are legendary proof of the disastrous effects of antisocial conduct.

Root, Phyllis. 1993. *Coyote and the Magic Words.* Illustrated by Sandra Speidel. New York: Lothrop, Lee & Shepard.

   Once all words were magic words, but by the time Coyote is through making mischief, words have lost all of their magic.

Stevens, Janet. 1993. *Coyote Steals the Blanket.* New York: Holiday House.

   Stevens retells this Ute story of how Coyote receives his comeuppance when he tries to take something that does not belong to him.

Taylor, Harriet Peck. 1993. *Coyote Places the Stars*. New York: Bradbury Press.
This is a retelling of a Wasco Indian legend in which Coyote shoots arrows at the stars, rearranging them in order to make pictures in the night sky. When you hear Coyote's howls, he is calling you to go to your window to gaze at his star pictures and to sharpen your imagination.

Zim, Herbert S., and Donals F. Hoffmeister. 1987. *Mammals: A Guide to Familiar American Species*. Revised ed. Illustrated by James Gordon Irving. New York: Golden Press, 160 pp.
This book covers 218 mammals of North America.

Articles

Alcock, John. 1990. The Cost of Coyote Meat. *Wilderness* 53(188):14, 16-17.
Summarizes the expenses versus the benefits of controlling coyotes.

Beasley, Conger Jr. 1993. Killing Coyotes. *Buzzworm: The Environmental Journal* 5(1):36-41.
Discusses the environmental consequences of predator elimination and the history of the Animal Damage Control program.

Brocke, Rainer H. 1992. A Taste for Venison. *Natural History* (May):50-51.
Describes the food habits of coyotes in the Adirondacks.

Halfpenny, James C. 1991. The Cold Facts of Winter. *Natural History* (December):50-61.
Discusses how coyotes and other animals deal with the rigors of winter in Yellowstone National Park.

Kiliaan, Hendrik P. L., Charles Mamo, and Paul C. Paquet. 1991. A Coyote, *Canis latrans*, and Badger, *Taxidea taxus*, Interaction Near Cypress Hills Provincial Park, Alberta. *Canadian Field-Naturalist* 105(1):122-23.
Describes one interaction between a coyote and a badger and discusses other records of these two species.

Milstein, Michael. 1991. Yellowstone's Top Dog. *National Parks* 65(34):24-29.
Describes research on coyotes in Yellowstone National Park.

Minta, Kathryn A., and Steven C. Minta. 1991. Partners in Carnivory. *Natural History* (June):60-63.
Describes coyote-badger interactions.

Parker, Warren. 1990. Investigating the Potential for Reintroducing Red Wolves into the Great Smoky Mountains National Park. *Endangered Species Technical Bulletin* 15(6):3.
Discusses how coyotes threaten the recovery of red wolves in the wild.

Randall, Dick. 1992. Wanted Dead or Alive? *BBC Wildlife* 10(2):16-23.
A former trapper for the Animal Damage Control branch of the U.S. Fish and Wildlife Service describes problems with coyote eradication programs.

Records and Tapes

Elliott, Lang. 1992. *A Guide to Night Sounds*. Ithaca, N.Y.: NatureSound Studio.
Use this tape to hear the howls of coyotes as well as other night-active creatures.

Chapter **12**

ANTS

Go to the ant, thou sluggard; consider her ways and be wise: Which having no guide, overseer or ruler, provideth her meat in the summer, and gathereth her food in the harvest.

Proverbs 6:6-8

FOLKLORE

The King, the Storyteller, and the Ants

There once lived a king who loved nothing so much as listening to stories. Every moment of his time was spent listening to the tales told by the storytellers of his land. His hunger for stories became known in the neighboring kingdoms. Wandering singers and traveling storytellers came to the land of the king to be rewarded for the new tales they could bring.

But the more tales the king heard, the fewer were left that he had not heard. Finally, in desperation he decreed that whatever storyteller could make him cry, "Enough! No more!" would be given a large part of his kingdom and the title of Ras, or prince.

Many people came to tell him stories but he always sat and listened eagerly without ever protesting that he had heard too much. One day a farmer came and offered to tell the king stories until he would cry out, "Enough! No more!" The king just smiled at this.

"The best storytellers in Ethiopia have come and gone without telling me enough. You in your simple innocence to win the land and the title of Ras do not know what is ahead. Well, begin, you may try."

And so the humble farmer settled himself comfortably on a rug and began. "Once there was a peasant who sowed wheat. He mowed it when it was grown, threshed it, and put all the precious grain in his granary. It was a rich harvest. In fact, it was one of the best he had ever had. But, this is the irony of the story. In his granary there was a tiny flaw. It was a hole big enough to pass a piece of straw through. When the grain was all stored an ant came and went through the hole and found the wheat. He carried away a single grain of it to his anthill to eat."

"Ah-ha! This is actually a story that I have never heard!" roared the king in delight.

"The next day another ant came and carried away a grain," continued the farmer.

135

"Ah-ha!"

"The next day still another ant came and carried away a grain."

"Yes, yes," interrupted the king. "I understand. Let us get on with the story."

"The next day another ant came and carried away another grain. And the next day another ant came and carried away another grain."

"Let us not dally with the details. The story is the thing," declared the king impatiently.

"The next day another ant came."

"Please, please," begged the king.

"But there are so many ants in this story. And the next day another ant came for a grain of wheat, and. . . ," but the farmer was interrupted by the king.

"No, no! It must not be so," demanded the king.

"Ah, but it is the crux of the story. And the next day another ant came and took away a grain . . ."

"But I understand all of this. Let us pass over it and get on with the plot," pleaded the king.

"And the next day another ant came and took his grain. And the next day. . . ."

"Stop! I want no more of it!" shouted the king.

"The story must be told in the proper way," explained the farmer. "Besides the granary is still nearly full of wheat and it must be emptied. That is the story. And the next day. . . ."

"No, no! Enough, enough!" roared the king.

"And the next day another ant . . . ," said the farmer before he was once more interrupted by the king.

"Enough, enough! You may have the land and the title of Ras!" proclaimed the king.

So the clever farmer became a prince and owned much land.

—African
Adapted and retold by Norma J. Livo

There are many references to ants in literature. Aesop's fables include several ant stories, such as the following:

The Ants

Once ants were human beings and made their living by farming. Busy as they were, they weren't content with the results of their own work and they were always looking with longing eyes upon the crops and fruits of their neighbors. In fact, they stole from them whenever they got the opportunity. At last their greediness made Jupiter so angry that he changed them into ants. Though their forms were changed, their natures remained the same. And that is why to this day they go about the fields and gather the fruits of others' labor and store them up for their own use.

The moral of this story is that you may punish a thief, but his bad character remains.

The Ant and Fly

The Ant and the Fly were in an argument over who was the most important creature. The Fly said that he was the greatest because all the temples and places were open to him. He also claimed that he was the taster to the gods and princes in all their sacrifices and entertainments. The Fly further pointed out that all of this was without either money or pain. His final boast was that he also trampled upon crowns and kissed whatever ladies' lips he wanted to.

The Ant called him a vain boaster and asked the Fly if he didn't know the difference between the access of a guest and that of an intruder. The Ant flung out more insults, such as the fact that people didn't like the Fly's company and would kill him as soon as they could catch him. The Ant called the Fly a plague to everyone. "Your very breath has maggots in it and for the kiss you brag of, what is it but the perfume of the last dunghill you touched upon, once removed?" The last taunt flung to the Fly was, "For my part," said the Ant, "I live upon what's my own and work honestly in the summer to maintain myself in the winter whereas you, filthy Fly, only cheat one half of the year and starve the other."

Moral: Honest mediocrity is the happiest state a person can wish for.

The Ant and the Grasshopper

A grasshopper sang happily throughout the summer. In the winter she went to the ants and asked for a little of the food they had stored. The ants asked the grasshopper what she had done all summer. When she replied that she had sung all day long, they told her that she could dance for the winter and refused to give her food.

Moral: In time of plenty provide for want.

The Ant and the Caterpillar

A Caterpillar met a lively Ant in one of the alleys of a beautiful garden. The Ant scornfully told the Caterpillar to get out of the way. "How dare you presume to obstruct the paths of your superiors by wriggling along the road, you poor creeping animal?" The Ant also told the Caterpillar that he looked like a thing that was half-made, which was left unfinished by Nature.

The humble Caterpillar was stunned by such distainful language and went to work winding himself up in a silken cell. When the time was right, the Caterpillar came out of his cocoon as a beautiful Butterfly. The Ant just happened to be passing by. The Butterfly told the ant never to despise anyone for their lowly condition since there is none so ugly that one day they may not be in a better state and in fact able to look down upon the one who had been so full of contempt.

Moral: Those of unpromising appearance often become great.

There are also stories from mythology that are similar to the African story of the king and the storyteller. When the jealous Venus, offended by the homage given to Psyche because of her beauty, sent her son Cupid to punish her, the two fell in love. Even though Cupid was with her only at night, when she could not see him, Psyche was happy until her malicious sisters convinced her that he might be a monster.

When Cupid saw her distrust he left her. To regain Cupids's love and to beg forgiveness of Venus for having accidentally wounded her son with the hot oil from her lamp, Psyche went directly to Venus. Psyche was given tasks to fulfill to prove her worth. One of them was to separate before evening all the wheat, barley, millet, vetches, beans, and lentils Venus used as food for her pigeons. Psyche was full of despair, but Cupid took pity on her and got the leader of the anthill to help Psyche. The ants sorted the pile grain by grain and then vanished.

The peoples of West Africa believed that the ant was the messenger of their serpent god. Both African witch doctors and physicians in India sutured wounds with the help of ants. Ants were placed along the length of a wound where they bit into the surrounding flesh, at which time the surgeon snapped off their bodies. The heads and clamped jaws were left behind as stitches. The Indian doctors used giant black Bengali ants for internal as well as external wounds. The fomic acid in the ants served as an antiseptic that helped safeguard against infection.

Other folk remedies include the Alabama black people's use of a bag filled with coarse white sand and large red ants. A healing salve includes the dirt from a red ant's hole as one of the main ingredients. A southern cure for whooping cough is a tea made from white ants (which are actually termites, another type of insect).

A widespread southern omen is that a row of ants crawling in your house, especially in your fireplace, indicates that you will soon move out. To dry up the mother's milk after weaning, throw some old rusty nails in an old ants' nest and when the ants go down, the milk will dry up.

Other ant beliefs are about love. An old English love recipe includes a frog that has been placed in an ant's bed until the flesh is removed from the bones. One particular bone is then used to hook the one you love. Other ant lore says to discourage an undesirable suitor, put his tracks in an ant bed.

Ants also have a part in weather predictions. A Native American proverb says:

> When buffalo band together,
> The storm god is herding them.
>
> When sheep collect and huddle,
> Tomorrow will become a puddle.
>
> An open ant hill indicates good weather;
> A closed one, an approaching storm.

Another old saying about ants is:

> When ants travel in a straight line, expect rain;
> When they scatter, expect fair weather.

Another belief is that if you step on an ant it will rain.

NATURAL HISTORY

At least 8,800 ant species have been described throughout the world, and about 580 species live in the United States and Canada. They are members of the order Hymenoptera. *Hymen* is from the Greek for *membrane*, and *ptera* is from the Greek for *wing*, so insects in this order, which includes bees and wasps, are "membrane wings." All ants are in the family Formicidae, which derives its name from the formic acid produced by some ants.

Description

An individual ant seems a rather ordinary insect: a body divided into three main parts; eyes, mouthparts, and a pair of antennae on the head; six legs on the trunk; and a bulging abdomen or gaster, often with a stinger at the end. But ants don't live solitary lives. Instead, they are members of complex insect societies with specialized functions and sophisticated forms of communication. Some biologists consider the colony more as a *superorganism*, with different castes of ants in the colony functioning something like organs in the body. Indeed, the colony seems to possess an intelligence of its own. Writer and scientist Lewis Thomas put it this way:[1]

> A solitary ant, afield, cannot be considered to have much of anything on his mind;
> indeed, with only a few neurons strung together by fibers, he can't be imagined to
> have a mind at all, much less a thought. He is more like a ganglion on legs. Four ants
> together, or ten, encircling a dead moth on a path, begin to look more like an idea. . . .
> It is only when you watch the dense mass of thousands of ants, crowded together
> around the Hill, blackening the ground, that you begin to see the whole beast, and
> now you observe it thinking, planning, calculating. It is an intelligence, a kind of live
> computer, with crawling bits for its wits.

The life of the colony depends on specialization, where each ant performs a specific type of work. Ant colonies consist almost entirely of female ants; males appear only fleetingly in most ant colonies. New queens and worker ants develop from fertilized eggs, and males develop from unfertilized eggs. Both the new queens and males possess wings. They use these wings to fly into mating swarms. Males live only a short time after the breeding season. The mated queens, however, try to start new colonies (or, in some cases, return to their original colony).

Each colony has its beginning with a queen. A young queen, newly mated during her nuptial flight, sheds her wings and finds a place to make her home. She lays eggs and raises the first ants for the colony by herself.

Ants are among the insects that undergo *complete metamorphosis*. That is, they have four discrete stages in their lives: egg, larva, pupa, and adult. Once the eggs laid by the queen develop into adult ants, they take over all the work in the colony except for egg laying, which remains the queen's job.

Worker ants—by far the most numerous ants in a colony—are sterile females. There are many different jobs to do in a colony, including caring for the queen, tending the larva and pupa, enlarging the colony, foraging, removing dead ants, and protecting the colony from enemies.

Worker ants may change jobs as they age. For example, a young ant may start out by tending the queen and her offspring. Later she may begin working as a forager, wandering far from the colony in search of food.

Ant colony, including winged individuals and pupae.

Different jobs sometimes require specialized body types, or *castes*. Soldier ants, large workers involved in the defense of their colonies, are among the most familiar of ant castes. In another example, leaf-cutting ants have large workers that trim pieces of vegetation and bring them back to the nest. In the nest itself are smaller workers that chop the vegetation into tiny pieces. Even smaller workers make a pulp from the plants and use it to cultivate the fungus gardens that supply the colony with food.

Some worker ants have bizarre jobs. One type of worker ant in the genus *Myrmecocystus*, called a honeypot or replete, acts as a living food storage container. During seasons of plenty, worker ants in these colonies continuously feed young adults sweet secretions from plant galls and insects. The abdomens of the young adults expand to hold all this incoming food. Ultimately, these living honeypots hang from the ceilings of the nest, their abdomens stretched to about the size of peas. As many as 1,500 of these honeypots were found in a single colony of about 15,000 individuals.

For a colony to survive and flourish, members of the colony must be able to communicate. Much of the communication in an ant colony depends on *pheromones*, or chemicals released by one ant that other ants can smell or taste. When an ant foraging away from the nest finds food that is too much for it to handle alone, it lays down a scent trail that other ants follow. Ants can distinguish the scents of colony members from those of other colonies. Other pheromones function as attractants during mating swarms, as alarms when a colony is invaded, and as a way to recognize different castes.

Range

Ants make their homes nearly everywhere, from the Arctic Circle to the deserts, swampy coasts to high mountains, but are most common in warm areas. The only places that lack native ants are Antarctica, Iceland, Greenland, and some remote Pacific and Atlantic islands.

Around the world, ants show marvelous specializations. One type of ant living in Africa's Namib Desert likes it hot. These ants scurry around on sand that reaches temperatures of more than 150° F (66° C). To keep their body temperatures just inside the roasting range, they occasionally climb onto grass to cool off for a few moments before resuming their frenzied search for food—mostly other insects that died in the heat.

And some of the animals that depend on ants demonstrate equally canny adaptations. In Latin America, caterpillars of some butterflies "sing" to attract ants. The ants protect the caterpillars from parasitic wasps, and the caterpillars reward the ants with a highly nutritious fluid.

North America has its share of oddities. Leaf-cutter ants extend as far north as Louisiana, and honeypot ants thrive in the southwestern United States. Carpenter ants make extensive galleries in downed logs. Trap-jaw ants studied in Arizona have the fastest recorded movements of any animal. When a prey animal brushes against "trigger hairs" on the ant's jaw, the jaws close within as little as 0.33 milliseconds.

Interactions

Perhaps you think of ants as ruining picnics, forming crumb-carrying lines through the nooks and crannies of kitchens, and swarming onto our shoes and legs when we inadvertently step on one of their colonies. Or maybe you consider them examples of industry and forethought, as they are characterized in the folktale about the grasshopper and the ant.

However you regard ants, they have developed a most unusual set of answers to the challenges of survival and succeeded well enough that incredible numbers and kinds range throughout the world.

Scientists who study ants—*myrmecologists*—often find uncanny parallels between ant behaviors and behaviors we consider human. For example, some ants wage war with nearby colonies. Depending on the species, the winning ants may eat the eggs of the victims or capture pupae and "enslave" them. Others types of ants are "farmers," tending and harvesting underground fungi gardens. Still other ants act like herders, guarding "flocks" of aphids and "milking" them for the sweet honeydew the aphids produce. Weaver ants of Africa, Asia, and Australia use leaves to make their nests. Adult workers hold the leaves together like pins holding fabric; other workers move the larvae back and forth, releasing the silk that binds the leaf edges together.

All these activities require numerous ants acting in coordination. And that teamwork with others of their kind is the true innovation that ants evolved, an apparently selfless cooperation for the good of the colony.

Lowly little ants are more important than they might seem. In New England, they bear as much responsibility for moving and aerating the soil as earthworms. In the western states, harvester ants often collect tiny fossil teeth and bones from the surface and add them to their conical mounds, a service much appreciated by paleontologists.

Many plants depend on certain types of ants to disperse their seeds. These ants don't haul just any seed back to their colony but instead favor seeds with a special type of coating (called an elaisome). The ants feed this coating to their larvae, then dispose of the seeds in the piles of dead ants and other refuse from the colony. Although the refuse is mere garbage to the ants, it is a nutrient-rich site for a germinating seed. Since the ants also move the seeds away from the plant that produced them, the seeds have less competition from established plants.

Several animals specialize in eating ants. In Central and South America, anteaters seek out ant and termite colonies. They use their long, sticky tongues to catch their small prey.

However, ants are often equipped with stingers or the ability to produce a spray of poison, and ant predators must somehow deal with these toxins. One way to deal with the toxins is to avoid them. For example, blind snakes feed on ant eggs and termites. When attacked by ants, a blind snake coils into a ball and streaks fluid from its cloaca onto its body, which appears to repel the ants.

Ant lions, or doodlebugs, are the larvae of a flying insect. They show another way of avoiding ant poisons. The doodlebugs make cone-shaped traps in sandy soil, often beneath rocky ledges, then lie in wait at the bottom. Ants and other small insects wander into the traps. Even though they try to escape, they gradually slip and slide to the bottom as the sand beneath them rolls from under their legs. Once an ant is within reach, the doodlebug clamps onto the ant's body with its massive jaws. The jaws are also hollow and permit the doodlebug to inject the ant with a poison that turns the inside of an ant into a liquid that the doodlebug can suck out.

Depressions made by ant lions ("doodlebugs") are protected by the overhang of rock.

Doodlebugs are irritated by the formic acid spray that ants normally use for defense. However, ants need to bite something before they attempt to use their poison spray. Because doodlebugs capture ants in a way that prevents the ants from biting, the ants never get around to trying their poison. A doodlebug eating this kind of ant also manages to leave the ant's poison sac intact.

In other cases, ant predators have adapted to tolerating ant poisons. Horned lizards—chunky lizards that are especially common in the Southwest—specialize in eating ants. A single Texas horned lizard might consume as many as 100 ants a day. These lizards simply sit near an ant mound or along a foraging trail and lap up ants as they pass. Horned lizards that routinely eat harvester ants (which defend themselves with a venomous sting) can tolerate 1,500 times the amount of ant venom that would kill a mouse.

Some animals, especially birds, put ants to use in an unusual way. In a behavior called "anting," birds let ants crawl over their bodies to remove mites and other parasites, or they smear ants onto their feathers. The formic acid and other chemicals from the ants may help the birds in a couple of ways. First, the chemicals might repel mites and other parasites. Second, the ant chemicals may inhibit the growth of molds.

Ants can cause real problems, however. Fire ants, for example, have been a growing pest in the southeastern United States ever since their accidental introduction in about 1918 to Mobile, Alabama. This species now inhabits approximately 250 million acres and continues to spread.

Fire ants earned their common name from the stings they can deliver. A single sting from a fire ant isn't too bad—but a fire ant typically stings repeatedly. Even worse, fire ants don't have any natural predators or diseases in the southeastern United States, so their populations can skyrocket out of control. Compared to native fire ants, the imported fire ants have more mounds per acre and more ants per mound. Some parts of Texas are dotted by as many as 400 fire ant mounds per acre, compared to 4 or 5 mounds per acre for the native fire ants. (Marshall, Texas, even has an annual fire ant celebration.) This superabundance decimates populations of native ants. Because native ants often serve to disperse plant seeds, those plants and the other organisms that depend on them may be living on borrowed time. Even ant predators can be affected. In Texas, some biologists blame an apparent decline in horned lizards on infestations by fire ants.

Ants have been on earth since at least the time of the dinosaurs. Eighty-million-year-old ants from the Cretaceous have been found preserved in ancient amber in present-day New Jersey. Other ants sealed in amber tombs have been found in Alberta, Canada, and in Siberia. If you weighed all the social insects, including ants, termites, and bees, they would weigh about seven times as much as the combined weight of all land vertebrates. "Bugs are not going to inherit the earth," said Thomas Eisner, an entomologist. "They own it now."[2]

ANT ACTIVITIES

1. See what kinds of ants live in your neighborhood or in a nearby nature preserve by looking for their homes. Try looking in the following places:

   Fallen logs (carpenter ants make their colonies in these situations).

   Under rocks. (Turn rocks carefully. You don't want to be bitten or stung by ants or other creatures that might live under the rocks. Also, make sure to replace the rock so that it can continue to be a home for small animals.)

   Mounds in open areas. Often the ants remove all the vegetation near their mound, making a circular clearing around their colony.

2. Find an ant colony that is easy to visit near your home or school. Each time you visit the colony, keep records of the time of day and temperature and make notes on the types of ant activity that you observe.

   a. How many ants can you count near the colony in a one-minute time period?

   b. Determine how fast the ants are moving. For five different ants, try measuring how far they travel in five seconds. If you can do this on several different days, plot your results against the temperature that you measure.

   c. Do you ever observe ants with wings? (These are young queens and males that have not yet left the colony.) Do you ever observe mating swarms from the colony? Describe them.

   d. Experiment by placing different kinds of foods near the anthill: bread crumbs, cracker crumbs, popcorn, peanut butter, and so on. Predict ahead of time what food you think will be the favorite of the ants. Were you right?

   e. Find an active ant trail. See what happens when the trail is blocked. First, try blocking the trail with something the ants can move, such as a very small piece of paper. Next, try blocking it with something the ants cannot move, such as a rock. Observe the activities of the ants. Next, predict what would happen if you blocked the trail with grass clippings, some water, a piece of clay, a card with holes punched in it, or other objects. Will the ants go over an object, go around an object, or move the object? Test your predictions.

   f. At an ant trail, use a stick or leaf to pick up a single ant. Move it about one yard (one meter) away and watch. Does the ant find the trail? If so, how long does it take? What tactics does the ant seem to use?

   g. Find a dead ant near an active anthill. Transfer that dead ant to another active hill. Observe the ants as they encounter the dead ant from a different colony.

3. Rewrite the story "The King, the Storyteller and the Ants" into a readers theatre script. Present it to another school class, a retirement center, or other community group.

4. Pretend you are a newspaper reporter. Your assignment is to get a story from an active ant colony. Watch the colony work for about 10 minutes. Decide on an angle to your story, then write it in newspaper-reporting fashion (answering questions such as who, where, when, what, and why).

5. Drop some sand, one grain at a time, near the opening of an anthill. What are the ants' reactions? What do they do to solve the problem?

6. Ants can show us exceptional models of cooperation. Put a fairly large crumb of a favorite ant food near a colony, then observe as the ants work together to move the food. Write an essay that uses the ant cooperation as a basis for suggesting that people could get more done if they learned to work together.

7. Purchase an ant farm kit with a transparent frame that allows observations of the ants as they work underground. Describe their work habits. What do they do? Do different chambers of the colony have different uses? Do the ants ever rest?

8. A "bug box" is a good investment for the avid ant watcher. These plastic boxes with a built-in magnifier can let you get a close-up view of an ant—or any tiny creature—under excellent conditions. Remember, it can get very hot in the bug box, particularly in the sun, so keep your observation time short and make your observations in the shade. After studying your ant, release it where you found it.

9. Ants often invade our picnics. Turn the tables. Pretend that ants are having a picnic and invade them. Write a short account of your adventure.

10. Ant lions, or "doodlebugs," are found in many parts of the world. As their name suggests, they prey on ants. Ant lions construct small indentations in loose sand, hollowing out a structure about 1 inch (2.5cm) deep and about 2 inches (5cm) in diameter. The doodlebug waits under the sand at the bottom of its trap. A hapless ant walks into the trap; once inside the small crater, the ant finds that it cannot escape. As the ant tries to walk up the steep wall, the sand gives way and the ant slides back toward the bottom of the trap. At the right moment, the doodlebug emerges, grasps the ant in its mandibles, and quickly scoots under the sand again. The geometry of the trap is interesting to study. Devise a way to measure the slope of doodlebug traps. Make a graph that shows the variation of the slopes in various traps.

11. You can get a close look at a doodlebug by enticing it to come out of its home. Touch a small weed or broomstraw against the side of the trap so that grains of sand start sliding to the bottom. Watch the doodlebug emerge, thinking it has captured a meal. A nursery rhyme accompanies this activity:

> *Doodlebug, Doodlebug,*
> *Come out of your home.*
> *Your house is on fire*
> *And your children will burn.*

From *Of Bugs and Beasts*. © 1995. Teacher Ideas Press. (800) 237-6124.

12. Capture an ant lion and observe it in your bug box. How is it like the ant upon which it preys? How is it different? List the unique adaptations the ant lion has to do its job.

13. M. C. Escher was a famous graphic artist who lived from 1898 to 1972. One of his works, called *Möbius Strip II*, shows several ants crawling on the surface of a Möbius strip. If possible, look at a copy of this work (one source is a book called *The Graphic Work of M. C. Escher*, published by Ballantine Books in 1971). As shown in this illustration, Möbius strips appear to have only one surface. Construct a Möbius strip by cutting a narrow rectangle of paper, put one twist in it, then tape the ends together. If you can find some plastic ants at a toy store, glue them onto your Möbius strip to make it look like Escher's illustration.

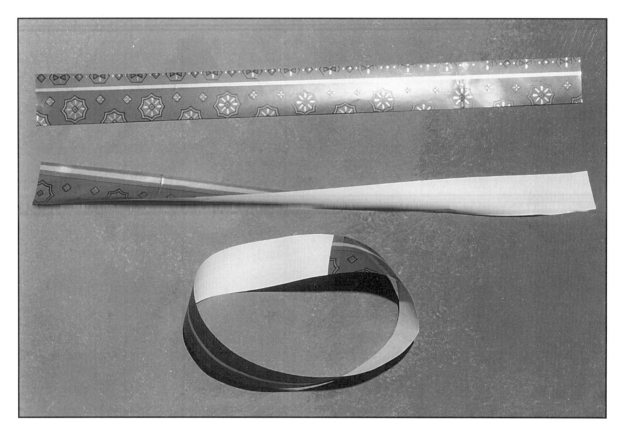

Construction of a Möbius strip.

From *Of Bugs and Beasts*. © 1995. Teacher Ideas Press. (800) 237-6124.

NOTES

1. Lewis Thomas, *The Lives of a Cell: Notes of a Biology Watcher*. New York: Viking Penguin, 1971. Although Thomas refers in this essay to individual ants as "he," all the worker ants— the ones you see crawling about—are actually females.

2. Thomas Eisner, quoted in *Science* 246, no. 4931 (November 10, 1989): 754.

BIBLIOGRAPHY

Books

Dorson, Richard M. 1975. "Why Ants Eat Termites." In *Folktales Told Around the World*, 375-77. Chicago, Ill.: University of Chicago Press.
    This book contains a broad collection of folktales.

Hepworth, Cathi. 1992. *Antics! An Alphabetical of ANThology*. New York: G. P. Putnam's Sons.
    Young readers will *ant*icipate the visual puns involving ants.

Hölldobler, Bert, and Edward O. Wilson. 1990. *The Ants*. Cambridge, Mass.: Belnap Press, 732 pp.
    Although the book is rather technical, it probably contains the answer to any question you may have about ants.

Milne, Lorus J., and Margery Milne. 1980. *Insect Worlds*. New York: Charles Scribner's Sons.
    A guide for humans on making the most of the environment.

Mound, Laurence. 1993. *Amazing Insects*. New York: Alfred A. Knopf.
    The world of insects is introduced through text and photographs.

———. 1990. *Insects*. New York: Alfred A. Knopf.
    A photo essay about insects and their crucial role in the lives of other living things.

Royston, Angela. 1992. *Insects and Crawly Creatures*. New York: Macmillan Aladdin Books.
    This Eye-Opener book uses brief text and photographs.

Articles

Adams, Daniel B. 1984. A Fossil Hunter's Best Friend Is an Ant Called "Pogo." *Smithsonian* 15(4):99-104.
    Describes how red harvester ants retrieve small fossils and concentrate them on their hills.

Bailey, Paul. 1992. Under the Dome. *Nature Canada* 21(1):20-25. (Winter)
    Profiles thatching ants of North America.

Beattie, Andrew J. 1990. Ant Plantation. *Natural History* (February):10, 12, 14.
    Describes how many plants use ants to disperse their seeds.

Conniff, Richard. 1990. You Never Know What the Fire Ant Is Going to Do Next. *Smithsonian* 21(4):48-52, 54, 56-57.
Discusses how the introduced fire ant is continuing to expand its range.

Eisner, Thomas, Ian T. Baldwin, and Jeffrey Conner. 1993. Circumvention of Prey Defense by a Predator: Ant Lion vs. Ant. *Proceedings of the National Academy of Science* 90(14):6716-20.
Ant lions are able to subdue ants so that the ants don't defensively spray their formic acid on these predators.

Gronenberg, W., J. Tautz, and B. Hölldobler. 1993. Fast Trap Jaws and Giant Neurons in the Ant *Odontomachus*. *Science* 262(5133):561-63.
A technical article describing the fast closure time of jaws on trap jaw ants.

Letourneau, Deborah K. 1993. Ants That Pay the Piper. *Natural History* (October):4, 6, 8.
This article describes the unique ecological interactions between the tropical piper tree and the *Pheidole* ants that make their homes in these trees.

Marsh, Alan C. 1993. Ants That Are Not Too Hot to Trot. *Natural History* (August):43-44.
Describes the frenzied activity of the Namib ants of southwestern Africa.

Moffett, Mark W. 1989. Trap-Jaw Ants: Set for Prey. *National Geographic* 175(3):394-400.
Small colonies of tropical trap-jaw ants have oversize jaws used for preying on springtails.

Morris, John R., and Kenneth L. Steigman. 1993. Effects of Polygyne Fire Ant Invasion on Native Ants of a Blackland Prairie in Texas. *Southwestern Naturalist* 38(2):136-140.
Describes the decline in native ant populations after fire ants invade an area.

Schmidt, Patricia J., Wade C. Sherbrooke, and Justin O. Schmidt. 1989. The Detoxification of Ant (*Pogonomyrmex*) Venom by a Blood Factor in Horned Lizards (*Phrynosoma*). *Copeia* 1989(3):603-7.
This technical article examines how horned lizards cope with a potentially lethal venom from the ants they prey on.

Wilson, Edward O. 1990. Empire of the Ants. *Discover* 11(3):44-48, 50.
In this article, famed entomologist E. O. Wilson relates how his interest in ants developed and discusses some of his favorites.

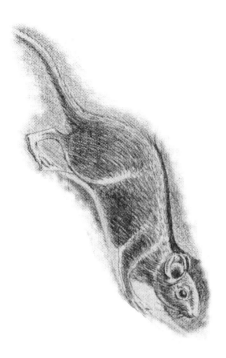

Chapter **13**

PACKRATS

*[Packrats] construct elaborate dens by drag-
ging sticks and other accouterments back to
a central location. The dens are passed along
from generation to generation, with each one
adding to the architecture.*

O. H. Reichman
Konza Prairie

FOLKLORE

Taking off Pitch Gloves

One day when Fox and Rabbit were in the hills looking for food, they found a piñon tree oozing lots of pitch.

Rabbit started to gather the pitch until he had a big pile of it. "What are you going to do with it?" asked Fox. "I am going to make a pair of gloves for you," said Rabbit. Then Rabbit put pitch all over Fox's hands and took her over to the pinon tree.

"Now hit the tree with your right hand," said Rabbit. Fox hit the tree as hard as she could, and her hand stuck to the tree. "What shall I do now?" asked Fox. "Hit the tree hard with your other hand," laughed Rabbit. Fox's other hand also stuck to the tree. Then Rabbit put gloves on Fox's feet also, and soon all of Fox's hands and feet were stuck to the pinon tree.

Rabbit went away laughing, but after a while he felt sorry for Fox and came back to the tree. He tried to get Fox loose, but the pitch was too sticky and it held Fox fast to the tree. So Rabbit went for help.

Soon Rabbit returned with Wood Rat, who said he could free Fox from the pinon tree. Wood Rat chewed on some animal fat and smeared it on Fox's hands and feet. Soon the pitch loosened, and Fox was free.

—Ronald M. Lanner
"Taking off Pitch Gloves"
(a Paguate Pueblo story)

149

A tall tale about packrats appeared in a newspaper on May 28, 1876. From this newspaper, the story spread all over the country and across the sea to Europe. John Thomas O'Keefe, a sergeant in the U.S. Army Signal Corps caused this national furor. He served as a signalman atop Pikes Peak when Colorado was still the Colorado Territory. His story was made up in cahoots with a local journalist and got picked up by the *Rocky Mountain News*. Here is the article as it appeared on the front page of the newspaper.

Killer Rodents on the Rampage! An Awful and Almost Incredible Story— A Fight for Life with Rats on Pikes Peak—An Infant Child Eaten!

Printed in the *Rocky Mountain News*

The vast number of packrats inhabiting the rocky crevices and cavernous passages at the summit of Pikes Peak have recently become formidable and dangerous. These animals are known to feed upon a saccharine gum that percolates through the pores of the rocks, apparently upheaved by some volcanic action.

Since the establishment of the government signal station on the summit of the peak, at an altitude of nearly 15,000 feet, these animals have acquired a voracious appetite for raw and uncooked meat, the scent of which seems to impart to them a ferocity rivaling the fierceness of the starved Siberian wolf.

The most singular trait in the character of these animals is they are never to be seen in the daytime. When the moon pours down her queenly light they may be seen in countless numbers trooping around among the rocky boulders that crown the barren waste, and during the warm summer months they may be seen swimming and sporting in the waters of the lake, a short distance below the peak, and on a dark, cloudy night, their trail in the water is marked by a sparkling light, giving the lake a bright and silvery appearance.

A few days since, Mr. John T. O'Keefe, one of the government operators at the signal station upon the peak, returned to his post, taking with him upon a pack animal a quarter of beef. It being late in the afternoon his colleague, Mr. Hobbs, immediately left with the pack animal for the Springs. Soon after dark, while Mr. O'Keefe was engaged in the office, he was startled by a scream from Mrs. O'Keefe, who had retired for the night to an adjoining bedroom, and who came rushing into the office screaming: "The rats! The rats!"

Mr. O'Keefe immediately encircled his wife with a scroll of zinc plating, such as is used in roofing, which prevented the savage creatures from climbing upon her person, and although his own body and limbs were being covered with them, he succeeded in encasing his legs each in a joint of stovepipe, and then with a heavy war club, preserved at the station with other Indian weapons captured at the battle of Sand Creek, began a desperate struggle for the preservation of his life.

Hundreds of animals were killed on every side by the rapid and well-aimed blows of the murderous bludgeon, yet still they seemed to swarm in with increasing numbers from the adjoining room, the door of which had, by a fatal oversight, been left open. The entire quarter of beef was devoured in less than five minutes, but it seemed only to sharpen their appetites for still fiercer attacks upon Mr. O'Keefe, whose hands, face, and neck were already lacerated.

In the midst of the warfare, Mrs. O'Keefe managed to reach a coil of electric wire hanging near the battery, and being a mountain girl, familiar with the throwing of the lariat, she hurled it through the air, causing it to encircle her husband, making unnumerable spiral waves along which she poured the electric fluid from the heavily charged battery with all the fullness of its power.

In an instant the room was ablaze with light, and whenever the rats came in contact with the wire they were hurled through the air to an almost instant death.

The sudden appearance of daylight, made such by the coruscations of the heavily charged wire, caused the ravenous creatures to abandon their attack and take refuge in the crevices and caverns of the mountain, making their exit by way of the bedroom window through which they had forced their entrance.

But the saddest part of this night adventure upon the peak is the destroying of their infant child, which Mrs. O'Keefe thought she had made secure by a heavy covering of bed clothing. But the rats had found their way to the infant (only two months old) and left nothing of it but the peeled and naked skull.

Doctors Horn and Anderson have just returned from the peak. It was thought at first that the left arm of Sergeant O'Keefe would have to be amputated, but they now believe it can be saved.

(There was no Mrs. O'Keefe or baby Erin O'Keefe. The grave of Erin O'Keefe withstood the stormy trials of existence on the mountaintop. In the 1930s, the grave marker was stolen. The weather station on Pikes Peak was abandoned in 1899.)

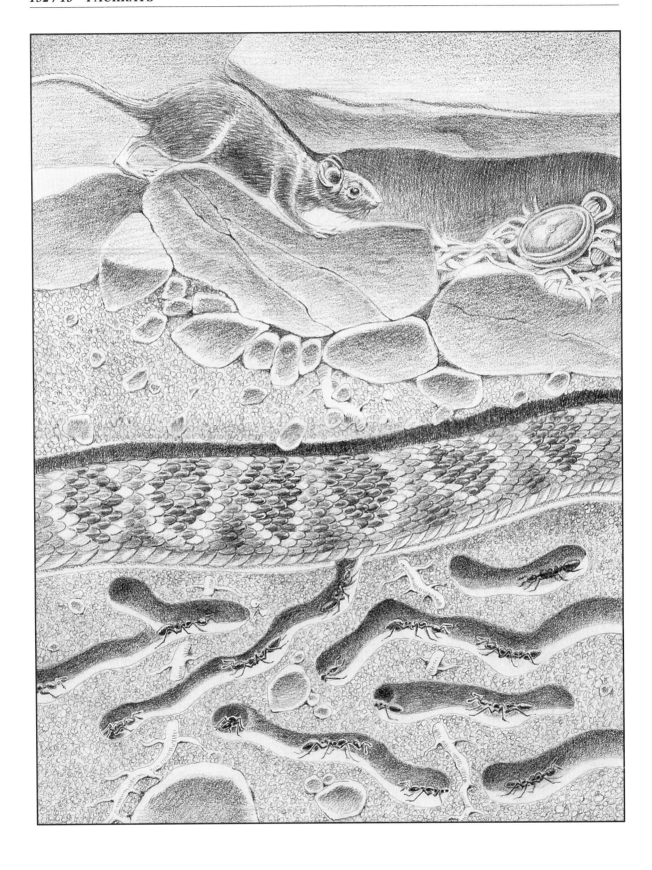

Ancient Romans believed that it meant good luck to see a white rat. However, if the white rat gnawed at your clothes or working equipment, that meant bad luck. Rather obvious, eh?

According to American Ozarks lore, if a rat comes into your house, you can be rid of it by writing it a polite note requesting that it leave. Then place the note in the entrance to the little animal's hiding place.

Men who sailed the seas were quick to see good and bad fortune in all the things around them. High among their pet hates were rats. Sailors believed that when rats abandon a ship just before sailing time, that ship is doomed. In *The Tempest*, Shakespeare wrote:

> *A rotten carcass of a boat, not rigg'd,*
> *Nor tackle, sail, nor mast; the very rats*
> *Instinctively had quit it.*

Because ancient beliefs held that rats were linked with the souls of the dead and consequently were blessed with insights into the future, they were able to warn their human neighbors of death and misfortune. Rats in mines, instead of being shunned, were welcome because they could sense danger. Miners even made pets of them. A miner's proverb was "When the rats move out, so does the miner." According to Myriam Friggens, "Sometimes they even alerted sleeping miners by tugging with their teeth on the men's clothes"[1] just before a cave-in or an explosion. There are many tall tales (a tall tale is a lie that has attained the dignity of age) about packrats leading miners to riches as well as taking rich gold nuggets and hiding them in their nests. At any rate, the packrats and miners were friends.

NATURAL HISTORY

Biologists know the rodents in the genus *Neotoma* as woodrats, but most people refer to them as packrats. At night, these rodents emerge from their dens and go forth to collect odds and ends, which they add to their messy accumulations of material. Perhaps, while carrying a bone back to its den, a packrat encounters an interesting tidbit, such as a watch left out by campers. The packrat may very well drop the bone and take the watch instead. The next morning, the camper finds the discarded bone "traded" for the watch, a habit that has earned packrats the nickname "trade rats." According to one writer, in the 1890s packrats stole snowgoggles, a teapot lid, and an aneroid barometer from naturalist John Muir, who woke up to discover a packrat trying to pull away—"with might and main"—an ice hatchet.

Description

Packrats look like overgrown mice. Most have bulging eyes, large ears, white feet, and furry tails. The bushy-tailed packrat has an especially furry tail, which looks like the tail of a squirrel.

In comparison, the troublesome Norway rats have smaller eyes, smaller ears, and scaly tails. Norway rats are closely associated with cities and towns; packrats more often live in wild areas where people seldom encounter them. John J. Audubon wrote about packrats, "They were mild in their dispositions, and much less disposed to bite when pursued than the common and more mischievous Norway rat."[2]

A Mexican packrat sits on a rocky ledge.

Because packrats don't hibernate, they store food in their dens to eat during periods of especially bad weather. The food habits of packrats affect the variety of material they bring back to their dens. Packrats frequently retrieve bones and items such as owl pellets that contain bones. They may use these as sources of calcium.

Packrats live in several kinds of dens. Most, such as the bushy-tailed and Mexican packrats, prefer to live in rocky crevices and talus slopes. Where cliffs and rocky outcrops aren't available, packrats sometimes make do with other building material. In the desert, bristly piles of cholla and prickly pear cactus may protect the entrance to a packrat den located under a large cactus. Some types of packrats occasionally make their dens in trees. They usually make one or more soft, grass-lined nests inside their dens.

Packrats depend on their dens in many ways. A den is a place to store food, a place that offers shelter from bad weather, a place for a female packrat to raise her young, and a place that offers defense from predators that regard packrats as tasty morsels. When a packrat dies, another often acquires the den. The same den can be used by countless generations of packrats, sometimes of the same species, sometimes of different species, each adding to the refuse heap, or midden.

Packrats also use the midden as a latrine. Over time, the feces and urine build up like molasses over the objects in the midden. In some sites, the middens contain several bushels of material.

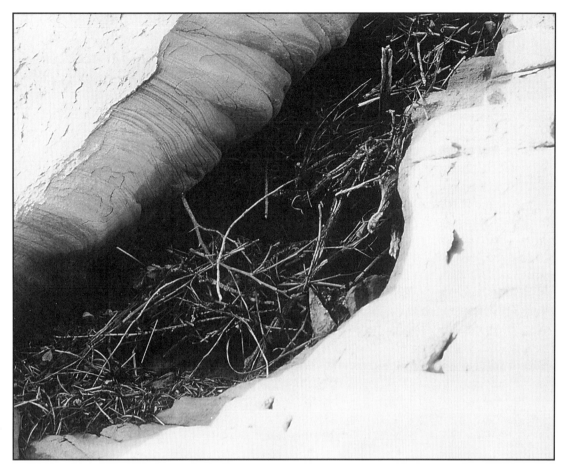

Packrats carry plants and other objects to their dens.

Except during the breeding season or when a female is raising young, packrats lead solitary lives. They have strong territorial instincts and defend their dens from other packrats. Females have one to six young per litter and up to four litters per year. After staying with their mother for about two months, the young leave to find dens of their own.

Range

More than 20 species of packrat occupy North America. Some species live as far south as Central America; northern populations of the bushy-tailed packrat approach the Arctic Circle in Canada's Northwest Territories. As a group, packrats occupy habitats from below sea level (near the Salton Sea of California) to over 14,000 feet (4270m) high (in Colorado's Rocky Mountains).

Altogether, about nine packrat species live in the United States and Canada. Often, more than one packrat lives in the same area, especially in the southwestern United States. In these situations, each species tends to specialize. For example, in rocky areas where Mexican and bushy-tailed packrats occur together, the Mexican packrats prefer horizontal crevices and the bushy-tailed packrats tend to occupy vertical cracks. The smallest species tend to live in desert areas. The bushy-tailed packrat, which occupies northern and high-elevation habitats, is one of the largest packrats; males sometimes reach weights of about a pound (0.45kg).

Interactions

Because they grow to larger sizes than mice, packrats have the unfortunate word *rat* as part of their name. Rats, such as the Norway rats introduced to North America, have had a long history as pests that destroy food stores and bring diseases to people. In contrast, packrats, though they sometimes make their dens in abandoned buildings, usually cause few problems for humans.

Packrats are probably stuck with the word *rat* as part of their name. However, it is interesting to speculate on whether their public image would improve if they were bestowed with a more endearing label; almost all mammalogists (biologists who study mammals) consider them attractive and fastidious creatures. Some researchers jokingly have proposed names such as the Pennsylvania pika, the Allegheny rock squirrel, and the long-tailed boulder bunny for the Allegheny woodrat.

You would expect to find a packrat in its den. Many other animals, though, also find packrat dens good places to live, at least part time. Box turtles, lizards, snakes, cottontail rabbits, chipmunks, mice, and skunks are among the other animals that biologists have found living in packrat dens. These animals don't depend on the packrat, and the packrat doesn't depend on them. This type of relationship, where one animal lives with another without either being much affected, is called a commensal relationship.

Native Americans would sometimes raid packrat dens for the piñon seeds accumulated there. Dens sometimes contain several pounds of the tasty and nutritious "pine nuts." (Note: Never take piñon seeds from a packrat den. First, the packrat worked hard for them and may need them to survive periods of bad weather. Second, it is possible that you would be exposed to disease organisms. Deer mice, which can carry a serious disease called Hantavirus, sometimes live in packrat dens.)

Packrats are herbivores (plant eaters). Some kinds, such as the bushy-tailed packrat, consume a variety of plants. Others depend on plants that other animals can't or won't eat. For example, the desert packrat survives on creosote leaves, especially in winter. The dusky-footed packrat eats oak leaves, and the white-throated packrat feasts on cactus. The most specialized is Stephen's packrat, whose diet consists almost entirely of juniper leaves. Each of these plants contains chemicals—such as tannins, alkaloids, and resins—that most other herbivores avoid.

Packrats don't travel far from their dens in their nightly forays, so the accumulated material gives scientists a snapshot of the plants in the area of the den. By analyzing contents of packrat middens, scientists have learned about changes in vegetation over long periods of time. They estimate, using carbon-14 dating methods, that some middens are more than 40,000 years old.

One group of researchers has even used packrat middens to investigate changes in the amount of cosmic radiation that bombards the earth. They found that cosmic-radiation levels were 41 percent higher 21,000 years ago, probably because the earth's magnetic field has grown stronger since then.

The U.S. Fish and Wildlife Service lists a packrat living on Key Largo, Florida, as an endangered species. Dangers affecting the Key Largo packrat include predation by dogs and cats, competition from introduced rats, and habitat loss from the increasing human population.

For some unknown reason, eastern packrats have suffered precipitous declines, especially in the northern parts of their range. Biologists have begun to study surviving populations to see if they can pinpoint the reasons for the declines elsewhere in the animal's range. Maybe they will find a new parasite or disease that is fatal to packrats. Or maybe some subtle change has occurred in packrat habitats. Biologists just don't know yet.

Some eastern packrats have been captured so that biologists can start breeding programs. In the future, young packrats produced in these programs may be used to repopulate areas where packrats have disappeared.

PACKRAT ACTIVITIES

1. Find out which packrat species live in your area. Check a field guide, such as *A Field Guide to the Mammals,* in the Peterson Field Guide Series. Or check a mammal field guide that concentrates on your state or province.

2. See how a packrat's den can protect it from extremes of weather. You need a large basket, sticks and leaves, two identical jars with lids, a thermometer, paper and pencil, and some water. On a cool day, start with hot water. On a warm day, start with cold water.

    Gather about a bushel of sticks and leaves in a large basket. Fill both jars with water. Measure and record the water temperature. Put the lids on the jars. Go outside and cover one jar with the sticks and leaves. Set the other jar on the ground beside it. After 20 minutes, measure the air temperature and the water temperature in the two jars. Record this information on your paper.

3. Use the information from the previous activity to make a chart that shows how the temperatures in the two jars of water change over time. Which jar changes temperature faster?

4. Both packrats and people collect things. (We hope people are more thoughtful about what they collect, however.) Make a list of things collected by people in your classroom or family.

From *Of Bugs and Beasts.* © 1995. Teacher Ideas Press. (800) 237-6124.

NOTES

1. Myriam Friggens, *Tales, Trails and Tommyknockers*, Boulder, Colo.: Johnson Books, 1979, p. 93.

2. V. H. Cahalan, ed. T*he Imperial Collection of Audubon Animals: The Quadrupeds of North America*. Original text by J. J. Audubon and J. Bachman. New York: Bonanza Books, 1967, p. 158.

BIBLIOGRAPHY

Books

Betancourt, Julio, Thomas R. Van Devender, and Paul S. Martin. 1990. *Packrat Middens: The Last 40,000 Years of Biotic Change*. Tucson: University of Arizona Press, 467 pp.
    Packrat ecology and research involving packrat middens are the topics covered in this technical book.

Burt, William H. 1976. *A Field Guide to the Mammals*. 3d ed. Illustrated by Richard P. Grossenheider. Boston: Houghton Mifflin, 289 pp.
    Illustrations of the animals and range maps help you identify mammals you encounter in North America.

Friggens, Myriam. 1979. *Tales, Trails and Tommyknockers*. Boulder, Colo.: Johnson Books.
    This book contains stories, legends, and lies from history.

Lanner, Ronald M. 1981. "Taking off Pitch Gloves." In *The Pinon Pine, A Natural and Cultural History*, 83-84. Reno: University of Nevada Press.
    Chapter 11 contains numerous myths pertaining to the piñon pine.

Zim, Herbert S., Donald F. Hoffmeister, and James G. Irving. 1987. *Mammals: A Guide to Familiar American Species*. Revised ed. Illustrated by James Gordon Irving. New York: Golden Press, 160 pp.
    This book covers 218 mammals of North America.

Articles

Betancourt, J. L., W. S. Schuster, J. B. Mitton, and R. S. Anderson. 1991. Fossil and Genetic History of a Pinyon Pine (*Pinus edulis*) Isolate. *Ecology* 72(5):1685-97.
    For this technical article, the authors used packrat middens to determine the history of an isolated piñon grove.

Dollar, Tom. 1992. The Desert's White-Throated Wood Rat. *Arizona Highways* 68(8):38-39. (August)
    Briefly profiles the white-throated woodrat, including photos.

Grayson, Donald K., and Stephanie D. Livingston. 1989. High-Elevation Records for *Neotoma cinerea* in the White Mountains, California. *Great Basin Naturalist* 49(3):392-95.
    In this technical article, the authors summarize information about bushy-tailed packrats at high elevation sites.

Hays, John P. How Many Species of Woodrats? *Conservationist* 43(5):39. (March-April)
    Discusses how research into the genetic relationships among packrats affects conservation decisions.

Hicks, Alan. 1989. Whatever Happened to the Allegheny Woodrat? *Conservationist* 43(5):34-38. (March-April)
    Describes the unexplained decline of the Allegheny woodrat in New York; includes photos of the woodrat.

Livo, Lauren J. 1992. The Pinon and the Packrat. *Colorado Outdoors* 41(5):20-23. (September-October)
    Summarizes the use of packrat middens in determining the origins of an isolated piñon grove.

Meyer, Michael W., and William H. Karasov. 1989. Antiherbivore Chemistry of *Larrea tridentata*: Effects on Woodrat (*Neotoma lepida*) Feeding and Nutrition. *Ecology* 70(4):953-61.
    This technical article investigates how toxic chemicals in plants affect packrat feeding strategies.

Murphy, Alexandra. 1993. Montana's Eclectic Collectors. *Montana Outdoors* 24(5):30-33. (September-October)
    The author describes her personal encounters with packrats. The article is accompanied by photos.

O'Keefe, John Thomas. "Killer Rodents on the Rampage!" *Rocky Mountain News*, May 28, 1876.
    A wonderful and creative tall tale.

Pack Rat's Liquid Legacy. 1992. *Science* 255(5041):155.
    Discusses cosmic ray research using information from packrat middens.

Chapter 14

SKUNKS

As a general rule, any animal large enough to kill a skunk is also smart enough not to bother.

David M. Armstrong
Lions, Ferrets & Bears

FOLKLORE

Skunk

Skunk and Coyote lived near each other on the prairies. Many prairie dogs also lived nearby. When Skunk became hungry, he killed quite a few prairie dogs with his skunk juice. He would then gather them up and carry them to his big bonfire made of branches and bushes. The bonfire was built near a pond because he always became thirsty after a big meal of prairie dogs.

When the fire ashes were hot enough, Skunk put the prairie dogs in them, placing them carefully side-by-side and alternating head and tail, head and tail, head and tail . . .

One day, Coyote dropped by. He was bored and had nothing to do so he challenged Skunk to a race. "My, my, Skunk. You have those prairie dogs cooking so nicely! Let's say that whoever wins our race shall get to feast on them!"

Skunk agreed, and they took off, digging their paws into the dirt and raising dust as they ran. Coyote took a strong lead at first, but Skunk was able to keep up with him for quite a distance. When Coyote began to put more distance between them, Skunk turned around and went back to where the prairie dogs were cooking.

Ah, they smell so good, he thought. Skunk decided to pick out the fattest, juiciest ones for himself. He then carried them to a hole that he had decided would be the perfect hiding place. Because the hole was quite a distance from the bonfire where the other prairie dogs were cooking, Skunk decided to stay by the hole and see what happened.

Coyote returned to the cooking prairie dogs, huffing and puffing. "Ha," he said. "My friend is still running. It will be a long time before he gets here. Skunk will really be hungry and thirsty when he arrives."

160

Coyote gazed down at the cooking prairie dogs. He picked one up with a stick. It was a little one. He picked up others and saw that they also were little. "There is nothing here but little dogs," he exclaimed. "I need to find Skunk and talk about this with him."

Coyote found Skunk sitting beside the hole. Skunk popped into the hole when he saw Coyote coming toward him. Coyote looked into the hole. "Dear friend, all of this running has made me very hungry. Please let me have one of those large prairie dogs to eat."

"No!" Skunk replied.

"Well," Coyote said. "I will just have to smoke you out of that hole then."

"What are you going to smoke me out with?" Skunk asked.

"I will use a nasty weed," answered Coyote.

"That's just fine," Skunk replied. "I eat that kind of weed regularly."

"I will get some pine gum then," Coyote announced. "Surely, that will not be pleasant for you!"

"Oh, are you going to kill me?" asked Skunk.

Coyote went off to a grove of pine trees to collect the pine gum. He scratched the bark of the trees and caught the gum as it oozed out. He returned with the pine gum and promptly deposited it into the hole. Coyote then built a fire, allowing the smoke to waft down into the hole.

"Hey, Coyote, put some more on. You are killing me. More, more," snorted Skunk. Tricky Skunk was moving closer to the entrance of the hole as he said this. Coyote was bending over the fire, continuing to blow more smoke down the hole.

"Keep on blowing," taunted Skunk.

Coyote moved even closer to the fire, putting his nose down and blowing as hard as he could.

About this time, Skunk was very close to the hole entrance, too. Suddenly, he shot his fragrant skunk juice right into Coyote's face and eyes. Coyote was completely covered with it. His eyes burned and he could not see anything.

As Coyote continued to rub his eyes, Skunk escaped, laughing as he went.

—Ute
Adapted and retold by Norma J. Livo

In the early days of the Old West, there existed a mutual dislike between cattlemen and sheepherders. The cattlemen insisted the sheepherders looked disreputable, but worst of all they smelled. In fact, they stunk!

There is an old story about a carnival that came to town. One of the carnival tents displayed a huge sign in front of it that read, "Five dollars if you can stay in this tent five minutes!" A cattleman, a farmer, and a sheepherder stood outside of the tent. Deciding to accept the challenge, the cattleman swaggered into the tent with cocky assurance. In two minutes he stumbled out, spluttering, coughing, and hacking. He dared the farmer beside him to try it.

The farmer ventured into the tent, but within one minute he burst out in distress. Knowing it was now his turn, the sheepherder ambled in while the other two caught their breath. One minute passed. Then two, three, four. Just as the cattleman and the farmer were preparing to go in and rescue the sheepherder, a large, virile, and highly disgusted skunk ran out from under the tent flap and made for the creek.

Folktales explain how things came to be. Among the stories from the Thompson Indians of British Columbia, there is one that explains why skunks are plentiful in Shuswap country. It started when Skunk invited all the animal neighbors over and incited them to war on the Shuswap Indians.

Skunk was their chief and guide on this warpath. He tricked them all into a large pit the Shuswap used for trapping. When the animals were all in the pit he let loose his obnoxious fluid all over them and thought he'd killed them. He returned home, where he lied about what happened to the animals. However, the warrior animals had revived after a few days. They returned home and put Skunk in a basket with a lid and threw him into the river with the curse, "From now on, you'll never be a chief, you'll never be able to betray your friends. You'll be shunned by all men and animals because you stink!" Skunk scrambled ashore in Shuswap country, and that is why skunks are plentiful there, even today.

An Abenaki (northeastern tribe) story explains how Skunk became as he is today. In the old days Skunk's coat was made of long, silky, pure white fur. He was one of the most beautiful of animals. He talked Gluskabe, the transformer and trickster hero, into being his companion. They had a falling-out and Skunk tied the Day Eagle's wings closed. Because the Day Eagle could not open his wings, there was no daylight. Gluskabe discovered what Skunk had done. Gluskabe was only able to free one of Day Eagle's wings, which is why only half the world has daylight at any time. The Day Eagle must keep turning around on his hilltop to share the daylight with all the world.

Gluskabe punished Skunk as he emptied the ashes from his pipe over Skunk's head, making his white coat black. Gluskabe drew two white stripes to remind Skunk of how beautiful he had once been. Then he blew smoke on Skunk to make him bad-smelling so that no one would want to be near him. That explains why Skunk usually comes out when it is dark. He is ashamed of his sooty coat and fears the Day Eagle will seek revenge for what he did long ago.

Odor alone can identify the presence (and degree of agitation) of a skunk. Even people who have never seen a living skunk can recognize the pungent smell.

Plants such as skunkweed, skunkleaf (usually called Jacob's Ladder), and skunk cabbage acquired their common names because of their milder, but still unpleasant, fragrances.

In human terms, an unpleasant person may be considered a skunk. In cribbage, you get skunked when you lose by 30 or more of the 120 total points. A "double skunking" is even worse because you've lost before you cross the 60-point line.

NATURAL HISTORY

Skunks belong to the Mustelidae, the same family that includes such creatures as mink, weasels, otters, and badgers. Mammals in this group have anal scent glands—a feature especially well developed for defense in skunks. These black-and-white animals can spray their foul-smelling fluid a dozen feet (3.7m).

The English word for *skunk* comes from an Algonquian term, *segonku*, meaning "one who squirts." Some people refer to skunks as "polecats," but this term best pertains to a European ferret. Spotted skunks are sometimes called "civet cats." However, civets (which aren't cats either) are members of the mongoose family that lives in Africa and Asia.

Description

Biologists arrange skunks into three groups: striped skunks (genus *Mephitis*), spotted skunks (genus *Spilogale*), and hog-nosed skunks (genus *Conepatus*). All skunks have distinctive black and white fur, although the patterns vary. Striped skunks usually have two white stripes on the back. Spotted skunks have patches of white on the head and broken lines of white fur on the back. Hog-nosed skunks have piglike noses and a broad white band of fur on their backs and tails.

Skunks forage at night, searching for mice and other small mammals, insects, birds and their eggs, carrion, and fruits. Spotted skunks have a weasel-like build and often climb trees in their search for food.

Although skunks don't hibernate, they may remain inactive during harsh winter weather. Several skunks may share a winter den site.

The western spotted skunk mates in late summer. This species has delayed implantation, so the embryos don't begin to develop until the next spring. Most other skunks mate in late winter and the females give birth to young skunks in May or June.

Litter sizes range from one to nine young. The female takes care of her blind and helpless babies by herself. After about a month, the babies' eyes open. By the time the baby skunks are about seven weeks old, they can spray. At maturity, spotted skunks weigh as little as a pound (0.45kg) or so; striped skunks can reach weights as high as 14 pounds (6.3kg).

Range

As a group, skunks range from Canada to South America. About 10 species of skunks occupy the United States and Canada, with striped skunks the most common and wide-ranging of the skunks. Striped skunks are found throughout the United States and southern portions of Canada. Spotted skunks have nearly as broad a distribution. The most restricted North American range belongs to the hog-nosed skunks, which occupy portions of the southwestern United States.

Interactions

Biologists believe the vivid black-and-white patterns on skunks serve as warning signals to potential predators. Skunks derive further protection from their threat displays. In *Trials of Life*, David Attenborough writes of the spotted skunk: "First it stamps vigorously with its front feet and erects its bristling tail. If you walk closer, it does a hand-stand, hoisting its hind legs in the air and pointing its tail over its head towards you. If that does not deter you, it drops back on all fours, turns its back on you and squirts."[1]

Threat displays of other skunk species differ. A striped skunk, for example, raises its furry tail when it becomes mildly disturbed. If further provoked, the skunk keeps its tail up and exposes the anal scent glands. Just before a striped skunk sprays, it bends its tail forward over its body. Skunks have good aim. If the spray gets in the eyes, it can temporarily blind a predator.

One bit of folklore suggests that skunks can't spray when they are held off the ground by their tails. Biologist Richard Van Gelder discovered an element of truth in this assertion. If someone picks up a striped skunk by the tail *before* the skunk exposes its anal scent glands, the skunk can't spray. However, a striped skunk can spray from any position once it has exposed the scent glands. Spotted skunks can spray at any time from any position.

Aroma also varies from species to species. The odor of a striped skunk endures for a long time—up to two weeks—compared to the shorter-lived odor of a spotted skunk. One of the few animals that seem unbothered by skunk odor is the great horned owl. These large birds occasionally prey on skunks.

Perhaps because their defenses are so effective, skunks don't seem to pay too much attention to things going on around them. Roger Knutson, in his book *Flattened Fauna*, describes the skunk's unfortunate interaction with traffic this way: "This peaceable, gentle creature has refused to come to terms with highway traffic and continues to behave as if roads, cars, and trucks do not exist. Armed as it has always been with an odorous repellent strong enough to turn away any potential predator, it hops along totally unafraid, which is as fatal as overly aggressive behavior on the road." [2]

Skunks can help control mice and other agricultural pests. However, skunks can also cause problems. Skunks sometimes have rabies; in fact, since 1961 they are the most common animal reported with the disease. This causes obvious public health concerns in areas with a high incidence of rabid skunks. Also, when a skunk—even a healthy one—makes its den under or near buildings, the odor (or its threat) can be a problem to the human inhabitants.

Enterprising humans have found inventive uses for skunk spray. Rocky Mountain Wildlife Enterprises sells a skunk-based product called Scrooge Christmas Tree Protector. Park managers and others spray the tree protector on pine trees or other shrubs that might be tempting targets for Christmas tree poachers. The smell discourages would-be tree thieves.

For some reason, spotted skunk populations have declined throughout most of their range. Because of this, wildlife departments in many states have begun to monitor skunk populations. One method, used by Minnesota's Nongame Wildlife Program, is posting "wanted posters" that illustrate spotted skunks. People who observe the skunks are asked to contact the Nongame Wildlife Program. This information helps biologists get an idea of the distribution and abundance of the animals.

SKUNK ACTIVITIES

1. Not everyone likes the same odors. In fact, not everyone can even smell some odors. Before conducting this classroom activity, collect 10 or more small (8-oz.) plastic yogurt containers and lids. With a needle, poke a small hole in each lid. Number the lids with a dark marker. Put different "scent sources" in each of the containers and cover with lids. Have kids sniff and react.

    Some scent ideas: coffee grounds, perfume or cologne, raw chicken (when left out for 1-2 days, said to be one of the worst odors), dill pickle juice, lemon or orange rind, tap water, distilled water, fur brushed from a pet, a piece of chocolate, needles from a pine tree, a drop or two of household ammonia, vanilla, and small pieces of soap.

2. Visit a local river or creek and make plaster of paris casts of mammal tracks. Match these with tracks in a field guide.

From *Of Bugs and Beasts*. © 1995. Teacher Ideas Press. (800) 237-6124.

NOTES

1. David Attenborough. 1990. *Trials of Life*. Boston: Little, Brown, pp. 88, 90.

2. Roger M. Knutson. 1987. *Flattened Fauna: A Field Guide to Common Animals of Roads, Streets, and Highways*. Berkeley, Calif.: Ten Speed Press, p. 70.

BIBLIOGRAPHY

Books

Bruchac, Joseph. 1988. "Gluskabe and Skunk." In *The Faithful Hunter*, pp. 5-7. Greenfield Center, N.Y.: Greenfield Review Press.
> Stories of the Abenaki.

Greenblat, Rodney A. 1993. *Slombo the Gross*. New York: HarperCollins.
> When the Swamp Beast's only food source is threatened and he drives hordes of skunks into town, only the disgusting Slombo the Gross can restore the ecological balance.

Hilbert, Vi. 1985. "Skunk's Important Information." In *Haboo, Native American Stories from Puget Sound*, 165-66. Seattle: University of Washington Press.
> A collection of 33 stories from oral storytelling in the original Lushootseed language and transcribed and edited by Vi Hilbert, a member of the Skagit Indian group and now an elder in that society.

Yolen, Jane. 1994. "The Skank." In *How Beastly! A Menagerie of Nonsense Poems*, p. 18. Illustrations by James Marshall. Honesdale, Pa.: Boyds Mills Press.
> A collection of the author's nonsense poems about beastly creatures. As Yolen says, "The Skank: A tense ancestor of the skunk."

Articles

Backlund, Doug. 1992. The Plains Spotted Skunk. *South Dakota Conservation Digest* 59(4):18-19.
> Profiles the life history of the spotted skunk.

Dollar, Tom. 1993. The Dauntless Skunk, Affable Camp Companion. *Arizona Highways* 69(1):32-33. (January)
> Describes the brazen campground behavior of some spotted skunks—including one that walked across the author while he was in his sleeping bag.

Gremillion-Smith, Catherine, and Alan Woolf. 1988. Epizootiology of Skunk Rabies in North America. *Journal of Wildlife Diseases* 24(4):620-26.
> A technical paper that describes patterns of rabies outbreaks in skunk populations.

Schuster, Larry. 1992. The Spray That Inspires. *National Wildlife* 30(5):34-39. (August-September)
> Skunk odor has a variety of applications. This article details some of its uses.

Van Gelder, Richard G. 1990. An Uplifting Tail. *Natural History* (August):6, 8-10.
> The author describes some of his personal encounters with skunks.

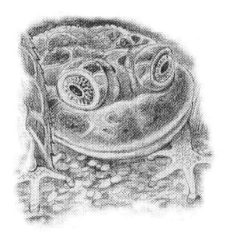

Chapter 15

TOADS

Sweet are the uses of adversity, which like the toad, ugly and venomous, wears yet a precious jewel in his head.

William Shakespeare
As You Like It

FOLKLORE

The Three Feathers

There was once a King who had three sons. Two of them were considered wise and prudent but the youngest, who said very little, appeared to others so silly that they gave him the name of Simple. When the King became old and weak and began to think that his end was near, he knew not to which of his sons to leave his kingdom.

So he sent for them and said, "I have made a determination that whichever of you brings me the finest carpet shall be King after my death."

They immediately prepared to start on their expedition and that there might be no dispute between them, they took three feathers. As they left the castle each blew a feather into the air, and said, "We will travel in whatever direction these feathers take." One flew to the east and the other to the west, but the third soon fell on the earth and remained there. Then the two eldest brothers turned one to the right and the other to the left and they laughed at Simple because where his feather fell he was obliged to remain.

Simple sat down after his brothers were gone, feeling very sad. Presently he noticed near where his feather lay a kind of trapdoor. He rose quickly, went toward it, and lifted it up. To his surprise he saw a flight of steps down which he descended, and reached another door. Hearing voices within he knocked hastily. The voices were singing:

> *Little toads, crooked legs,*
> *Where do you hide?*
> *Go and see quickly*
> *Who is outside.*

167

At this the door opened of itself, and the youth saw a large fat toad seated with a number of little toads round her. On seeing him the large toad asked what he wanted. "I have a great wish for the finest and most beautiful carpet that can be got," he replied. Then the old toad called again to her little ones,

Little toads, crooked legs,
Run here and there;
Bring me the large bag
That hangs over there.

The young toads fetched the bag, and when it was opened the old toad took from it a carpet so fine and so beautifully worked that nothing on earth could equal it. This she gave to the young man who thanked her and went away up the steps.

Meanwhile his elder brothers, quite believing that their foolish brother would not be able to get any carpet at all, said one to another, "We need not take the trouble to go further and seek for anything very wonderful. Ours is sure to be the best." And as the first person they met was a shepherd wearing a shepherd's plaid, they bought the large plaid cloth and carried it home to the King.

At the same time the younger brother returned with his beautiful carpet, and when the King saw it he was astonished and said, "If justice is done, then the kingdom belongs to my youngest son."

But the two elder brothers gave the King no peace. They said it was impossible for Simple to become King for his understanding failed in everything and they begged their father to make another condition.

At last he said, "Whoever finds the most beautiful ring and brings it to me shall have the kingdom."

Away went the brothers a second time and blew three feathers into the air to direct their ways. The feathers of the elder two flew east and west, but that of the youngest fell, as before, near the trapdoor and there rested. He at once descended the steps and told the great toad that he wanted a most beautiful ring. She sent for her large bag and drew from it a ring which sparkled with precious stones and was so beautiful that no goldsmith on earth could make one like it.

The elder brothers had again laughed at Simple when his feather fell so soon to the ground and forgetting his former success with the carpet, scorned the idea that he could ever find a gold ring. So they gave themselves no trouble, but merely took a plated ring from the harness of a carriage horse, and brought it to their father.

When the King saw Simple's splendid ring he said at once, "The kingdom belongs to my youngest son."

His brothers however were not yet inclined to submit to the decision. They begged their father to make a third condition and at last he promised to give the kingdom to the son who brought home the most beautiful woman to be his wife.

They all were again guided by blowing the feathers, and the two elder took the roads pointed out to them. But Simple, without hesitation, went at once to the toad and said, "This time I am to take home the most beautiful woman."

"Hey-day!" said the toad. "I have not one by me at present but you shall have one soon." So she gave him a carrot which had been hollowed out, and to which six mice were harnessed.

Simple took it quite sorrowfully, and said, "What am I to do with this?" "Seat one of my little toads in it," she said.

The youth on this, caught one up at a venture and seated it in the carrot. No sooner had he done so than it became a most beautiful young lady. The carrot was turned into a gilded coach and the mice were changed to prancing horses.

He kissed the maiden, seated himself in the carriage with her, drove away to the castle and led her to the King.

Meanwhile his brothers had proved more silly than he. Not forgetting the beautiful carpet and the ring, they still thought it was impossible for Simple to find a beautiful woman also. They therefore took no more trouble than before and merely chose the handsomest peasant maidens they could find to bring to their father.

When the King saw the beautiful maiden his youngest son had brought he said, "The kingdom must now belong to my youngest son after my death."

But the elder brothers deafened the King's ears with their cries, "We cannot consent to let our stupid brother be King. Give us one more trial. Let a ring be hung in the hall and let each woman spring through it." For they thought the peasant maidens would easily manage to do this because they were strong and that the delicate lady would no doubt kill herself. To this trial the old King consented.

The peasant maidens jumped first but they were so heavy and awkward that they fell. One broke her arm and the other her leg. But the beautiful lady whom Simple had brought home sprang as lightly as a deer through the ring and thus put an end to all opposition.

The youngest brother married the beautiful maiden and after his father's death ruled the kingdom for many years with wisdom and equity.

—Brothers Grimm

Perhaps because of their nocturnal habits, toads have an association with evil and witchcraft. In Shakespeare's *MacBeth*, the witches chant:

> *Round about the cauldron go;*
> *In the poison'd entrails throw.*
> *Toad, that under cold stone*
> *Days and nights hast thirty-one*
> *Swelter'd venom sleeping got*
> *Boil thou first i' the charmed pot.*
> *Double, double toil and trouble;*
> *Fire burn and cauldron bubble.*

Something about a toad just looks grumpy, and we may insult a person by calling them a toad. A "toady" is someone who flatters another person, hoping for a favor. "Toadstones" were charms thought to be antidotes to poisons. We still call poisonous mushrooms "toadstools."

People often think toads must feel slimy, but they usually feel dry to the touch. The "warty" bumps on their skin probably gave rise to the myth that toads cause warts. A virus that has nothing to do with toads causes warts on humans.

Toads, frogs, and snakes were thought to have a sacred influence over the weather. The toad and the frog, because their lives were spent in or near the water, were also associated with rain. Some cultures credited them with having given the world its water.

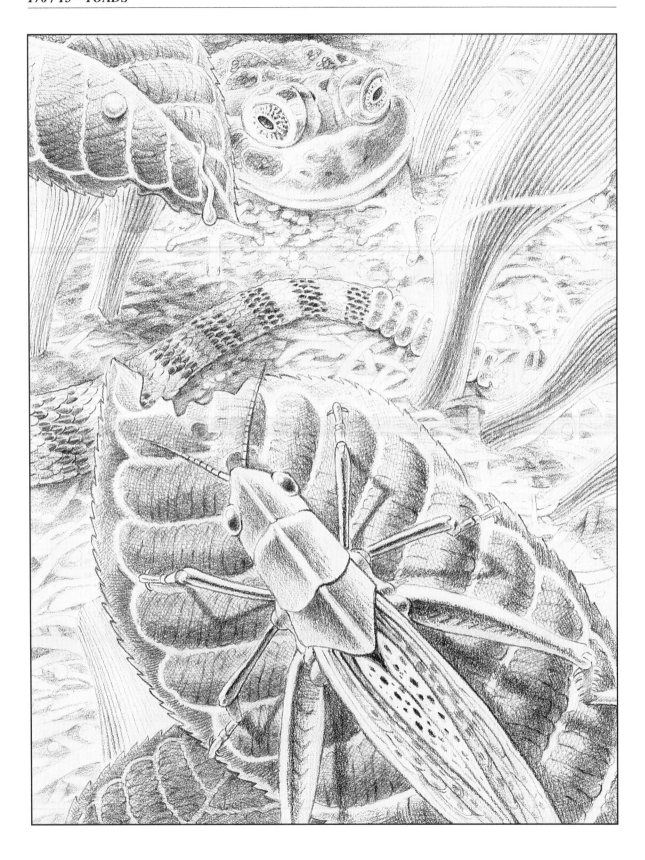

In many rural areas of the United States, toads are viewed as a sign of good luck. If newlyweds catch sight of a toad in the roadway, theirs will be a happy marriage. That superstition however, does not encourage throwing toads as the happy couple leaves the church.

As a folk medicine aid, boiled toads were known to help in cases of dropsy and leprosy. A promising remedy from a fifteenth-century leechbook specifies a bushel of barley and half a bushel of toads simmered in a lead cauldron until the flesh of the toads falls from the bones. The barley brew should be dried in the sun and then fed to newly hatched chicks. The chicks, roasted or boiled, may then be fed to the lepers as a cure.

Martin Luther, from sixteenth-century Germany, gave a recipe to draw the poison from any pestilent tumor: Run a stick through three toads, dry them out in the sun, and apply them to the tumor. The Chinese have used toad venom for its digitalis-like properties in treating heart ailments. A Chinese story tells of a man who had been suffering for months from a wound in his foot. He was told to apply a mashed toad three times a day. It drew the poisons from the wound and he got well. Toads are used in Central and South American shamanic cultures for healing.

The Chinese see not a man but a toad in the moon. According to legend, the Queen of Western Paradise gave the pill of immortality to the archer Shen. His wife stole the pill, swallowed it, and went to the moon to escape her husband's wrath. She was transformed into a three-legged toad. Shen still visits her on the 15th day of each month, which is why the moon is unusually brilliant at this time. Periodically the moon-toad attempts to swallow the moon itself, which causes an eclipse.

Pliny defined the toad as a frog who lives in brambles. He also told stories about how the presence of a toad will cause a meeting of people to fall silent; that a small bone in its right side will stop water from boiling; that a bone in its left side will repel the attacks of dogs, and that toads will act as an aphrodisiac if worn as an amulet.

Toads were once used to test the virtue of gems. A circle was drawn around a toad using the gem in question; then the gem was placed before the eyes of the toad. If the gem were flawed, it would break apart; if the gem were perfect, the toad would burst.

The Jamaicans tell a variation of the tortoise-and-hare story. In this story the king sets up a 20-mile race between a toad and a donkey. Before the race the toad plants one of his children at each of the 20-mile posts. Their taunts during the race cause the donkey to gallop and wear himself out.

Biologist Marth Crump tells us this about the golden frog, *Atelopus varius zeteki*, which is a type of toad: "According to the legends of the Panamanian Indians, anyone who manages to find the golden frog finds happiness; some people let the frog go, without recognising happiness when they find it, and others wish not to hold the frog because they fear happiness."[1] This beautiful amphibian is listed as an endangered species.

NATURAL HISTORY

True toads belong to the family Bufonidae, a group containing about 360 species and occurring throughout the most of the world. The only true toads native to the United States and Canada belong to the genus *Bufo*. Toads are amphibians, a group of animals with life cycles that generally include both an aquatic and a terrestrial stage. In fact, the word *amphibian* comes from the Greek *amphibios*, meaning "double life."

Frogs and toads are anurans, or amphibians without tails (in contrast to salamanders, amphibians that have tails). Frogs and toads are common animals in Europe, so both English and other European languages possess words for these amphibians. German, for example, has the word *frosch* for frog and *kröte* for toad. In French, *grenouille* means frog and *crapaud* means toad. *Sammakko* and *rupisammakko* mean frog and toad, respectively, in Finnish. However, many other types of anurans live elsewhere in the world. Are they frogs or are they toads?

Herpetologists (people who study amphibians and reptiles) have a saying: "All toads are frogs, but not all frogs are toads." This means that you can properly call any anuran a frog. The word toad usually refers to squat, warty amphibians.

Toads, such as this western toad, usually have warty skin.

When biologists gave scientific (two part) names to various anurans, they adopted the Latin words *rana* (frog) and *bufo* (toad) for two of the groups of amphibians. So, although you can call any anuran a frog, members of the genus *Rana* are "true frogs." And although you can call any squat anuran a toad, members of the family Bufonidae, and especially the genus *Bufo*, are true toads.

Although spadefoot toads and narrowmouth toads are not "true toads," people often refer to them as toads because of their squat bodies. The "horny toads" of western North America, by the way, are neither frogs nor toads. They are reptiles more properly called horned lizards.

Description

Toads in the genus *Bufo* have warty skin, stocky bodies, and raised areas behind the eye called parotoid glands. North American toads range in size from the tiny oak toad (three-quarters to one and five-sixteenth inches, or 1.9 to 3.3cm long) to the Colorado River toad (reaching lengths of 7.5 inches, or 19cm).

Each spring and summer, ponds and pools come alive with the trilling calls of male toads. A vocal sac under the lower jaw helps a male toad amplify the sound. Males often struggle with one another for the opportunity to mate with the females entering the breeding pools. When mating, a male toad firmly clasps the female with his front legs. As the female releases her eggs into the water, the male sheds sperm to fertilize them. Many toads' eggs look like small dark balls suspended in long, clear strands of jelly. Depending on the species, a female toad can deposit from a few thousand to more than 20,000 eggs at a time.

Although often called a horny toad, this animal is actually a horned lizard.

The Colorado River toad is one of the largest North American toads.

Over a week or two, the eggs develop into small tadpoles, which eventually wriggle out from the jelly and begin the aquatic part of their lives. For several weeks, the tadpoles graze on algae and other plant material in the water. Gradually, the tadpoles begin to change into little toads, a process called metamorphosis.

First, hind legs start growing where the tail and body meet. Then the front legs appear. While this is happening, the eyes and mouthparts begin to change into the form needed by a young toad. Soon the little animal reabsorbs its tail. Many toadlets are about the size of flies when they crawl out of the water and begin their lives on land.

A bump on the side of this tadpole indicates that a front leg is about to emerge.

Toads lack the teeth of wolves and the claws of lions but are predators just the same. A toad uses its sticky tongue as its hunting weapon. The tongue attaches to the front of the lower jaw, enabling the toad to quickly flick it out and snap up nearly any insects or other invertebrates small enough to swallow. Toads don't chew their food but swallow it whole.

Toads that live in cold areas must find shelter from winter weather. Some burrow into the ground below the frost line or seek shelter in rodent burrows. In the Rocky Mountains, at least some populations of the western toad find underground chambers where the air temperature stays above freezing all winter.

Although some toads hop about during the day, most prefer to come out only at night. This activity pattern lets the toad protect itself from drying out too much. Toads can even live in some dry desert areas by limiting most of their activity to nights after rains.

Adult toads live on land, but each year they return to water to call for mates and lay their eggs, beginning the cycle anew.

Range

Toads occupy habitats throughout the world except for New Guinea, Australia, New Zealand, South Pacific islands, and arctic regions. They are also absent from some extremely dry areas. About 18 native species of true toads (all in the genus *Bufo*) can be found throughout the United States and Canada. Their range extends as far north as the Alaskan panhandle and extreme southern Yukon and Northwest Territories. Toads occur as high as 11,940 feet (3,640m) in mountains.

Interactions

Toads participate in both aquatic food webs (as tadpoles) and terrestrial food webs (as adults). This makes them especially important members of the ecosystems in which they occur.

Because they eat large numbers of insects, toads help control pests. In the 1930s, people were looking for a way to control infestations of beetles and grubs that were destroying sugarcane crops. So they introduced giant toads (*Bufo marinus*) to sugar fields throughout the world on the theory that the toads would eat the beetles and grubs. This large toad has a native range that extends from South America to the southern tip of Texas. Introduced populations of the giant (or "cane") toad now exist in northeastern Australia, the Philippines, Taiwan, New Guinea, Hawaii and other Pacific islands, south Florida, and numerous Caribbean islands. The giant toads quickly adapted to their new homes. Unfortunately, though, they were not effective at controlling the beetles and grubs and have become major pests themselves.

Toads also participate in food webs as prey. When a toad encounters a potential predator, it often puffs itself up with air and stands on its legs to look as large as possible. Toads do possess a kind of venom. The warts on the toad's skin, particularly the large parotoid glands behind the eyes, can secrete irritating substances. These chemicals make the skin taste bad to predators and can irritate eyes and other mucus membranes. Because of this, you should always wash your hands after handling a toad. (Since toads potentially can absorb chemicals through their skin, you might also consider washing your hands before touching the toad to remove sunscreen or other substances that might harm the toad.)

Toads can not only taste bad but be dangerous to some predators that try to eat them. For example, occasionally pet owners report that their dogs were killed when they bit large toads such as giant toads or Colorado River toads. Some birds have learned the trick of neatly skinning a toad to avoid the poison glands. Hognose snakes have noses built for digging out toads, which are their favorite food, and have much larger adrenal glands than most other snakes. Biologists think that this latter adaptation helps the hognose snake counteract the poisons in toad skin.

Recently, a strange and disturbing trend has begun to affect some toads and other amphibians throughout the world. Sometimes the populations of these animals decline for easily observed reasons such as destruction of wetlands or local droughts. Other times the amphibians disappear without any clear reason. Even previously flourishing introduced populations sometimes show declines. For example, the giant toad appears to have undergone a major decline on the island of Kauai, Hawaii. These introduced toads were common there as recently as 1991.

On the mainland United States, Yosemite toads of the Sierra Nevada Mountains and the western toad of the southern Rocky Mountains are among the native amphibians that have suffered dramatic population declines. In addition, the U.S. Fish and Wildlife Service lists both the Wyoming and Houston toads as endangered. Some biologists believe that amphibians are especially sensitive indicators of environmental quality because their skin offers little protection against pollutants, acidic water, or changes in ultraviolet radiation.

These population declines have not affected all toads and frogs. In many places, these amphibians seem to be as common as ever.

Some toads, such as western toads in the Rocky Mountains of Colorado, are suffering unexplained population declines.

TOAD ACTIVITIES

1. Many organizations help survey toads and frogs. Check with a local museum or wildlife department to see if you can volunteer to help with any amphibian surveys they sponsor.

2. If toads or other amphibians live near your neighborhood, keep notes on what you observe.

3. Borrow a recording of amphibian calls and listen to the types of sounds that toads and frogs make.

4. Make an origami toad (or frog). Folds in construction paper are often too rough to make the smooth folds needed for origami. Craft stores sell paper for origami, or you can use pieces of gift wrap or other paper that holds smooth folds. A book by Toyoaki Kawai (listed in the bibliography) shows how to make numerous origami animals, including frogs, bats, snakes, and caterpillars.

5. Have races with origami toads. Drop dried beans near the back to make the toads "jump" to a finish line. Or give contestants identical numbers of beans and see how far they can make their paper toads jump.

6. In 1865 Mark Twain wrote an interesting story about a frog jumping contest, called "The Celebrated Jumping Frog of Calaveras County." With this story as inspiration, Calaveras County stages frog-jumping contests as annual events. Go to the library, read Twain's story, and see what you can learn about these current-day events.

   a. How are frog jumps measured? (Clue: One hop isn't enough.)

   b. How long have the Calaveras County frog-jumping contests been going on?

   c. How long is the record jump and when was it recorded?

   d. What is the difference between the current Calaveras record and the record of 32 feet, 3 inches set in South Africa in 1954 (by a frog called *Rana oxyrhynchus*)?

7. In 1990, the Calaveras County frog-jumping contest was clouded in controversy. Contestant Andy Koffman wanted to race goliath frogs (a huge frog native to Africa). A photo of Koffman and his frogs appeared in many local newspapers and the January 22, 1990, issue of *Time* magazine (page 27). The contest was scheduled for May 17-20. Try to locate stories about this event and report on the outcome. What is your position on allowing contestants to use giant imported frogs?

8. Obtain the GEMS teacher's guide, *Frog Math: Predict, Ponder, Play* (listed in bibliography) for a series of great activities about toads and frogs. Some of the activities include toy frog races, the speed of various frog contestants being determined by rolls of the dice. Toy frogs may be available at toy stores or science stores near you.

TOAD WORD SEARCH

A	H	T	X	Z	V	S	N	Q	J	Y	Y	W	K
A	N	E	O	E	F	I	W	K	Q	A	A	Y	S
M	I	U	R	A	X	R	O	E	W	R	D	I	P
P	L	F	R	P	D	K	M	I	T	A	S	I	R
H	O	U	M	A	E	O	Q	X	O	O	O	K	E
I	O	S	F	J	N	T	Q	T	H	P	F	A	D
B	T	E	O	U	T	I	O	P	U	H	B	W	A
I	S	S	C	Y	E	R	L	A	T	J	H	T
A	D	J	D	E	L	O	Z	M	O	E	I	B	O
N	A	U	R	O	M	G	Q	C	E	G	D	S	R
Z	O	P	P	A	V	Y	W	Z	U	G	I	U	Z
E	T	D	T	R	C	X	F	E	Y	N	O	S	P
P	A	E	C	F	U	O	G	J	U	W	F	R	T
T	M	P	Z	E	A	D	I	N	O	F	U	B	F

AMPHIBIAN	METAMORPHOSIS	TOAD
ANURAN	PREDATOR	TOADSTOOL
BUFONIDAE	PREY	TOADY
FROG	TADPOLE	WART
HERPETOLOGIST		

DIRECTIONS: Search for the words in the puzzle and circle them. Words can be found forward, backward, horizontally, vertically, or diagonally.

From *Of Bugs and Beasts*. © 1995. Teacher Ideas Press. (800) 237-6124.

NOTES

1. "Phive phrogophiles." 1992. Phrogophilia. *BBC Wildlife* 10, no. 6 (June 1992): 33-44.

BIBLIOGRAPHY

Books

Bellows, Cathy. 1990. *Toad School*. New York: Macmillan.
    A young toad sees no point in what she learns at school. She soon discovers, however, that the lessons are invaluable for getting through life.

Cogger, Harold G., and Richard G. Zweifel, eds. 1992. *Reptiles and Amphibians*. New York: Smithmark, 240 pp.
    Provides information about reptiles and amphibians throughout the world.

Cook, Francis R. 1984. *Introduction to Canadian Amphibians and Reptiles*. Ottawa: National Museum of Natural Sciences, 200 pp.
    A field guide to the amphibians and reptiles that occupy Canada.

DeGraaff, Robert M. 1992. *The Book of the Toad: A Natural and Magical History of Toad-Human Relations*. Rochester, Vt.: Park Street Press, 192 pp.
    Artwork and photographs enhance this book, which is strongest when describing folklore and toad-human relations.

Florian, Douglas. 1994. *Beast Feast*: *Poems and Paintings*. San Diego, Calif.: Harcourt Brace.
    Paintings and poems for 21 animals, including the toad.

Graham-Barber, Lynda. 1994. *Toad or Frog, Swamp or Bog?* Illustrated by Alec Gillman. New York: Four Winds Press.
    Explains the easily confusable animals and other elements in the natural world.

Grahame, Kenneth. 1933. *Wind in the Willows*. New York: Scribners.
    This milestone book in children's literature was first published in 1908 and introduces the wonderful character of Toad of Toad Hollow. The book is full of humor, kindliness, and warmth.

Halliday, Tim R., and Kraig Alder, eds. *The Encyclopedia of Reptiles and Amphibians*. New York: Facts on File, 143 pp.
    Provides information about reptiles and amphibians throughout the world.

Kawai, Toyoaki. 1970. *Origami*. Translated by Thomas I. Elliott. Osaka, Japan: Hoikusha, 135 pp.
    One of many books on the Japanese art of paper folding, or origami. There are enough animals in this little book to make an entire origami zoo.

Kopp, Jaine. 1992. *Frog Math: Predict, Ponder, Play*. Teacher's Guide. Great Explorations in Math and Science (GEMS). Berkeley: University of California at Berkeley, Lawrence Hall of Science, 100 pp.

Lewis, Stephanie. 1989. *Cane Toads: An Unnatural History.* New York: Dolphin-Doubleday, 98 pp.
    This book is based on the film of the same name. It takes a humorous look at the cane toad, which was introduced to Hawaii and subsequently to Australia to control sugarcane grubs.

Lobel, Arnold. 1970. *Frog and Toad Are Friends.* New York: Harper & Row.
    The adventures of Frog and Toad are told in five chapters.

———. 1971. *Frog and Toad Together.* New York: Harper & Row.
    Toad has lost his white, four-holed, big, round, thick button from his jacket. His best friend Frog helps him. Another collection of five of their adventures.

———. 1976. *Frog and Toad All Year.* New York: Harper & Row.
    Two friends share experiences in each season of the year.

———. 1979. *Days with Frog and Toad.* New York: Harper & Row.
    Frog and Toad spend their days together but find that sometimes it's nice to be alone.

Walton, Rick, and Ann Walton. 1991. *I Toad You So.* Illustrations by Susan Slattery Burke. Minneapolis, Minn.: Lerner.
    A collection of riddles about toads and frogs, including What game do toads play with a rope? and Tug-of-Wart.

Zim, Herbert S. 1950. *Frogs and Toads.* Illustrated by Joy Buba. New York: Morrow.
    A complete informational book on these amphibians.

Articles

Cowen, R. 1990. Vanishing Amphibians: Why They're Croaking. *Science News* 137(8):116.
    Summarizes some of the initial reports of declining amphibians.

Gelder, Jennifer. 1993. Frogs and Toads. *Outdoor Oklahoma* 49(2):26-32. (March-April)
    Discusses the frogs and toads living in Oklahoma.

Kingsmill, Suzanne. 1993. Is the Chorus Croaking? *Nature Canada* 22(2):22.
    Describes some of the questions biologists are asking concerning population declines noted for amphibians.

Livo, Lauren J. 1990. The Great Plains Toad. *Colorado Outdoors* 39(4):810.
    Describes an odd encounter on a windy night with Great Plains toads.

———. 1991. In Very Cold Blood. *Colorado Outdoors* 40(6):710.
    Describes how toads and other amphibians and reptiles survive winter.

O'Brien, James P. 1992. Amphibians Under Siege. *Outdoor California* 53(3):1-4. (May-June)
    This article, accompanied by photographs by Ed Ely, describes some of the amphibians of special concern in California.

Out of Africa—Superfrogs! 1990. *Time*, January 22, p. 27.
    A brief article tells about Andy Koffman, his Goliath frogs, and the conflicts brewing with the Calaveras County frog-jumping contest.

Sherman, Cynthia Kagarise, and Martin L. Morton. 1984. The Toad That Stays on Its Toes. *Natural History* 93(3):72-78. (March)
    Describes the mating strategies of the Yosemite toad.

Records and Tapes

Elliott, Lang. 1992. *The Calls of Frogs and Toads: Eastern and Central North America*. Ithaca, N.Y.: NatureSound Studio.
    This tape introduces listeners to the calls of 42 species of frogs and toads.

————. 1992. *A Guide to Night Sounds*. Ithaca, N.Y.: NatureSound Studio.
    Nighttime sounds can be spooky and mysterious. This tape will help you identify the animals, including toads, that make some common night sounds.

Rana, Ritual, and Revelations: The Music of Anne LeBaron. Kew Gardens, N.Y. (Box 375): Mode Records.
    This CD includes the New Music Consort performing LeBaron's "Concerto for Active Frogs," a composition inspired by the calls made by frogs and toads.

EDIBLE ANIMALS

How lucky the frog. He eats what bugs 'im.

Anonymous

At chili cook-offs held in southwestern states of the United States, the names of chili recipes are sometimes interesting in terms of the implied ingredients. One year a chili recipe was called "Buzzard's Breath Chili." "Road Kill Chili" was an entry at one contest. The titles of these recipes are probably not indicative of the actual contents but are used simply for humor, the attention-getting potential, and shock value.

But consider the menu of the centennial banquet of the New York Entomological Society in May 1992: chocolate cricket torte, mealworm ganoush, wax worm fritters with plum sauce . . . and more. Most of us shudder at the prospect of consuming these culinary delights. We would excuse ourselves, leave the banquet, and stop by some fast-food restaurant on the way home—if we still had an appetite. Or we might not accept an invitation to dine with the society to begin with. John Rennie noted in his article about this banquet in *Scientific American* that most participants accepted the banquet offerings with relish, particularly honeypot ants, whose transparent abdomens were filled with peach nectar. However, the large Thai water bugs—which evidently bore too much resemblance to cockroaches—were eschewed by even these adventurous diners.

North Americans and Europeans seem a little finicky about their diets compared to the rest of the world. Specifically, few members of these groups eat insects, and most are very selective concerning the vertebrates they eat.

In Australia, from November to January, Aborigines collected moths aestivating in rock crevices in the Bogong Mountains of New South Wales. Before they were eaten, the moths were "cooked in sand and stirred in hot ashes, which singed off the wings and legs."[1] In central Australia, women and children collected witchety grubs by digging them up from around the roots of acacia bushes. The grubs, said to have an almondlike taste when cooked, are loaded with calories, protein, and fat. The repletes of honeypot ants provided sweet nectar.

Native American tribes in California would prepare a fire in a hole, then drive swarms of grasshoppers into the hole. They would eat the grasshoppers roasted or grind them into a flour for later use. During winter these tribes collected the larvae of wood-boring insects and ate them raw. Strong winds washed great numbers of fly pupae onto the shores of Mono Lake (California), where Native Americans could collect bushels of them. Called koo-cha-bee, the fly pupae were dried and resembled an oily grain of rice. Another favored item was the caterpillar of the pandora moth. These caterpillars, which feed on pine trees, were collected by clearing an area from under the tree, then making a smoky fire beneath the tree so that the mature caterpillars would drop to the ground from the branches.

Yet nowadays North Americans rarely eat insects, except inadvertently. And eat insects inadvertently we do. The Food and Drug Administration dictates just how many insect parts per milliliter are allowed in foodstuffs but doesn't expect that our consumed grains will ever be free of some contamination by insects. How can this be?

The mealworm, for example, is one of those ubiquitous creatures found among grains because grains are their food source. Mealworms exist in all stages of their life cycle within wheat crops. As wheat is harvested, many insects or parts of insects survive to the flour mill. Mealworm parts and possibly some surviving eggs are packaged with the flour. Under favorable conditions, the eggs hatch, the tiny mealworms grow through many molts and, unless the flour is used in a timely manner, may metamorphose into the pupa and then the adult darkling beetles. The usually unseen remains of mealworms are baked into our bread and other products that use flour. We eat these none the wiser and also without any particular health risks.

Almost everyone has, at one time or another, found a mealworm or the shed molt of a mealworm in a container of flour, oatmeal, or other cereal. If such an event occurs, we sometimes toss out the contaminated foodstuff in disgust. However, if evidence of insect infestation is found in some samples of grain, it doesn't take much logic to imagine that insects or insect parts exist in virtually all grain samples.

In some parts of the world, foodstuffs are less rigorously inspected than in the United States. In some countries, the buyer of a roll may find a whole mealworm inside. If the buyer is North American or European, he or she may discard the roll, eat around the mealworm, or ask for money back. Natives of countries in which this is a common occurrence simply eat the roll, mealworm and all, and consider that they have just received an extra bonus of protein.

Exotic foods are available in many markets for the daring. One can buy, for example, chocolate-covered ants and french-fried grasshoppers and feel quite adventurous in eating these. A company called Dale's Exotic Game Meats sells items like Cajun Style Alligator and Smoked Rattlesnake. Restaurant owners in Zimbabwe have found that tourists are eating much exotic food while on their safaris. Fried flying ants, field mice casserole, and grasshopper gravy are a few of the items that have been successfully sold. Crocodile tail, hippo burgers, and roasted warthog are other popular items in Zimbabwe cuisines.

An upscale restaurant in Mexico City, Don Chon, offers dishes that Aztecs were eating before the arrival of Spaniards. The most popular dishes here are reported to be *chapulines tostaditos* (toasted crickets), *gusanos de maguey* (maguey plant worms), *escamoles a la mantequilla* (ant eggs sauteed in butter, also known as Mexican caviar), *huevos ahuatle* (fried fly larvae), and *rata de campo* (field rat).

In what Whit Gibbons describes as an all-consuming passion, herpetologists at the Savannah River Ecology Laboratory in Georgia have "herp dinners" that feature delights such as snapper turtle salad (served on crackers), fried mole salamander, breaded amphiuma, and "swamp oysters"—appetizers made of water snake testes collected during a study of the male reproductive cycles. *A Herpetological Cookbook: How to Cook Amphibians and Reptiles* by Ernest A. Liner features additional "tempting recipes."

The movie *Never Cry Wolf*, based on a book by Farley Mowat, is about a naturalist who is convinced that arctic wolves are not severe predators on caribou but subsist chiefly on field mice. To test his thesis, he prepares and eats mice to determine if a large carnivore could get enough nutrition from such a source. The scenes in the movie depicting this act are not for the squeamish. Mice seem, to western tastes, a little bit too exotic.

People in many parts of the world, however, still eat foods such as the ones previously described not on a dare or in a spirit of adventure or even as a necessity but because they enjoy the flavors. People in other parts of the world favor much more variety in their diets, and most consume at least some insects. Colombians, for example, eat roasted ants like many of us eat popcorn. More than 60 percent of the dietary protein for some Africans comes from insects. In Nigeria, various tribes consume caterpillars, termites, crickets, and palm weevil larvae. Children are forbidden to eat some of these insects—not because the food is harmful but rather because they are such treats. The adults believe that the children, who are needed to work in the fields, would spend all their time searching for morsels such as termite queens and palm weevil larvae.

Simply from a nutritional standpoint, an argument can be made for including insects and other exotic fare in the diet. Dried insects contain a higher percentage of protein than "conventional" meat. Grubs and caterpillars are high in unsaturated fats. Plus, insects are rich in vitamins. Chinese scientists are developing an extract from maggots for use as a nutritional supplement. According to one source, 1,000 grams of the maggots yield 500 grams of protein and 200 grams of low-fat oil and amino acids.

Sometimes consumption of insects and other wildlife goes too far. The French, for example, are eating Roman snails at such a rate that extinction seems a possibility unless something changes. To many in the world, escargot remains an undiscovered delicacy, probably by prejudicial choice. Fruit bats, or "flying foxes," are considered a delicacy by the Chamorros of Guam, with prices ranging from $25 to $40 per bat. However, only about 500 of these fruit bats remain, and they continue to be threatened with extinction as Chamorros continue to catch them.

The Chinese frequently use wild animal parts as ingredients in potions for traditional healing methods. Prescriptions can contain items such as ground badger bones in wine for a cough, turtle shells or rhinoceros horns for fever, and sloth brains for rheumatism. Many times, endangered species are used in these traditional medicines. In addition, restaurant menus frequently offer wild animal dishes, including those featuring endangered species. One survey of restaurants in Canton, China, found that endangered species were served in about half of them.

Our biases against many invertebrates aside, we do find a number acceptable, and even extremely desirable, as foods in our culture. These include lobster, crab, and shrimp. Mollusks such as clams and scallops are also treats. And honey, the "sweet touch" for many a meal, is a product of an insect, the bee.

NOTES

1. Ron Cherry. 1993. Use of Insects by Australian Aborigines. *Cultural Entomology Digest* 1, no. 1: 14-15.

BIBLIOGRAPHY

Books

Clayton, Mary Ann. 1992. *Critter Cuisine*. Photography by Al Clayton. Atalanta, Ga.: Longstreet Press, 54pp.
From "Armadillo Asado Ahumar" to "Winged Victory," the photographs and text provide both a spoof on food styling and a commentary on our food prejudices.

Essig, E. O. 1965. *A History of Entomology*. New York: Hafner, 1,029 pp.
    Chapter 2 in this book describes how Native Americans in California collected and prepared various insects as food.

Monroe, Lucy. 1993. *Creepy Cuisine*. New York: Random House, 79 pp.
    This Halloween cookbook for kids uses traditional ingredients (no real insects) but produces dishes such as "tongues on toast," "spaghetti and eyeballs," and "pus pockets."

Mowat, Farley. 1963. *Never Cry Wolf*. New York: F. Watts.
    A story that takes its title from one of Aesop's fable.

Taylor, R. L, and B. J. Carter. 1976. *Entertaining with Insects: Or: The Original Guide to Insect Cookery*. Santa Barbara, Calif.: Woodbridge, 159 pp.
    A cookbook with a nontraditional approach to menu planning. Because of their availability, crickets and honey bees are featured as ingredients (the authors prefer the taste of the greater wax moth, but these aren't commercially available). An appendix contains some recipes that use earthworms.

Articles

Briscoe, David. 1993. Guam Tribe's Cuisine Endangered Fruit Bats. *Denver Post*, Thursday, September 2, p. 17A.
    The Chamorro custom of catching and eating fruit bats has endangered the increasingly rare bats.

Cherry, Ron. 1993. Use of Insects by Australian Aborigines. *Cultural Entomology Digest* 1(1):14-15.
    Insects were important items in the diet of Australian Aborigines.

China Eats Animals in Jeopardy. 1993. *Denver Post*, Sunday, November 14.
    Describes how many restaurants in China serve endangered animals. The article also lists some of the folk medicines that contain animal parts.

Chinese Menus May Add Maggots. 1994. *Rocky Mountain News*, Sunday, February 13, p. 2A.
    Summarizes research of an extract from maggots for use as a nutritional supplement.

Fasoranti, J. O., and D. O. Ajiboye. 1993. Some Edible Insects of Kwara State, Nigeria. *American Entomologist* 39(2):113-16.
    Describes how Nigerian tribes make use of a number of insects as food.

Gibbons, Whit. 1985. Reptilian Repast. *Science 85*, 6 (7): 74-75. (September)
    In this article, the author enthusiastically describes the "Herp Dinners" at the Savannah River Ecology Laboratory in Georgia.

Group Champions Creepy-Crawlies. 1983. *Denver Post*, Thursday, November 24, p. 12CC.
    This article mentions the consumption of Roman snails by the French.

Jellyfish Still Needs Fine-Tuning, 1993. *Denver Post*, Wednesday, December 1.
    Briefly describes research into using jellyfish as food.

Oppenheimer, Andres. 1992. Off the Eaten Path: Mexico Restaurant Specialized in Creepy Crawlers.
    Denver Post, Monday, December 28.
    The renowned restaurant features the food items that the Aztecs once ate.

Rennie, John. 1992. Entomophagy: A Meal of Cooked Insects Offers Food for Thought. *Scientific
    American*, 267 (2): 20. (August)
    This article describes the banquet items featured at a meeting of the New York Entomological
Society.

Salisbury, Laney. 1990. Getting a Taste of Africa: Tourists Love Crocodile Tail, Hippo Burgers,
    Roasted Warthog. *Denver Post*, May 10, p. 24A.
    When tastes run to exotic vacations, they also can encompass exotic meals.

Movie

Never Cry Wolf
    Based on the book of the same title by Mowat, this movie depicts the trials and tribulations of
a young naturalist alone in the arctic wilderness, attempting to show that wolves do not primarily
chose caribou as prey.

ANIMAL CLASSIFICATION

Classifications both reflect and direct our thinking. The way we order represents the way we think. Historical changes in classification are the fossilized indicators of conceptual revolutions.

Stephen Jay Gould
Hen's Teeth and Horse's Toes

Throughout the book we occasionally use the terms *class*, *family*, and *genus*. These are names that biologists use to organize, or classify, living creatures into hierarchical groups. Three examples using the biological classification are shown below.

	Coyote	Toads	Jellyfish
Kingdom	Animalia	Animalia	Animalia
Phylum	Chordata	Chordata	Cnidaria
Class	Mammalia	Amphibia	Scyphozoa
Order	Carnivora	Anura	
Family	Canidae	Bufonidae	
Genus	*Canis*	*Bufo*	
Species	*latrans*		

In this example, all the creatures belong to the kingdom Animalia (animal kingdom). Because coyotes and toads both have backbones, they belong to the phylum Chordata. Jellyfish belong to a phylum with a very different body plan, the Cnidaria. Biologists recognize 32 phyla within the kingdom Animalia.

The coyote profile discusses a single species with the scientific (two-part) name *Canis latrans*. The first part of the scientific name, *Canis*, is the genus name. The second part, *latrans*, is the species name. Biological conventions dictate capitalization of the genus name; the species name appears with all lowercase letters. In addition, the scientific name should appear in italics or be underlined. Whenever you see a two-part name in this book that appears in italics, it is the scientific name of a single organism. A single organism may have numerous common names—or none at all—but it has only one scientific name, which no other organism shares.

The toad and jellyfish accounts aren't about single species. Instead, they cover groups of related species. In the case of the toad, the group is the genus *Bufo*. For the jellyfish, the group is the class Scyphozoa.

Because this classification system is hierarchical, animals in the same genus are more closely related to one another than animals in different genera but the same higher group, such as family or order. This means that the coyote (*Canis latrans*) is more closely related to the wolf (*Canis lupus*) than either is to a striped skunk (*Mephitis mephitis*), although all are in the order Carnivora. In a similar way, toads and coyotes, in the same phylum, are more closely related to one another than either is to animals in other phyla, such as jellyfish in the phylum Cnidaria.

Many of the terms used in scientific nomenclature (scientific naming) come from Latin or are Latinized words from other languages. Because of this, the words follow Latin rules for making the singular and plural forms. For example, the word *genus* is singular, *genera*, plural. The word *phylum* is singular; *phyla*, plural. The word *species* is used for both singular and plural—there is no such thing as a "specie."

Where possible, we indicate the number of species described for the various groups of animals. Different authorities sometimes disagree about how to define species. In addition, new species continue to be found for many groups of animals. For example, although about 205 toad species have been described by scientists at this writing, additional species are discovered and described each year, especially from tropical areas. The numbers cited are the best in our judgment.

The table on the following page shows the taxonomic categories for each of the animals or groups of animals profiled in this book.

This book discusses organisms in the "animal" kingdom. Biologists now recognize at least four additional kingdoms: Plantae, Protoctista, Monera, and Fungi. For a book that illustrates all the recognized phyla, see: Margulis, Lynn, and Karlene V. Schwartz. 1982. *Five Kingdoms: An Illustrated Guide to the Phyla of Life on Earth*. San Francisco: W. H. Freeman, 338 pp.

CLASSIFICATION OF PROFILED ANIMALS

	Kingdom	Phylum	Class	Order	Family	Genus	Species
Ants	Animalia	Arthropoda	Insecta	Hymenoptera	Formicidae		
Bats	Animalia	Chordata	Mammalia	Chiroptera			
Buzzards	Animalia	Chordata	Aves	Falconiformes	Cathartidae		
Clams	Animalia	Mollusca	Pelecypoda				
Coyotes	Animalia	Chordata	Mammalia	Carnivora	Canidae	*Canis*	*latrans*
Jellyfish	Animalia	Cnidaria	Scyphozoa				
Leeches	Animalia	Annelida	Hirudinida				
Moths	Animalia	Arthropoda	Insecta	Lepidoptera			
Packrats	Animalia	Chordata	Mammalia	Rodentia	Cricetidae	*Neotoma*	
Skunks	Animalia	Chordata	Mammalia	Carnivora	Mustelidae		
Slugs	Animalia	Mollusca	Gastropoda	Stylommato-phora			
Snakes	Animalia	Chordata	Reptilia	Serpentes			
Razorback suckers	Animalia	Chordata	Osteichthyes	Cypriniformes	Catostomidae	*Xyrauchen*	*texanus*
Tarantulas	Animalia	Arthropoda	Chelicerata	Aranea	Theraphosidae		
Toads	Animalia	Chordata	Amphibia	Anura	Bufonidae	*Bufo*	

Note: Not all authorities agree on the names for the groups listed in this table. For example, the class Pelecypoda is sometimes called Bivalvia.

In addition, each of the levels in this table can be further grouped or divided. For example, all the animals on this table that belong to the phylum Chordata also belong to the subphylum Vertebrata. As another example, skunks—along with weasels, otters, and other animals—are members of the family Mustelidae. However, only skunks are members of the subfamily Mephitinae.

ANIMAL PREFERENCE SURVEY

As part of our selection of animals to profile in this book, we wanted to get an idea of animal likes and dislikes. We conducted a survey to assess which animals people preferred and which they disliked.

METHODS

We created a simple, pictorial survey form that illustrated both species we anticipated would be disliked along with other animals we thought would be more popular. The survey form illustrated 40 animals, including 28 vertebrates and 12 invertebrates:

Vertebrate classes illustrated		Invertebrate phyla illustrated	
Fish	2	Arthropods	6
Amphibians	4	Mollusks	3
Reptiles	4	Cniderians	1
Birds	5	Annelids	2
Mammals	13		
		Total Invertebrates	**12**
Total Vertebrates	**28**		

The arthropods included three insects, two crusaceans, and an arachnid. The animals represented varying levels of specificity (for example the general term *snail* versus the narrower term *snapping turtle*).

The front of the survey form contained instructions and boxes for 16 animals. The back of the form contained boxes for 24 animals. Each box for an animal contained an illustration, the name of the animal, and three icons to designate the preference score for the animal. The smiling-face icon was scored as 3, the empty circle as 2, and the frowning-face icon as 1. If respondents were unfamiliar with an animal, they were to draw an X through the box, and the animal wasn't scored. Also, no score was recorded for boxes left blank. Thus, scores for an individual animal could vary from 1 to 3.

THINKING ABOUT ANIMALS

We would like to know what you think about animals. The pictures below show different animals. If you really like an animal, circle the ☺. If you really dislike an animal, circle the ☹. For in-between feelings, circle the ◯. Put an X through the box if you don't know the animal.

The animals I like most are: _____

The animals I hate most are: _____

My age is _____
If adult, circle one: (21-35) (36-50) 51+

I am a (girl/woman) (boy/man)

Ant	Armadillo	Bat	Bear
☺ ◯ ☹	☺ ◯ ☹	☺ ◯ ☹	☺ ◯ ☹
Bluebird	Box turtle	Buzzard	Clam
☺ ◯ ☹	☺ ◯ ☹	☺ ◯ ☹	☺ ◯ ☹
Coyote	Crayfish	Deer	Dog
☺ ◯ ☹	☺ ◯ ☹	☺ ◯ ☹	☺ ◯ ☹
Dragonfly	Eagle	Fox	Frog
☺ ◯ ☹	☺ ◯ ☹	☺ ◯ ☹	☺ ◯ ☹

From *Of Bugs and Beasts*. © 1995. Teacher Ideas Press. (800) 237-6124.

Respondents were also asked to fill in a blank with the animals they "like most" and those they "hate most." The categories were scored individually by vertebrate class, invertebrates, and miscellaneous. An individual's response could contain several examples of animals from the same category, such as "deer and dogs." In this situation, only a single score was added to the category "mammal." Other times, a single response contained examples from different categories, such as "snake and tarantula." In this situation, a score was added to "reptile" and another added to "invertebrate."

In summer and fall 1993, we distributed the survey to four groups with a total of 344 people. The group characteristics are described below:

General Population (n=121)

Ages varied in this group from age 3 to over 50. Slightly more than half (n = 64) were adults (21 or older). Among the respondents were teachers in graduate programs, their children, spouses, friends, and students, and 40 urban families in a weekend camping experience in the mountains above Evergreen, Colorado. In this group were 44 males and 72 females; gender was not recorded for 5 respondents.

Middle School Students (n=108)

Students in this urban middle school sample varied in age from 12 to 15, with age 13 as the mode. This group had 54 males and 46 females; gender was not recorded for 8 students.

Pre-IB (n=54)

Students in this urban high school population, consisting of freshmen enrolled in biology, ranged in age from 13 to 15, with the mode at age 14. These students were in a pre-International Baccalaureate program and thus represent a high-performance group. The freshman biology course was not an elective for these students. This group had 19 males and 29 females; gender was not recorded for 6 students.

IB (n=61)

Students in this urban high school population, consisting of juniors and seniors, ranged in age from 15 to 17, with the mode at age 16. These students were in an International Baccalaureate program and thus represent a high-performance group. Additionally, they were enrolled in environmental systems and/or biology courses, which are electives for these students. This group had 17 males and 41 females; gender was not recorded for 3 students.

Results

Most respondents completed both the front and back of the survey form; six individuals noted preferences only on the front. The number of scorable results for individual animals varied from 344 (100 percent) for the bluebird to a low of 214 (62 percent) for the hellbender (a large, aquatic salamander). Other animals with relatively low numbers of scorable results included the razorback sucker (276 scores, or 80 percent scorable) and the horseshoe crab (287 scores, or 83 percent scorable).

The table below displays the average scores for the 10 least popular and 10 most popular animals. Higher mean scores indicate greater preference.

10 Least Popular Animals		10 Most Popular Animals	
Animal	**Mean Score**	**Animal**	**Mean Score**
leech	1.29	eagle	2.85
slug	1.45	dog	2.85
ant	1.67	deer	2.84
jellyfish	1.71	fox	2.74
tarantula	1.73	mountain lion	2.72
moth	1.75	bluebird	2.71
buzzard	1.78	bear	2.69
razorback sucker	1.78	coyote	2.65
skunk	1.80	robin	2.64
worm	1.88	box turtle	2.62

The next table (see page 198) contains a more complete breakdown of results. The lowest standard deviations in mean animal preference scores were for the deer and dog (SD=0.46). The highest standard deviations in mean animal preference scores were for the snake and tarantula (SD=0.88).

Among the three groups with relatively small variation in age, the average preference score increased slightly. The middle school group had an average preference score of 2.05, the pre-IB group a score of 2.17, and the IB group a score of 2.28.

Most respondents filled in blanks for animals they "like most" and those they "hate most." Many wrote the names of more than one animal; some left one or both questions unanswered. Consequently, there were 374 rather than 344 responses scored for the "like most" section and 263 for the "hate most" section.

A total of 260 respondents, or 70 percent, indicated or implied that one or more mammals were among the animals they liked most. In addition to giving straightforward responses for specific mammals (such as dogs, horses, "kitties," or wolves), some respondents wrote things such as "mammals," "pet type animals," and "wildlife (fuzzy)." A few mentioned animals such as packrats and bats that are otherwise generally regarded as unpopular.

Animal Preference Survey Results

ANIMAL	Gen. Pop.			Middle School			Pre-IB			IB			Mean		
	n	Avg	SD	n	Avg	SD	n	Avg	SD	n	Avg	SD	n	Avg	SD
ant	121	1.70	0.76	106	1.57	0.77	53	1.74	0.65	62	1.73	0.77	342	1.67	0.75
armadillo	115	2.20	0.70	103	1.93	0.81	50	2.26	0.63	61	2.28	0.61	329	2.14	0.72
bat	120	1.95	0.85	108	2.03	0.92	52	2.04	0.79	62	2.10	0.78	342	2.01	0.85
bear	121	2.72	0.59	108	2.62	0.67	53	2.70	0.54	61	2.75	0.43	343	2.69	0.59
bluebird	121	2.88	0.43	108	2.56	0.71	53	2.64	0.62	62	2.69	0.53	344	2.71	0.59
box turtle	119	2.72	0.55	107	2.53	0.74	53	2.55	0.64	62	2.65	0.58	341	2.62	0.64
buzzard	117	1.74	0.77	103	1.87	0.82	52	1.60	0.72	62	1.84	0.73	334	1.78	0.78
clam	117	2.26	0.74	107	1.72	0.75	53	2.08	0.65	61	2.26	0.70	338	2.06	0.76
coyote	120	2.58	0.68	108	2.70	0.57	53	2.60	0.63	62	2.74	0.48	343	2.65	0.61
crayfish	119	2.12	0.85	103	1.71	0.82	50	1.86	0.81	61	2.13	0.81	333	1.95	0.84
deer	120	2.89	0.41	108	2.77	0.56	53	2.79	0.49	62	2.92	0.27	343	2.84	0.46
dog	121	2.89	0.40	108	2.79	0.55	52	2.81	0.53	62	2.89	0.32	343	2.85	0.46
dragonfly	119	2.15	0.85	108	1.73	0.86	52	1.92	0.79	62	2.13	0.80	341	1.98	0.85
eagle	119	2.92	0.36	108	2.73	0.62	53	2.83	0.47	62	2.92	0.27	342	2.85	0.47
fox	120	2.76	0.57	107	2.64	0.65	53	2.72	0.53	62	2.87	0.34	342	2.74	0.56
frog	120	2.45	0.73	108	1.90	0.86	52	2.40	0.69	62	2.37	0.71	342	2.25	0.80
hellbender	78	1.90	0.71	67	1.82	0.82	26	2.12	0.65	43	2.19	0.70	214	1.96	0.75
heron	113	2.46	0.68	87	2.13	0.77	47	2.45	0.62	57	2.56	0.60	304	2.38	0.70
horseshoe crab	109	1.99	0.74	84	1.69	0.79	41	1.95	0.71	53	2.19	0.68	287	1.93	0.76
jellyfish	114	1.74	0.84	101	1.52	0.83	49	1.86	0.84	60	1.83	0.83	324	1.71	0.84
leech	116	1.35	0.66	102	1.30	0.70	49	1.18	0.53	61	1.25	0.57	328	1.29	0.64
lizard	119	2.34	0.82	105	2.34	0.81	50	2.52	0.68	61	2.48	0.77	335	2.39	0.78
moth	118	1.97	0.86	105	1.59	0.82	49	1.41	0.61	61	1.85	0.85	333	1.75	0.84
mountain lion	118	2.75	0.55	105	2.68	0.63	50	2.64	0.66	61	2.77	0.50	334	2.72	0.59
newt	111	2.13	0.83	96	2.09	0.85	47	2.38	0.71	59	2.34	0.82	313	2.19	0.82
packrat	117	1.87	0.84	102	1.91	0.89	49	2.06	0.85	61	2.05	0.83	329	1.95	0.85
porcupine	118	2.38	0.79	102	2.04	0.84	49	2.20	0.74	61	2.34	0.73	330	2.24	0.80
raccoon	121	2.64	0.67	102	2.46	0.74	50	2.58	0.67	61	2.54	0.70	334	2.56	0.70
razorback sucker	105	1.89	0.79	85	1.59	0.82	38	1.68	0.66	48	1.98	0.73	276	1.78	0.78
robin	119	2.82	0.50	105	2.49	0.77	50	2.54	0.68	61	2.66	0.57	335	2.64	0.65
slug	117	1.54	0.76	101	1.28	0.65	48	1.50	0.71	61	1.54	0.74	327	1.45	0.72
skunk	114	1.91	0.85	104	1.54	0.80	49	1.90	0.74	61	1.97	0.80	328	1.80	0.82
snail	117	2.28	0.79	105	1.53	0.81	49	1.80	0.74	61	2.00	0.77	332	1.92	0.84
snake	121	2.07	0.87	106	2.24	0.91	50	2.14	0.83	61	2.08	0.90	338	2.14	0.88
snapping turtle	117	2.30	0.81	105	2.31	0.85	49	2.10	0.71	61	2.41	0.74	332	2.30	0.80
tarantula	91	1.56	0.83	133	1.93	0.91	50	1.62	0.88	61	1.64	0.82	335	1.73	0.88
toad	120	2.21	0.81	104	1.67	0.84	49	2.12	0.70	61	2.30	0.76	334	2.04	0.83
trout	121	2.68	0.62	104	2.05	0.90	50	2.28	0.76	61	2.46	0.65	336	2.38	0.78
weasel	118	2.38	0.81	104	2.55	0.74	50	2.40	0.78	61	2.46	0.72	333	2.45	0.77
worm	121	2.19	0.81	104	1.53	0.78	49	1.86	0.76	61	1.89	0.82	335	1.88	0.84
Avg. Preference		2.26			2.05			2.17			2.28			2.18	

Another 44 respondents (12 percent) indicated that birds were among their favorite animals. For most of these individuals, raptors were particularly popular, although one respondent indicated "birds (not of prey)." Penguins, bluebirds, waterfowl, and buzzards were among the other specific birds listed.

Approximately 8 percent of the respondents (29 responses) indicated a reptile, including snakes, turtles, and lizards, as a most-liked animal. Even smaller numbers indicated amphibians (9 individuals) or fish (7 individuals).

There was considerable variability among respondents who indicated invertebrates as preferred animals. Responses of 13 individuals included worms, snails, slugs, jellyfish, and insects, including butterflies, ants, dragonflies, and termites.

Of the miscellaneous responses in the "most liked" category, 4 individuals stated that they liked all or almost all animals, 1 individual liked "none," and 7 others offered responses such as "deadly," "those without rabies," "weird ones," and "small, with no more than 4 legs."

Few people expressed a preference for invertebrates; many (98, or 37 percent of responses) disliked one or more invertebrates. A wide variety of invertebrates was mentioned, including such creatures as mosquitoes, leeches, ants, "intestinal parasitic worms," and slugs. Arachnids, with 60 individuals mentioning them, was the single most frequent response in the "hate most" category.

Sixty-four people (24 percent) disliked mammals, usually bats, rats, rodents, "rabid dogs," and skunks. Birds such as buzzards and pigeons were mentioned by 12 people (5 percent).

Reptiles were mentioned in 45 "hate most" responses; of these, snakes, with 36 responses, were the single most-mentioned dislike. Amphibians had 7 responses and fish 6 responses. Comments in the total of 31 miscellaneous responses included "creepy crawly," "slimy ones," "animals with more than four legs or none at all," "those that are dead," and "don't hate any animals."

DISCUSSION

The coyote was among the 10 most popular animals in this survey (ranked as number 8). Because most of our survey participants are urban, their attitudes might be quite different from other population groups. For example, coyotes were among the least liked from a group of 33 animals in a survey conducted by Stephen Kellert (1989). However, Kellert's study was conducted prior to 1980, so it is possible that attitudes regarding coyotes have changed because of increasing exposure to well-publicized issues involving coyote management.

Preferences often varied substantially between taxonomically similar animals. For example, box turtles ranked 10th, compared to 16th for snapping turtles. Snails ranked 30th, compared to the less popular snails known as slugs (39th). Eagles and "buzzards" are raptors, but eagles tied for first on the preference list; "buzzards" were 34th. Weasels and skunks are both mustelids, but weasels ranked 12th compared to 32nd for the skunk. Porcupines and packrats ranked 18th and 27th, respectively. Regarding the latter pair of animals, perhaps packrats look more like typical rodents than porcupines.

The most popular animals tended to have low standard deviations for the mean preference scores; nearly everyone agreed that they liked the animals. The leech, ranked as the least-liked animal, also had a relatively low standard deviation. Perhaps surprisingly, snakes were not among the 10 least popular animals. These animals, along with tarantulas, had the highest standard deviations for the mean scores, indicating that individuals tended to like or dislike them, with relatively few people having neutral feelings.

The slight trend toward higher mean preference scores in the middle school, pre-IB, and IB groups may be due to increasing self-selection for an interest in animals among the respondents or a factor such as gender, which we did not examine.

For all subgroups, the 10 most popular animals were vertebrates, and except for the box turtle, all were mammals or birds. As is obvious from the table on page 197, invertebrates fared more poorly in terms of popularity than vertebrates, accounting overall for 7 of the 10 least popular animals. This is despite the fact that invertebrates represented only about a third of the animals illustrated on the survey. Both overall and within groups, all invertebrates scored in the lower half of the popularity list (the overall highest score for an invertebrate belonged to the clam, which placed at number 22 out of 40). This corresponds with Kellert's observations that "most invertebrates are viewed with attitudes of fear, antipathy, and aversion."[1]

Within groups, the "most popular" (or "least unpopular") invertebrate varied:

Most popular invertebrate:	
General population	snail
Middle School	tarantula
Pre-IB	clam
IB	clam
Overall	clam (number 22)

The fill-in-the-blank section of the survey paralleled the trends exhibited in the scoring of illustrated animals, with vertebrates being highly preferred over invertebrates.

Varying preferences for different animals can have practical consequences. For example, one survey observed that 90 percent of respondents would stop a hypothetical dam project to protect endangered wolves. About 85 percent would halt the project for a bird such as a bald eagle. Species that garnered less than 50 percent support were all "cold-blooded," except for a rat.

A recent opinion poll by Don Coursey (1994) indicated that more than 60 percent of the respondents considered preservation of threatened or endangered species "important" or "extremely important." However, about two-thirds of the people polled were much less willing to fund recovery of creatures such as rodents, arthropods, snakes, and snails. Actual expenditures for species recovery corresponded in large part to the animal preference poll, meaning that animals people "liked" were more likely to receive a disproportionate share of recovery funds compared to equally endangered but less popular animals.

However, as Stanley Temple, an ecologist at the University of Wisconsin, Madison, notes, "Many ecosystems could continue to function without any vertebrates. On the other hand, removing invertebrates would collapse most ecosystems rapidly."[2]

NOTES

1. Stephen Kellert, Values and Perceptions of Invertebrates, *Conservation Biology* 7, no. 4 (1993): 851.

2. Stanley A. Temple, Appreciating Our Cold-Blooded Nature, *Wisconsin Natural Resources* 16, no. 1 (February 1992): 5.

BIBLIOGRAPHY

Coursey, Don. 1994. The Revealed Demand for Public Goods: Evidence from Endangered and Threatened Species. Paper presented at annual meeting of the American Association for the Advancement of Science, San Francisco, February 1994.

Gerhardt, Gary. 1994. Imperiled, Slimy Critters Losing Funding Race. *Rocky Mountain News*, Tuesday, February 22, p. 24A.

Kellert, Stephen R. 1989. "Perceptions of Animals in America." In *Perceptions of Animals in American Culture*, edited by R. J. Hoage. 5-24. Washington, D.C.: Smithsonian Institution, 151 pp.

———. 1993. Values and Perceptions of Invertebrates. *Conservation Biology* 7(4):845-855.

Temple, Stanley A. 1992. Appreciating Our Cold-Blooded Nature. *Wisconsin Natural Resources* 16(1):4-11. (February)

APPENDIX D

SOLUTIONS TO PUZZLES

Animal Place-Names (*from p. 54*)

Answers: A-14, B-7, C-18, D-5, E-1, F-11, G-17, H-19, I-12, J-8, K-13, L-20, M-3, N-15, O-6, P-2, Q-16, R-9, S-10, T-4.

Jellyfish Crossword Puzzle (*from p. 82*)

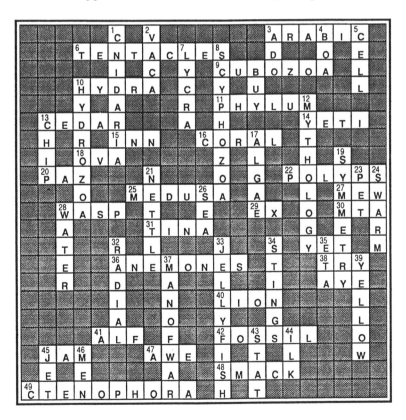

203

Slug Crossword Puzzle (from p. 110)

Coyote Word Search (from p. 131)

Toad Word Search (from p. 178)

GLOSSARY

aestivate: to become dormant in summer or the dry season.

anuran: an amphibian without a tail; a frog or toad.

bilateral symmetry: refers to a form having only one plane of symmetry, that is, the left side is a mirror image of the right side.

bromeliad: a type of plant that grows in the American tropics.

byssal threads: gluelike strands that bivalves produce to anchor themselves to hard surfaces.

carnivore: an animal that eats other animals.

caste: a type of structural and functional specialization of a group of organisms in a colony of social insects, such as the soldier caste in a colony of ants.

caterpillar: the larval stage of a butterfly or moth.

cephalothorax: the united head and thorax of an arachnid.

clitellum: a glandular structure on leeches, earthworms, and other annelids that secretes a cocoon around fertilized eggs.

cloaca: the opening on a reptile or amphibian's body for waste products and reproduction. The portion of the body in back of the cloaca is the tail.

commensal: a type of relationship between two or more organisms of different species that live together without either positive or negative interactions.

complete metamorphosis: Insects that undergo complete metamorphosis have four distinct stages in their lives: egg, larva, pupa and adult. Compare to *simple metamorphosis*.

crèche: normally, a day nursery. Biologists use this term to mean a maternity colony of bats.

diurnal: active during daylight hours.

echolocation: the ability possessed by some animals, such as bats, that allows them to emit high-frequency sounds and analyze the sound's echo to perceive objects.

ectothermic: deriving body temperature from the external environment. Also see *endothermic*.

elaisome: a nutritious coating found on seeds of plants that depend on ants for dispersal.

endothermic: maintaining a relatively constant body temperature through the production of metabolic heat, circulatory adaptations, and other mechanisms.

filter feeding: feeding by removing small particles suspended in water; also called suspension feeding.

gaster: an ant's abdomen.

genital pore: the external opening of a female spider's sex organs.

genus (plural **genera**): the first name in the two-part scientific name. Closely related species are frequently assigned to the same genus.

hemipenes: the paired male sex organs of snakes and lizards.

herbivore: an animal that eats plant material.

hermaphrodite: an organism containing both male and female sex organs.

hibernation: winter dormancy, especially when an organism's metabolic processes slow and its body temperature drops.

instar: the period of time between an insect's molts.

Jacobson's organ: an organ present in snakes and some other reptiles, located in the roof of the mouth, that is used with the tongue to detect odors.

larva (plural **larvae**): an immature stage of an organism.

lateral line: a row of sense organs along the sides of fish and amphibian tadpoles. These organs help the animal orient itself in the water.

mantle: a fold of skin that covers all or part of a mollusk's body. On mollusks with shells, this organ secretes the material for shells.

medusa: a free-swimming Cnidarian, such as an adult jellyfish.

metamorphosis: a developmental change from one body form into another, such as the change from tadpole to toad or pupa to moth.

midden: refuse heap that can be created either by humans or animals such as packrats.

molt: the shedding of skin or exoskeleton.

mutualism: interdependence of two organisms.

nacre: the mother-of-pearl that lines the inner surfaces of clamshells.

nematocyst: stinging cells used by jellyfish and other Cnidarians for defense and collection of food.

nocturnal: active at night.

nuptial flight: the mating flight of a queen ant after she leaves the colony of her birth.

parasite: an animal that lives on or in another organism, obtaining its food from that organism.

pedipalps: leglike appendages on the cephalothrorax of a spider. In male spiders, pedipalps are adapted to transfer sperm to the female.

pheromone: a chemical secreted and released by an animal that is used to communicate with another animal. For example, in many species, female moths secrete a pheromone that attracts male moths.

pollination: the transfer of pollen from the male parts of a flower onto the female parts of a flower, a process that fertilizes the seeds.

polyp: the immature stage in the life cycle of most jellyfish. Unlike the free-swimming medusa stage, the polyp grows attached to the substrate.

pneumostome: the opening to the lung that looks like a hole in a slug's mantle.

proboscis: tubular mouthparts, such as those on moths or other insects that feed by sucking on liquids.

proleg: one of the fleshy "false legs" on the middle and rear parts of a caterpillar.

pupa (plural **pupae**): the "resting stage" of an insect that undergoes *complete metamorphosis*. The pupal stage takes place between the larval stage and the adult stage.

radial symmetry: refers to a form that has parts arranged around a central point, that is, a mirror image can be constructed using one of several lines through the center.

radio transmitter: an electronic device. Before the release of an animal, biologists may attach a radio transmitter to the animal. Later, the biologists can listen to signals from the transmitter and gather information about things such as the animal's movements and activities.

radula: a tonguelike organ in the mouth of mollusks such as snails and slugs. The radula contains numerous small teeth used to rasp food.

simple metamorphosis: the three-stage development of insects such as grasshoppers and dragon-flies, with egg, nymph, and adult stages. Compare with *complete metamorphosis*.

species (same word used for both singular and plural): usually, a group of organisms that interbreed under natural conditions. Each described species has a unique two-part scientific name.

spinnerets: silk-producing organs located near the rear of the abdomen on spiders.

stigma: the part of a flower that receives pollen. Pollen deposited elsewhere in the flower can't fertilize the seeds.

superorganism: colonial animals, such as ants, that are organized so that specific animals within the colony function somewhat like the organs of a body. That is, various castes are devoted strictly to reproduction (like gonads in a body), others to distributing food (like the circulatory system carrying nutrients), and so on.

tadpole: the larva of an anuran (frog or toad).

taxonomy: the scientific classification of organisms.

thermal: a body of air, usually warmed by the sun, that rises. Buzzards and other soaring birds "ride the thermals" to get to high elevations without having to flap their wings (and waste energy).

ultrasonic: a sound above the range of frequencies that humans can hear.

Index

ABOUT THE AUTHORS

Lauren J. Livo, a long-time Colorado resident and naturalist, received her B.A. in Biology from the University of Colorado at Boulder and her M.A. in Biology from the University of Colorado at Denver. When she is not writing about the natural history of reptiles, amphibians, and other small creatures, she and her husband venture to mountains, deserts, and plains on photographic and nature-watching expeditions. Their nature photographs have appeared in books, articles, museum exhibits, and calendars. In 1993, she was selected as an Artist-in-Residence at Rocky Mountain National Park. She is involved in conservation efforts for the boreal toad and other amphibians.

Glenn McGlathery received his B.S. in English at Texas Wesleyan College in Forth Worth and his M.Ed. and Ph.D. in science education from the University of Texas at Austin. He has taught in public schools in Texas and at the University of Texas in Austin. He was a professor of science education at the University of Colorado at Denver from 1968 until his retirement in 1994. He is married, the father of two, and the grandfather of four. He and Larry Malone wrote *Tons of Scientifically Provocative and Socially Acceptable Things to Do with Balloons Under the Guise of Teaching Science*. He and Norma J. Livo wrote *Who's Endangered on Noah's Ark? Literary and Scientific Activities for Teachers and Parents*. He was a founder of the Children's Museum of Denver. He received the Martha Kime Pipe award and was named Outstanding Southwest Science Educator of the Year, by Southwest Association for the Education of Teachers in Science in 1992.

Norma J. Livo received her bachelor's, master's and doctorate degrees from the University of Pittsburgh. She has been employed as a geophysical assistant with Gulf Research Laboratory, as a demonstration teacher at the Falk Laboratory School with the University of Pittsburgh, and as professor at the University of Colorado at Denver.

She has authored *Who's Afraid... ? Facing Children's Fears with Folktale*; *Storytelling: Process and Practice*; *Storytelling Activities*; *Folk Stories of the Hmong*; *Storytelling Folklore Sourcebook*; *and Who's Endangered on Noah's Ark?*, all published by Libraries Unlimited. Other books include *Joining In* with Yellow Moon Press, *Free Rein* with Allyn & Bacon, and *Hmong Textile Design* with Stemmer House.

She is a columnist for the *Rocky Mountain News* and has served on the board of directors for the National Storytelling Association. Norma has also been president of the Colorado Council of the International Reading Association and organizer of the Rocky Mountain Storytelling Conference. In 1995, the Governor of Colorado awarded Norma the Governor's Award for Excellence in the Arts.

She and her husband, George, are the parents of four fantastic young folks and the grandparents of seven perfect grandchildren.

Learning Through Folklore Series

Norma J. Livo, Series Editor

Of Bugs and Beasts: Fact, Folklore, and Activities. By Lauren J. Livo, Glenn McGlathery, and Norma J. Livo. 1995.

Fascinating profiles of nature's least-loved animals reveal their beneficial qualities, their vital role in the ecosystem, and their overlooked but inherent grandeur. Folk stories about bats, snakes, slugs, skunks, and other creepy creatures are coupled with natural histories and problem-solving projects that are perfect for science and environmental studies.

Who's Afraid...? Facing Children's Fears with Folktales. By Norma J. Livo. 1994.

Invite children to listen, share, and respond to popular folk tales that exhibit their most common fears. With the author's insightful commentary, suggestions for discussion and activities, and a bibliography of further resources, this powerful but nonintrusive approach helps transform children's fears into understanding and acceptance.

Who's Endangered on Noah's Ark? Literary and Scientific Activities for Teachers and Parents. By Glenn McGlathery and Norma J. Livo. 1992.

Build student awareness and their responsibility to the environment with traditional folk tales and extension activities based on endangered species. A captivating introduction to conservation and an integrated approach to teaching and learning about wolves, California condors, bears, bald eagles, northern spotted owls, whooping cranes, tigers, alligators, leopards, and elephants.

ORDER FORM

Complete Order Form and Send to:

TEACHER IDEAS PRESS
A Division of Libraries Unlimited, Inc.
Dept. B2
P.O. Box 6633
Englewood, CO 80155-6633
Fax to **303-220-8843** or call toll-free **1-800-237-6124**
and ask for Dept. B2

Name _____

Title/Grade Level _____

School or District _____

School Address _____

_____

City/State/Zip_____

With all personal orders prepayment is required.
____Prepaid (save postage & handling charges)
____Check enclosed (**Make check payable to Teacher Ideas Press.**)
____Please charge my VISA/MC Account:

Account #_____ Exp. date _____

Signature_____

CALL FOR CURRENT PRICES   *1-800-237-6124*

Author/Title	Quantity	Amount
_____	_____	_____
_____	_____	_____
_____	_____	_____
_____	_____	_____

Subtotal _____

Sales tax _____
(CO residents only, add 3.8%)

Please send a ☐ School Library Catalog
☐ Teacher Catalog

Shipping charges _____
(10% of total; free if prepaid)

TOTAL _____

Free Shipping (Book Rate)
with Prepaid Order

PLEASE PAY IN U.S. FUNDS